Essential ICT

for WJEC

WJEC
CBAC

A2 Level | Stephen Doyle

OXFORD
UNIVERSITY PRESS

OXFORD
UNIVERSITY PRESS

Great Clarendon Street, Oxford OX2 6DP

Oxford University Press is a department of the University of Oxford. It furthers the University's objective of excellence in research, scholarship,and education by publishing worldwide in

Oxford   New York

Auckland Cape Town Dar es Salaam Hong Kong Karachi
Kuala Lumpur Madrid Melbourne Mexico City Nairobi
New Delhi Shanghai Taipei Toronto

With offices in

Argentina Austria Brazil Chile Czech Republic France Greece
Guatemala Hungary Italy Japan Poland Portugal Singapore
South Korea Switzerland Thailand Turkey Ukraine Vietnam

Oxford is a registered trade mark of Oxford University Press
in the UK and in certain other countries

British Library Cataloguing in Publication Data

Data available

ISBN 978-1-85008-422-8

FD4228

10 9 8 7 6 5 4

Printed in Malaysia by Vivar Printing Sdn. Bhd.

Paper used in the production of this book is a natural, recyclable product made from wood grown in sustainable forests. The manufacturing process conforms to the environmental regulations of the country of origin.

This material has been endorsed by WJEC and offers high quality support for the delivery of WJEC qualifications. While this material has been through a WJEC quality assurance process, all responsibility for the content remains with the publisher.

Editor:	Geoff Tuttle
Project development:	Rick Jackman (Jackman Publishing Solutions Ltd) and Claire Hart
Concept design:	Patricia Briggs
Layout artist:	GreenGate Publishing Services
Illustrations:	GreenGate Publishing Services
Cover design:	Jump To! www.jumpto.co.uk
Cover image:	Courtesy of Chris Harvey/Fotolia.com

Acknowledgements

p.2, © petrafler/Fotolia; p.3, © drx/Fotolia; p.4, © Scott Maxwell/ Fotolia; p.5, © alphaspirit/Fotolia; p.7, © Nathalie Dulex/ Fotolia; p.7, © dechefbloke/Fotolia; p.7, © Dominique Luzy/ Fotolia; p.7, © Com Evolution/Fotolia; p.7, © jeff gynane/Fotolia; p.7, © Galyna Andrushko/Fotolia; p.7, © 2005 Sean MacLeay/ Fotolia; p.9, © Helder Almeida; p.10, Glasbergen; p.20, © Sean Gladwell/Fotolia; p.21, © treenabeena/Fotolia; p.22, © Guy Erwood/ Fotolia; p.23, © Aycan Zivana/Fotolia; p.24, © Onidji/Fotolia; p.25, © ktsdesign/Fotolia; p.25, © cbpix/Fotolia; p.25, © Sebastian Kaulitzki/Fotolia; p.26, © Petr Kratochvil/Fotolia; p.26, © e-pyton/ Fotolia; p. 27, © Andres Rodriguez/Fotolia; p.28, Glasbergen; p.29, © Mark Poprocki/Fotolia; P.40, © dotshock/Fotolia; p.41, © Ramona Heim/Fotolia; p.49, Glasbergen; p.50, © tetrex/ Fotolia; p.51, Sony; P.52, © godfer/Fotolia; p.53, © Stephen Coburn/ Fotolia; p.53, Glasbergen; p.54, © Konstantin Shevtsov/Fotolia; p.55, © Stephen Finn/Fotolia; p.55, © tetrex/Fotolia; p.62, © ewerest/ Fotolia; p.62, © Robert Paul Van Beets/Fotolia; p.62, © 2006 Ron Hudson/Fotolia; p.62, © NorthShoreSurfPhotos/Fotolia; p.62, © 2006 James Steidl, James Group Studios, Inc./Fotolia; p.62, © pattie/Fotolia; p.64, © Christopher Dodge/Fotolia: p.64, © alphaspirit/Fotolia; p.64, © Sean Gladwell/Fotolia; p.65, © Fotolia VIII/Fotolia; p.65, Lindy Electronics; p.65, © Secret Side/Fotolia; p.65, © robynmac/Fotolia; p.66, Glasbergen; p.67, Glasbergen; p.68, GreenGate Publishing Services; p.68, © Anette Linnea Rasmussen/Fotolia; p.70, © Clivia/ Fotolia; p.71, © Ana Vasileva/Fotolia; p.71, © Nikolai Sorokin/ Fotolia; p.71, © Paul Lockwood/Fotolia; p.71, © Andy Mac/Fotolia; p.71, © Yong Hian Lim/Fotolia; p.72, © Dasha Kalashnikova/Fotolia; p.72, © James Blacklock/Fotolia; p.74, Glasbergen; p.75, Glasbergen; p.77, © Cyrus Cornell/Fotolia; p.77, © Warren Rosenberg/Fotolia; p.94, © Amy Walters/Fotolia; p.111, Glasbergen; p.119, © Dimitrije Paunovic/Fotolia; p.120, © Doug Olson/Fotolia; p.120, © Emin Ozkan/Fotolia; p.120, © pressmaster/Fotolia; p.120, © Mark Aplet/ Fotolia; p.130, © Roland/Fotolia; p.131, © Helder Almeida/Fotolia; p.135, © Ronald Hudson/Fotolia; p.136, © Peter Galbraith/Fotolia; p.141, © endostock/Fotolia; p.141, Microtechware; p.146, Glasbergen; p.146, © George Dolgikh/Fotolia; p.155, © Dara/Fotolia; p.161, Glasbergen; p.163, © demarco; p.163, © tetrex/Fotolia;

Microsoft product screenshots reprinted with permission from Microsoft Corporation.

Every effort has been made to contact copyright holders of material used in this publication. If any copyright holder has been overlooked, we should be pleased to make any necessary arrangements.

Contents

Unit IT3 Use and Impact of ICT

Topic 1: Networks   1

Topic 2: The Internet   19

Topic 3: Human–computer interface   39

Topic 4: Working with ICT   47

Introduction to the A2 Units

There are two units for the A2 Information Communication Technology:

- Unit IT3 Use and Impact of ICT
- Unit IT4 Relational Databases

For A2 level the balance of the marks for the two units is:

Unit IT3 Use and Impact of ICT   60%
Unit IT4 Relational Databases   40%

Unit IT3

Use and Impact of ICT

Assessment for Unit IT3 Use and Impact of ICT

This consists of a question paper with answers written in an answer booklet which is marked externally by WJEC. The written paper is of 2 hr 30 min duration.

There are two sections to the pape

Section A

- All the questions from this section should be answered.
- Consists of structured questions designed to assess your breadth of knowledge of the IT3 specification.
- Quality of written communication (clarity of answer, grammar, spelling, and punctuation) may be assessed in some of the questions.

Section B

- You are required to answer one of two questions.
- Consists of structured questions designed to assess your breadth knowledge of the IT3 specificati
- Quality of written communicatic may be assessed in some of the questions.

The organisation of Unit IT3 Use and Impact of ICT

Unit IT3 is divided up into the following topics:

1. Networks
2. The Internet
3. Human–computer interface
4. Working with ICT
5. Security policies
6. Database systems
7. Management of change
8. Management information systems
9. System development life cycle

1 Networks

You covered the basics of networks in Topic 8 of the AS Unit IT1 and this unit

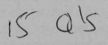

taken into account when designing a good user interface.

4 Working with ICT

This topic covers aspects of working with ICT such as telecommuting (teleworking and videoconferencing), codes of conduct, the contents of a code of conduct and the difference between legal and moral issues with respect to codes of conduct.

5 Security policies

In this topic you will learn about the potential threats and consequences for data misuse and understand the need for backup procedures.

You will learn about how ocedures can be adopted that can p prevent deliberate and accidental use. You will also learn about risk lysis and how an organisation can imise the risks.

Database systems

ic 11 of the AS Unit IT1 briefly ered an introduction to databases in particular the differences ween relational database systems flat files.

n this topic you will be looking etail at the creation of relational bases and the preparation of a cture for the data. Also covered is the use of distributed databases d their relative advantages and sadvantages.

Management of change

this topic you will be looking at w change can be managed when new ICT system is introduced into organisation. You will look at the aining required to learn new skills, e way the organisation structure ight need changing along with work atterns, internal procedures and orkforce.

8 Management information systems

In this topic you will learn about how management information systems are collections of people, procedures and resources designed to support the decisions of managers.

You will learn about the features of a management information system and their uses. You will also learn about the factors which can lead to a poor management information system.

9 System development life cycle

This topic covers the main components of the system development life cycle and how they may be applied to the development of an ICT system.

You will learn about all the stages in the SDLC such as system investigation, system analysis, system design, system implementation, system maintenance and system evaluation.

Unit IT4 Relational Databases

Assessment for Unit IT4 Relational Databases

This unit requires you to produce a project based around a relational database. Although the project you pick does not have to have an actual commercial context, it does still need to be realistic.

You need to look carefully at what is required for the project before you start, in order for you to produce a demanding enough project that will address all the assessment criteria.

Component 1: User requirements

For this component you have to put the problem you are going to solve into context by giving a general description of the chosen organisation.

Component 2: Design specification

This component is an essential component and a major source of the marks for the whole project. Without careful and considered design, the solution will not be an efficient solution and may not work properly. You need to work through all the design steps carefully and ensure that you have produced evidence for each step.

Component 3: Implementation

In this component you take your design and use the software tools to produce a working solution. If you need to alter the design in some way in order to implement it, this should be recorded.

Component 4: Testing

For this component you need to develop a test plan which compares actual outcomes with expected outcomes and

any remedial work that needs to be completed is recorded. All aspects of the system must be tested and you must provide evidence that this has been done.

Component 5: User documentation

User documentation is produced to help the user to use the system properly. Good user documentation will enable the user to use the solution with as little training as possible. The documentation should cover all aspects of the system and you should provide screenshots to help with explanations of the workings of the database.

Component 6: Evaluation

For this component you need to evaluate your solution against the user requirements to see how well matched the solution is. You also need to comment on the problems you encountered with your solution and the strategies you used to resolve them.

Component 7: Project planning

This component is completed throughout the project and here you need to show that you have managed your work effectively and you have successfully used a project time plan. You must supply evidence that you have planned and managed your project successfully.

Introduction to the features in the student book

The philosophy behind the student book

This student book has been based on extensive research from schools and colleges on the different ways ICT is taught and this book has been developed with all the findings in mind. As this is a new specification, many students and teachers/lecturers will be finding their way and the aim of the book is to provide a depth of coverage for all the material for Units IT3 and IT4. This book covers all the material for the A2 level in ICT.

This book should be used by the teacher/lecturer in conjunction with the teacher support materials. Of course this book can be used stand-alone, but if you are a teacher then there are many resources in the teacher support materials to help your students succeed and maximise their marks. The Teacher Support CD-ROM contains the following non-digital resources: Answers to the Questions, Activities and Case studies and also provides additional Questions and Case studies.

The Teacher Support CD-ROM also includes a wealth of digital materials such as PowerPoint presentations, multiple choice questions, missing word tasks and free text tasks. These will all help your students consolidate their understanding of the topics.

The structure of the student book

The WJEC A2 level consists of two units with each unit being divided into topics. In this book each topic has been further divided up into spreads. This allows division of each topic into bite-size easily digested chunks of material. For consistency and to make the student book easy to use, all topics are structured in the same way.

Topic introduction pages

The first page of each topic consists of an introduction to the material in the topic and includes the following features:

Topic introduction: just a couple of paragraphs introducing students to the subject matter in the topic.

Key concepts: this lists the key concepts covered in the topic. These key concepts are identical to those in the A2 WJEC specification.

Contents: the contents lists the spreads used to cover the topic and each spread covers key concepts.

Topic spreads

Introduction: introduces the content on the spreads.

You will find out: this tells you what you will learn from the content of the spreads.

The content: what you need to learn is presented in the content and this material has been written to give you the essential information in order to answer examination questions.

Key words: these are specialist terms used in the content spreads and it is important that you not only remember these words, but you can use them with confidence when describing aspects of ICT systems. There is also a glossary at the back of the book which can be used for reference.

Cartoons: relevant cartoons drawn by the cartoonist Randy Glasbergen add a bit of humour and fun to the topics.

Diagrams and photographs: brings the topic to life with relevant and carefully researched images.

Exam tips: useful tips based on the problems that students have when they answer questions on the topics.

Questions, Activities and Case study spreads

These are usually included at the end of the content spreads and are used to consolidate learning. There are some occasions where Activities or Questions are included within the content spreads. Each block of questions covers a certain number of pages and most of the time this will be a double-page spread. This allows you to look at the spreads and then practise the questions. The answers to all the questions are available in the teacher support materials, which are available separately on CD-ROM and complement the student text.

▶ Questions 1 | pp.

1 An organisation is thinking of networking its stand-alone computers to form a network.
   (a) Explain **three** factors that will influence their choice of network. (6 marks)
   (b) Write down a list of **five** questions you would need to ask before you could decide on a suitable network for them. For each of your questions you should briefly describe why the answers are needed. (5 marks)
2 When choosing a network for a company, the performance needed from the network will need to be taken into account.

State and explain **three** distinctly different performance issues which will need to be considered. (6 marks)
3 A school is upgrading its network. The head-teacher is worried that the security problems that occurred with the old network could occur with the new network.
   Outline **three** security issues which the new network should address. (3 marks)
4 An organisation is purchasing a new network. Describe **three** different hardware items that will need to be purchased and for each one explain why they are needed. (3 marks)

▶ Activity Network topologies

A network consultant visits a small business and finds that their 10 computers are in a stand-alone environment. After conducting a fact find and investigating the information flows within the business, the consultant has told them that they need a local area network. He also tells them that there are a variety of network topologies to choose from.
1   Explain what a network topology is.
2   The consultant has said that the following network topologies are available:
    Star
    Bus
    Ring
    Mesh
    Using the 10 computers in the head office, produce a diagram showing how the computers should be connected together for each of the different topologies listed above.
3   By looking at the diagram you have drawn for the mesh network, work out how many wires would be needed. Why can this be an advantage and a disadvantage for this topology?
4   The consultant says 'it is important to get the bandwidth right'. What is meant by this statement?

▶ Case study 4 | pp.

A terrorist attack

On a Saturday in June 1996 the police received a coded warning that a bomb had been planted at the Arndale Centre, which is Manchester's premier shopping area. Just over an hour after a speedy evacuation of the Centre and the surrounding area, the bomb exploded, injuring over two hundred people and destroying a large part of the Centre and ripping apart many of the business premises surrounding it. The bomb, which was the largest bomb explosion in peacetime Britain, caused extensive damage to the offices of the Royal and Sun Alliance insurance company where some staff were injured.

As these offices housed the company's mainframe computer, it was initially feared that the day-to-day operations of the company would be severely affected. The staff in the Liverpool office, which contained terminals that were networked to the mainframe, found that there was still some life in the system, even though

there was extensive damage to the building the computer was housed in. There was some optimism that the system could be recovered, but to prevent the likelihood of gas explosions from the ruptured gas mains, the fire brigade cut off the electrical power. Effectively most of the hardware had been irreparably damaged during the explosion. However, like most sensible companies, this one had a contingency plan and it involved having a contract with a specialist data recovery company who had similar hardware and copies of software being used by Royal and Sun Alliance. Because they needed staff who understood the Insurance business to operate the computer, the Royal's staff were transported to the offices of the recovery company and they set to work recovering the data from the backup media which was kept off-site. By Monday morning all the data had been recovered and a temporary switchboard had been set up and not a single day's trading was lost.

1   The Royal and Sun Alliance insurance company has an ICT security policy. As part of this policy they performed a risk analysis and also established a disaster recovery programme.
    (a) Explain what is involved in risk analysis. (2 marks)
    (b) Describe the techniques used in the disaster recovery programme to recover the data used by the ICT systems. (6 marks)

2   Backup and recovery procedures are an essential part of ensuring the security of ICT systems.
    (a) Explain the difference between backup procedures and recovery procedures. (2 marks)
    (b) Give **three** things that must be considered when choosing a backup procedure. (3 marks)
    (c) Explain why recovery procedures are essential if an organisation such as this insurance company wants to ensure the security of its data. (2 marks)

Questions: are included at the end of each topic and refer to the content in the spreads and are clearly labelled so that you can either do them after each double-page spread or all in one go at the end of the topic. The questions are designed to be similar to A2 examination questions and have marks to give students the opportunity to understand how answers are marked.

The answers to the questions are included in the Teacher Support CD-ROM.

Activities: offer interesting things for you to do which will help add to and reinforce the material in the spreads.

Case studies: real-life case studies are included that relate directly to the material in the topic. Case studies give a context in which you can answer the examination questions. Often examination questions on ICT ask not only for a definition or explanation but also an example. Case studies build up your knowledge of how the theory you learn about is used in practice.

Case study questions: will give you practice at answering questions which relate to real-life situations. The questions have been carefully constructed to be similar to the examination questions you could be asked and relate directly to the case study and other material contained in the content spreads.

If your teacher has the Teacher Support CD-ROM, they will have the answers to these case study questions.

Exam support

Worked example: is an important feature because it gives you an insight into how the examination questions are marked. At A2 level you can have the knowledge but still fail to get a good mark because you have failed to communicate what you know effectively. It is essential that you understand just what is expected of you when answering questions at A2 level.

Student answers: you can see an examination question which has been answered by two different students. For each student answer there is a corresponding Examiner's comment.

Examiner's comment: offers you an insight into how examiners mark student answers. The main thing here is to be able to see the mistakes that some students make and ensure that you do not make similar mistakes. By analysing the way answers are marked you will soon be able to get more marks for the questions that you answer by not making common mistakes.

Examiner's answer: offers some of the many possible answers and an indication of how the marks are distributed between the answers. It should be borne in mind that there are many possible correct answers to some questions and that any mark scheme relies on the experience of the markers to interpret the mark scheme and to give credit for answers that do not appear in the mark scheme.

Summary mind maps

Mind maps are great fun to produce and a very good way of revising. They are included here to summarise the material contained in the topic. Sometimes there will be only one mind map and other times there will be several – it all depends on how the material in the topic is broken down.

As well as using these mind maps to help you revise, you should produce your own.

Why not produce them using the computer. There are many good pieces of mind mapping software.

Worked example 1

1 When designing any ICT system, the human–computer interface is an important part of the system. Give the names of four factors that should be taken into account when designing a human–computer interface and for each factor describe why it is important. (8 marks)

Student answer 1

1 The ability to adjust the size of the text. For example, in a PDF file you can adjust the size of the document by magnifying it so that you people with poor eyesight will be able to see it.
The Next button or other buttons used to navigate should be in the same place on the screen so that users immediately know where they are on each screen.
On-screen help should be provided so that the users can type in a phrase or sentence and the software will do it for them.
The user should be able to adjust the colour combinations of text and background on the screen.

Examiner's comment

1 The factor and reason for the first point are correct. The second factor only gains one mark because the student has failed to state specifically why it is important. They should have stated what the importance is of having Next positioned at the same place on each screen.
The third factor only gets one mark for the mention of on-screen help. The reason is not a sensible one.
The final factor states what the factor is but fails to state why it is important. Maybe the student thought that the 'why' is obvious, but it still should be included to get the mark. **(5 marks out of 8)**

Student answer 2

1 The font size is important because the old and the very young need a large font, whilst other users can have a smaller font to enable more information to be seen on the page.
There should be a clear navigation structure so that the user can move forward and backward though the screens without wasting time.
The interface should be intuitive so that it is easy to use.
No bad colour choices for screen and background will make the screen easy to see, particularly for users with poor eyesight or who are colour blind, and in some packages or websites you can easily change the colour combinations.

Examiner's comment

1 There needs to be a full explanation of each factor and why it is important to gain the two marks for each factor. The first factor, the font size, has its relevance explained enough to gain two marks.
There are two explanations for the second factor, so two marks for this.
The third factor, although correct, has not been explained in enough detail so no marks are awarded here.
The final factor about the colour has been well explained and is worth two marks. **(6 marks out of 8)**

Examiner's answers

1 Just a statement of the factor gains no marks so students have to give further description of the factor and/or details of what makes the factor relevant to a good user interface for the two marks.
Any four of the following should be described in detail:
Font size – some users will want to see more on the screen so font size should be small (1) or young and old users with poor recognition or eyesight need a larger font (1).
On-screen help – important in case help is not available from other sources (1) as it is always available with the program (1).
Layout appropriate to task. Experts may prefer to type in commands rather than use a mouse (1). Less experienced users will prefer to use the mouse and GUI (1) as they do not have to learn commands.
Clear navigation structure. It should be clear for users how to get to the next step or screen (1) and navigational features (e.g., Next, Forward and Backward arrows) should be positioned in the same place (1).
Colour choice. Use combinations that allow contrast between text and background (1) and allow users to change the colours (1) so if they are colour blind, they can avoid the red/green combination (1).
Consistency of signposting and pop-up information. So that interface is intuitive (1) which makes the software easier to learn (1).

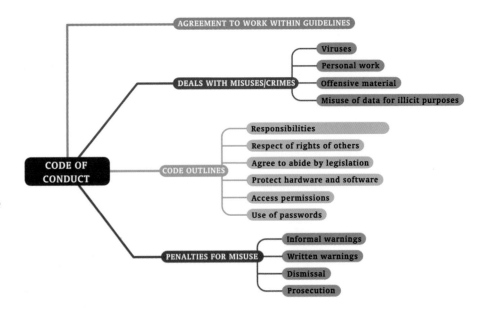

TOPIC 1: Networks

The basics of networks were covered in Topic 8 of the AS Unit IT1 and this topic seeks to expand this knowledge by looking at the factors which need to be considered when choosing a network for a company or organisation. This topic covers the two main types of network: peer-to-peer networks and client-server networks and also looks at the different ways in which computers can be arranged and the relative advantages and disadvantages of each type. Also covered in this topic are the software components that ensure the security of the system and enable the network to be administered.

▼ The key concepts covered in this topic are:

▶ Choosing a network for a company

▶ Types of network available and the use of associated hardware

▶ Software components

CONTENTS

Unit IT3 Use and Impact of ICT

Choosing a network for a company

▶ **You will find out**

▶ About the factors that influence the choice of a network

Introduction

Organisations and companies are of different sizes and have different networking requirements. For example, large companies such as airlines operate in many different countries and have totally different networking requirements from a small kitchen design company which only has a few employees all based in the same office.

Factors which influence the choice of a network

Factors which influence choice of a network include:
- cost of network
- size of organisation
- how the system will be used
- existing systems
- performance required
- security issues.

Cost of network

This can include costs of the server (if applicable), costs of cabling, costs of software and costs of third party communications services.

Cost is always a limiting factor with any network. For large organisations cost is not normally an issue but with smaller organisations one major cost is the cost of someone who is able to manage the network and deal with any problems and keep the network running. Wage costs are high compared to the costs of hardware and software, and this can be an issue for small organisations. Also finding someone who is suitably qualified at a price you can afford can be a problem.

Other costs are shown in the following diagram:

Size of organisation

This determines the complexity of the network. Large organisations may have users in many sites all around the world, so communication costs can be high because satellite links may have to be used. The size of the organisation will also determine whether a LAN or WAN is needed. Large networks need complex security measures and a range of specialist staff are needed to keep the network running.

How the system will be used

This will affect the scale of the network. Large retailers will need local area networks set up in each store with each one being connected to form a wide area network. This will allow each store to perform some local processing but still allow data communication with the head office. Some networks may allow employees to work from home using on-line databases, videoconferencing, etc.

Some tasks such as order processing or booking tickets are performed interactively by conducting a dialogue with the user. Networks used in this way need to be fast in order to reduce the response time.

Network maintenance costs (upgrades, adding terminals)

Staffing costs (e.g., network manager)

Hardware costs (cabling, file server, routers, etc.)

COSTS ASSOCIATED WITH A NETWORK

Training costs

Software costs (e.g., network operating system, network management software)

Cost of third party communication lines (e.g., BT, Virgin, etc.)

Costs associated with a network

A file server is an essential part of most networks

Some tasks such as payroll or the production of utility or credit card bills use batch processing, which means that all the inputs are collected together over a period and then processed in one go. Batch processing requires lots of processing power and this will slow the network down for other users, so it is best to perform batch processing when other users are not using the network interactively. Batch processing is therefore performed during less busy periods, usually at night.

Existing systems

When networks are introduced or expanded, they often have to work with the existing systems. Often the new or expanded network will need to work with the existing hardware and software, and because staff understand the systems, you are not introducing too many new things for them to learn. It also keeps the costs down if some existing systems can be re-used.

Performance required

This will determine the way that the computers and other hardware should be connected together (i.e., the topology used). The performance needed will also determine the type of server needed. Performance is also measured by how well the network supports the users; use of on-line help and ease with which users can get their work done using the user interface is a measure of performance. E-commerce systems will need to be fast otherwise users will get fed up waiting and choose to go elsewhere. It is essential that the network is reliable

Speed   Reliability

MEASURES OF NETWORK PERFORMANCE

Cost   Usability

Measures of network performance

and available to all users at all times, so reliability is also a performance issue.

Summarising, a high performance network will be:

- fast
- reliable
- as cheap as possible
- easy to use.

Security issues

Most networks offer a way of allowing users to access the Internet. In many organisations the Internet is an essential part of the network, so steps need to be taken to keep hackers out and make sure that customer financial details are not intercepted or revealed. If personal data is held, then appropriate security needs to be in place to prevent unauthorised access. Other issues include the introduction of viruses, users copying copyrighted material using their computers, sending offensive e-mails and so on.

Security requirements of one organisation will be different from another. For example, a school will be

worried about their pupils accessing certain sites or using chat rooms, whereas businesses will be more worried about making secure payments.

Here are some security issues which will need to be considered when choosing a network:

- access to illicit material (e.g., pornography, sites promoting racial hatred, etc.)
- whether users are free to use unlimited words in search engines or whether words should be restricted
- how hackers can be kept out (e.g., by the use of firewalls, etc.)
- how payment details can be protected when sending them over communication lines (e.g., encryption)
- problems when users connect to networks wirelessly
- the need to avoid viruses
- the need to restrict staff access to only certain files
- the blocking of downloading copyright material (e.g., films, music, etc.).

This small network is connected to the Internet via a high speed link called a backbone

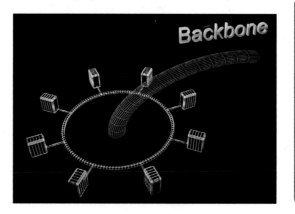
Backbone

Topic 1: Networks

Types of networks available and the use of associated hardware

You will find out

▶ About peer-to-peer networks

▶ About client-server networks

➥ KEY WORDS

Client-server – a network where several computers are connected to one or more servers

Peer-to-peer – a network arrangement where each computer is of equal status

Introduction

In this section you will look at the way the terminals in a network are linked. We use the word linked rather than connected, as many networks are wireless.

This section will also cover the two main types of network: peer-to-peer and client-server.

Peer-to-peer or client-server

Networks can be divided into two main types:

- peer-to-peer
- client-server.

Peer-to-peer (P2P) networks

Peer-to-peer networks are networks where each computer has the same status and they are able to communicate with each other on an equal footing. This means that every computer on this type of network can access all the resources of any of the other computers on the network.

Peer-to-peer networks are used for home networks. If you simply want to share files and printers using several computers in your home, then a peer-to-peer network will be fine.

P2P has become very popular with Internet users for the sharing of files between users. Each user is able to connect to another user's computer over the network so there is no central management. There have been many problems with this over the legality of sharing copyrighted music, video, images, etc.

P2P software systems such as Kazaa and Napster are one of the most popular software applications with users.

With peer-to-peer networks all the computers are of equal status and can access each other's resources.

Advantages of peer-to-peer networking:

- cost saving – no server is needed, so all the computers can be the same
- no network manager is needed – all users take responsibility for the network
- easy to set up – they are the simplest of computer networks, so they can be set up by anyone
- there is no reliance on a server – so no worry about the server breaking down
- lower operating costs – less setup and maintenance costs
- peer responsibility – users decide what resources other users can use on their computer.

Disadvantages of peer-to-peer networking:

- backups cannot be made centrally – this places responsibility on all the users to back up their own data; you cannot be sure that all users will do this

Peer-to-peer allows computers to share files

- users need more IT knowledge – as they will be responsible for the files on their own computers
- poorer security – resources are shared, so users have to decide what resources of theirs other users on the network can use
- some computers may run slowly – those computers that have resources on them that all users use will run very slowly
- users may experience difficulties in finding files as they are not organised and held centrally
- only suitable for very small networks with typically fewer than 15 networked computers.

Client-server networks

Client-server networks are the preferred choice for large networks. In a client-server network all the computers are not the same status. Usually a more powerful computer is used as the central computer, where all the files and programs are stored, and this computer is called a server. The other computers on the network are called clients.

As the server is such an important part of a client-server network, a person, called the network manager, is usually appointed to be in charge of it.

Advantages of client-server networks:

- security is better – because it is centralised and a person is given responsibility for it
- centralised data – data is all held on the file server which means that all users have access to the same set of data
- backups are taken centrally – regular backups are taken by the network manager which means data and programs are unlikely to be lost
- faster access to programs and files – servers are used which are powerful computers, so the whole network runs faster
- centralised administration – all the administration of the network (e.g., allocation of usernames and passwords, help, etc.) is performed centrally so users do not have to worry about it.

Disadvantages of client-server networks:

- more expensive – servers are expensive
- need specialist knowledge – need to have a person who understands the technicalities of a network in charge of the network
- software is sophisticated and expensive – network operating systems are expensive. For larger client-server networks it may be necessary to buy network management software.
- if the server breaks down it renders the network unusable until it can be repaired.

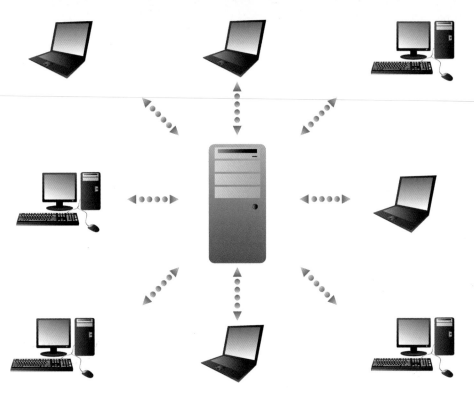

With client-server networks a more powerful computer is in charge of the networking facilities

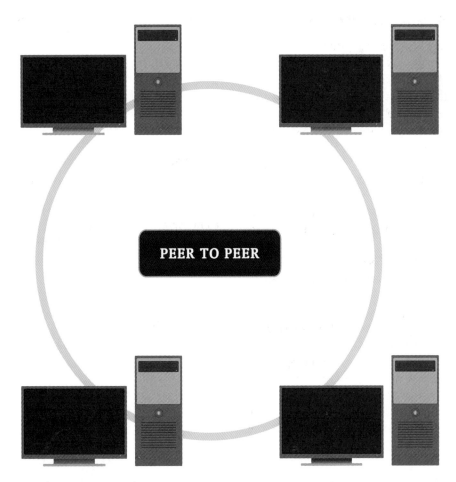

In a peer-to-peer network all the computers are of equal status

Types of networks available and the use of associated hardware *continued*

Network topologies

The devices in a network can be set up in many different ways and the way this is done is called the topology.

A network topology shows how the computers are connected when wires are used and if wireless (radio, infra-red and microwaves) is used, it shows how the devices in the network communicate with each other.

The ring topology

This is a ring network which is also a peer-to-peer network because there is no server.

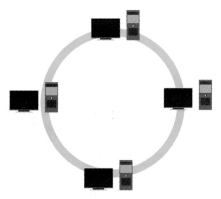

With the ring topology:

- all the computers are arranged in a circle
- data sent by one computer passes around the ring until it reaches the correct computer.

Advantages of ring networks:

- the network is not dependent on a central computer
- each computer has the same access as the others so no one computer can 'hog' the network.

Disadvantages of ring networks:

- if there is a break in the connection (wire or wireless), then the whole network fails
- faults are difficult to locate
- it is impossible to keep the network running whilst equipment is added or removed because there is only one path for the data to follow.

The bus topology

With a bus topology, all the devices connected to the network are connected to a common shared cable called the backbone. Signals are passed in either direction along the backbone.

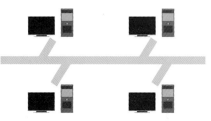

Advantages of bus topology networks:

- cost effective because of the small amount of cable needed
- simple cable runs makes it easy to install
- easy to add extra devices to the network.

Disadvantages of bus topology networks:

- if more than about 12 devices are connected to the network, then the performance of the network is degraded
- if there is a break in the backbone cable, then the network cannot be used.

The star topology

The star topology uses a central connection point to connect all the devices on the network together. The central connection point can be a hub, a switch or a router.

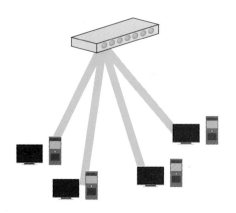

➡ **KEY WORDS**

Hotspot – a region where the Internet can be accessed wirelessly

Wi-Fi – a trademark for the certification of products that meet certain standards for transmitting data over wireless networks

Advantages of star topology networks:

- fault tolerant – if one of the cables fails, then the other computers can still be used
- load tolerant – extra computers can be added without much loss in performance because all computers have their own path to the hub
- easy to add extra computers – extra computers can be added without disturbing the network.

Disadvantages of star topology networks:

- higher cost – the large amount of cabling needed makes it a more expensive topology
- dependence on the central hub, switch or router – if the device at the centre of the network fails, then the whole network will fail.

Wireless networking

Many computers are now able to connect to the Internet or communicate with other computers in a local area network wirelessly. With wireless communication, the data transfer medium is the air through which the radio waves travel.

Wireless networks enable people to connect to the Internet or to a LAN wirelessly. This means they can work anywhere they can get a radio signal for their network.

Many people, especially people who travel a lot, need to access the Internet regularly. There are many public places where the Internet can be accessed wirelessly using a person's laptop computer or other portable devices such as mobile phone or PDA.

These places where you can access the Internet using Wi-Fi are called hotspots.

To set up a small Wi-Fi network you would need:

- a broadband connection to the Internet
- a router
- Wi-Fi enabled computers (most computers have a wireless adapter installed in them). You can buy wireless adapters for older computers.

How Wi-Fi works

1. The router is connected to the Internet by a high-speed broadband connection.
2. The router receives data from the Internet.
3. It transmits the data as a radio signal using an antenna.
4. The computer's wireless adapter picks up the signal and turns the radio signal into data that the computer can understand.

When sending data, the above processes work in reverse.

Advantages and disadvantages of wireless networks

Advantages of Wi-Fi:

- allows inexpensive LANS to be set up without cables
- allows people the freedom of working anywhere a signal can be received
- ideal for networks in old listed buildings where cables would not be allowed to be installed
- global set of standards – you can use Wi-Fi all over the world.

Disadvantages of Wi-Fi:

- power consumption is high – which means laptops soon exhaust their rechargeable batteries
- there may be health problems in using Wi-Fi
- there may be security problems even when encryption is used
- home networks have a very limited range (e.g., 150 ft)
- can get interference if wireless network signals start to overlap.

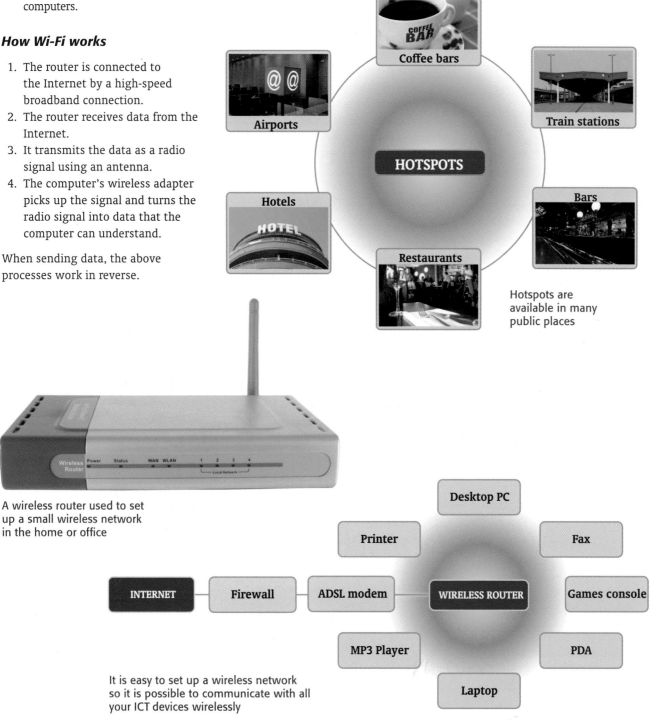

A wireless router used to set up a small wireless network in the home or office

It is easy to set up a wireless network so it is possible to communicate with all your ICT devices wirelessly

Software components

Introduction

The hardware of the network has been looked at in detail in the previous sections. This section is devoted to the software that allows all the hardware components to function correctly and each computer to communicate with others.

Networking software

Networks need software to tell the connected devices how to communicate with each other.

Network operating systems software

Small networks can be run using existing Windows software, but for larger client-server networks, specialist network operating systems software is needed.

Network operating systems have more complexity because they need to coordinate the activities of all the computers and other devices connected to the network.

Examples of network operating system software include:

- UNIX
- Linux
- Novell Netware – this is a very popular client-server network operating system.

Network management software

If you were the network manager responsible for a network consisting of several hundred computers, you would need help in looking after them all to keep the network running.

Luckily there is software called network management software that will help you do this.

Some tasks the network management software would help with include:

- Making sure that all the computers have up-to-date software with the latest security patches, so that hackers cannot get into the network.
- Keeping track of the software being run on each computer and checking that there are licences for all the software being used.
- Keeping all application software up-to-date.
- Providing remote control facilities so that help-desk staff can sort a user's computer problem out by seeing exactly what is on the user's screen.
- Check that bandwidth is being used correctly.
- Finding out if a user has installed non-licensed software without permission on a networked computer.
- Checking the speed of the processor and the memory used for a particular computer on the network. This can be useful to identify computers that need upgrades.

User accounts and logs

User accounts and logs are an important part of network software and prevent misuse of the network by users. Should misuse still occur then it is very easy using this software to determine the culprit.

User accounts

Everyone who uses a network is given a user account. The user account is set up by the network administrator or network manager.

At the time the account is created the network administrator or network manager will allocate the user certain rights, which are things that the user is allowed to do using the network. All users of a network are able to:

- change their password
- change desktop settings (i.e., they can personalise their user interface)
- manage their own files in their storage area.

It is then up to the person controlling the network to decide:

- which software the user can access
- which shared files the user has access to

- if a user is allowed to copy files
- if a user is allowed to install software.

User logs

When a user logs in they supply their username and then their password. The system then allocates network resources to the user. When a user no longer requires access to the network they can log out. As well as making sure only authorised users are allowed access to the network, the log-in procedure can provide an audit trail as to who has used what resources on

▼ You will find out

▶ About networking software

▶ About network operating systems software

▶ About network management software

▶ About user accounts and logs

▶ About security strategies

▶ About configuration management

▶ About remote management

▶ About disaster planning (i.e., backup and restoration)

▶ About auditing (keeping logs)

KEY WORDS

Log-in – identifying yourself to the network in order to gain access

Log-out – informing the network you want to close access to the network facilities until the next log-in

Password – a sequence of characters (which is kept secret from others) that the user enters to gain access to the network

Username – a unique series of characters the user or the network manager chooses. Quite often it will be the user's name or perhaps a nickname

the system. This is done by providing a user log, which is a record of the successful and failed logins and also the resources used by those users who have access to network resources.

User log-in screen

Security strategies

The use of networks exposes organisations to a range of security threats, so strategies regarding the use of networks need to be developed to minimise these threats.

There are a number of ways in which software can help with a security strategy:

- Use of passwords and user-IDs – used to authenticate a user of a network. Ensures that access is restricted to authorised users.
- Virus checkers – all computers have the latest virus checking software loaded which scans the computer and all files, e-mails and instant messages for viruses. If viruses are detected, they can be removed automatically.
- Firewalls – can be software, hardware or both and protect the network from hackers.
- Encryption – used to keep data secret when being sent over networks. Used for financial details (e.g., bank details, credit card details, etc.) when being sent over the Internet.

Configuration management

Once a network has been created, it is necessary to configure it to maximise its performance. Network configuration management is the process of organising and maintaining all the information about a network.

When a network needs modification, repair, expansion or upgrading, the network manager/administrator will refer to the network configuration database to determine the best course of action. The network configuration database contains the locations and network addresses of all hardware devices used in the network and also information about the programs, versions and updates of the software installed on the networked computers.

The advantages in using configuration management software are:

- It is much easier to repair, expand or upgrade the network.
- The network will be optimised and so will run faster.
- There will be less network downtime owing to better management of the network.
- Network security will be optimised.
- It is possible to roll back changes to a previous configuration if changes made to a network adversely affect its performance.
- It keeps records of all the changes made to a network so you do not need to write down the new settings.

Remote management

There are many tasks that a person in charge of a network can do on their terminal. Network managers/

administrators can use remote management to:

- see which users are using the network
- check on e-mails being sent in company time
- check on the Internet sites visited by employees
- check on the hardware (disk drives, processor, etc.) to see if upgrades are needed
- check to make sure that the number of allowed users as per the licences for software are not being exceeded
- guide users through problems they may be having
- check to make sure users do not have any unauthorised software loaded on their computers
- log a user off their computer if they have left their computer while logged on
- see if components on the networks are failing
- shut down stations that are not functioning correctly
- rebuild stations by adding software.

Disaster planning (backup and restoration)

Sooner or later most companies will have to cope with a situation that will cause the loss of hardware, software, data or communications services or a combination of these. This loss could be caused by:

- hardware failure
- software bugs
- natural disasters (e.g., floods, fire, earthquakes, hurricanes, etc.)
- deliberate damage (malicious damage by staff, viruses, hacking, vandalism, terrorist bombs, etc.)
- accidental damage (e.g., accidental deletion of files, accidental damage to equipment, etc.).

Disaster planning is needed:

- to minimise the disruption caused
- to get the systems working again in the shortest possible time
- to ensure that all staff know what to do to recover data, programs, etc.

Software components *continued*

Backup

Loss of programs and hardware is not too much of a problem as these can be replaced. Data, however, if there is no backup, cannot easily be replaced and such a loss could cause companies so much financial loss that they may go out of business.

Backing up data on a network is extremely important. Backups should be:

- taken on a regular and routine basis or even taken automatically
- kept away from the computer in a locked fireproof safe or preferably kept off-site
- taken using the grandfather, father and son principle in the case of batch processing systems
- used with a RAID (random array of inexpensive disks) system.

Restoration

It is no use taking backup copies of files and not checking that the original files

can be recovered using the backup. It is important that staff understand what they need to do to recover the lost or damaged data. Occasionally, organisations should do a mock of a disaster recovery to check it actually works.

Restoration can be done on a smaller level. For example, a computer crash may mean that the existing copy of a file has become corrupted. Most software contains a way of restoring such files. It is also possible to re-create files that have been deleted by accident.

Auditing (keeping logs)

Auditing keeps a record of who has done what on the network. Auditing keeps records of:

- usernames
- the times they logged on and off
- details of programs they used
- details of files accessed
- details of changes made.

Auditing is used to identify abuses of the systems by authorised staff and also to investigate instances of unauthorised access (i.e., by hackers).

Copyright 2005 by Randy Glasbergen.
www.glasbergen.com

GLASBERGEN

"We back up our data on sticky notes because sticky notes never crash."

▶ Questions

1 A local business uses a local area network and it is an essential part of their business.
   (a) Staff using the network are given user accounts. Describe the function of user accounts. (2 marks)
   (b) A network manager is placed in charge of the network. The network manager is responsible for managing the users of the network. The network manager makes use of both configuration management and remote management to help manage the network.
   Describe **two** functions of configuration management and **two** functions of remote management. (4 marks)
   (c) It is essential that the security of the network is ensured.
   Explain the part played by auditing in ensuring the security of data stored on a network. (3 marks)

2 A local dentists' surgery uses a network to manage patient records, appointments, staff pay and all the financial functions. The administration manager is worried about the confidentiality of the patient records.
   (a) Explain why the surgery should have a security strategy and give **two** examples of what this security strategy should contain. (4 marks)
   (b) Discuss the use of user accounts and logs as a way of ensuring the confidentiality of patient records. (3 marks)

3 A company is introducing a new network and the company are looking at the security issues that the new network presents.
   Discuss the issues involved in ensuring the security of the network. (10 marks)

Questions

▶ Questions 1 | pp. 2–3

1 An organisation is thinking of networking its stand-alone computers to form a network.
   (a) Explain **three** factors that will influence their choice of network. (6 marks)
   (b) Write down a list of **five** questions you would need to ask before you could decide on a suitable network for them. For each of your questions you should briefly describe why the answers are needed. (5 marks)

2 When choosing a network for a company, the performance needed from the network will need to be taken into account.

State and explain **three** distinctly different performance issues which will need to be considered. (6 marks)

3 A school is upgrading its network. The head-teacher is worried that the security problems that occurred with the old network could occur with the new network.
   Outline **three** security issues which the new network should address. (3 marks)

4 An organisation is purchasing a new network. Describe **three** different hardware items that will need to be purchased and for each one explain why they are needed. (3 marks)

▶ Questions 2 | pp. 4–5

1 (a) Explain **two** main differences between a client-server network and a peer-to-peer network. (2 marks)
   (b) A large network is to be built for a college. State which of the two types of network mentioned in part (a) would be best and give **two** reasons for your statement. (3 marks)

2 A company is thinking of networking its stand-alone computers.
   (a) Give **two** advantages of networking the computers. (2 marks)
   (b) Discuss the relative merits of server-based networks and peer-to-peer based networks. (6 marks)

3 At the office of a kitchen design company there are six employees. Each employee has a stand-alone computer system and printer. The company would like to network these computers. A network expert has indicated that it would be more efficient if the six PCs were formed into a peer-to-peer network.
   (a) State **three** benefits that the company would gain from networking their computer systems as a peer-to-peer system rather than a server-based system. (3 marks)
   (b) What additional hardware would be needed to connect the six stand-alone computer systems as a peer-to-peer network system? State why each item of hardware is required. (4 marks)

▶ Questions 3 | pp. 6–7

1 A company is installing a new network in an old building and they have decided to use a wireless network.
   (a) Describe **two** advantages and **two** disadvantages of them using a wireless network. (4 marks)
   (b) The wireless network will be a LAN.
      (i) What is meant by a LAN and give **two** reasons why the network chosen is a LAN. (2 marks)
      (ii) Name **one** topology suitable for a LAN and give **one** advantage of the topology you have chosen. (2 marks)

2 Ring and star are two types of network topologies.
   (a) Give the name of **one** other type of network topology and draw a diagram or explain using words how the computers are arranged in the topology. (2 marks)
   (b) Compare and contrast the relative advantages and disadvantages of the ring and star topologies. (6 marks)

Case study and Activity

▶ **Case study 1** | pp. 8–10

Network procedures at a university

All universities, colleges and schools use networks and having a set of procedures for staff and students helps prevent problems.

This document sets out the network procedures. Read these procedures carefully and then answer the questions that follow.

1 Usernames and passwords

(a) All staff and students need a username and password to log on to the network.

(b) Usernames are the member of staff's employee number and for students it is their student number.

(c) Passwords should be at least 7 characters and contain at least 3 numbers.

(d) Passwords should be changed every three months.

2 Unauthorised use

(a) Do not share your password with anyone.

(b) Any unauthorised use of the network must be reported to the network manager so that they are able to assess the network for damage.

3 Confidentiality

(a) Staff should not allow students to enter or view other students' electronic grades or records.

(b) Periodic directory maintenance is performed by network administration staff to help ensure the network performance and integrity. They will only view information related to file size, number of files, etc.

(c) When network administration staff need to troubleshoot a user problem, or need to access or view a user's files, they will obtain the user's permission first.

4 Student use

(a) Students must be monitored/supervised when using the network.

(b) Students should only log in to the network with their own username and password.

(c) All data must be saved on the student's area on the network. Data must not be stored on the local hard drive.

(d) Students are not allowed to install software on the hard drives or the network.

5 Logging out

(a) When staff leave their work area they should log out of the network.

(b) All computers should be turned off at the end of the day.

(c) Always log out before turning off computers.

6 Viruses

(a) If you bring media from home or another place, scan it for viruses.

(b) All hard drives will be scanned for viruses by support staff before they are connected to the network.

(c) When using laptops on the network, make sure that there is a current copy of a virus scanner installed on them and ensure that this is updated regularly.

(d) If files are downloaded from the Internet, make sure that they are downloaded as a temporary file which you should then scan before opening the file.

7 Backups

(a) The network is backed up every day. It is also best if you take your own backup copies of your personal work on removable media.

8 Software

(a) Your amount of storage is limited. You should therefore maintain your files by copying them to removable media and deleting them off the network.

(b) Staff but not students are able to install legal and original software on the hard drive of their computer.

(c) Software can only be added to the network by the network manager.

9 Copyright

(a) All staff and students must comply with current copyright laws.

(b) Software on the network should not be copied.

(c) Non-copy-protected audio (e.g., MP3) and video files for personal use should not be stored on the network.

10 Hardware

(a) All networked hardware must remain on-site and must be kept connected to the network.

(b) Computer and other equipment must not be borrowed and taken home.

(c) Hardware must be modified or repaired only by the network technicians.

11 Removable media

(a) Care must be taken when pen drives are inserted into or removed from computers.

(b) Keep magnetic media away from magnetic fields (top of screen, metal cabinets, etc.).

12 Problem solving

(a) All help requests should be referred to the help-desk.

(b) Help is available 7 days per week from 8.00 am to 6.00 pm.

See over for questions.

► Case study 1 (continued) pp. 8–10

Questions: Network procedures at a university

All the following questions refer to the case study.

1 This question concerns usernames and passwords which are needed to log on to this network.

   (a) Explain why usernames are displayed whilst passwords are never displayed on the screen. (1 mark)

   (b) Explain the purpose of:
      (i) a username (1 mark)
      (ii) a password (1 mark)

   (c) The network manager has said that users of the network need more guidance about choice of passwords. Describe **four** different things users should bear in mind when choosing passwords. (4 marks)

   (d) To be effective, passwords need to be changed regularly. For this network, the passwords should be changed every three months. Give **one** reason why the network manager might be opposed to a proposal to make users change their password every week. (1 mark)

2 (a) Give **one** reason why the network manager will only allow students to store data on the network and not the local hard drive of the computer they are working on. (2 marks)

   (b) Explain why the procedures make it a requirement for students to maintain their own storage area on the network. (2 marks)

3 Some networks in businesses do not allow removable media to be inserted into networked computers.

   (a) Give **one** reason why this is done. (1 mark)

   (b) Explain why this is not a real option for a network for a college or university. (1 mark)

4 Explain why software should only be added to the network by the network manager. (2 marks)

5 Students are able to use removable media to store their work for backup purposes.

   (a) Give the names of **three** examples of removable media which the students could use. (3 marks)

   (b) Students are able to bring in pen-drives and other media from home. Give **one** danger that this presents to the network and state what can be done to minimise the risk. (2 marks)

► Activity Network topologies

A network consultant visits a small business and finds that their 10 computers are in a stand-alone environment. After conducting a fact find and investigating the information flows within the business, the consultant has told them that they need a local area network. He also tells them that there are a variety of network topologies to choose from.

1 Explain what a network topology is.

2 The consultant has said that the following network topologies are available:

   Star

   Bus

   Ring

   Using the 10 computers in the head office, produce a diagram showing how the computers should be connected together for each of the different topologies listed above.

3 The consultant says 'it is important to get the bandwidth right'. What is meant by this statement?

Topic 1: Networks

Exam support

Worked example 1

1 (a) Other than the cost of the network and the size of the organisation, explain **four** factors which influence the choice of a network for a company. (8 marks)

(b) There are two main types of network that a company could choose: peer-to-peer and client-server networks. Compare and contrast these **two** types of network. (4 marks)

Student answer 1

1 (a) How many employees the company has, as this will determine how many computers are needed.

How much money there is to spend on a network. If there is little money, then a simple network will be needed.

The number of people who have used a network before, as this will determine how complicated the network can be.

The layout of the site or sites. If the company is based on more than one site then a WAN would be needed, but if based on only one site they could use a LAN.

(b) A peer-to-peer network is cheaper because no server is needed.

Peer-to-peer networks are simpler to operate so no one person is needed to manage the network.

Peer-to-peer networks are much simpler to set up than client-server networks.

Client-server networks use centralised data, which means that all the users can access the same data. This improves data consistency.

Whether client-server network backups are taken centrally, which means that they are more likely to be done as someone has responsibility for it.

One disadvantage with a client-server network is that if the server breaks down, then it renders the network unusable.

Examiner's comment

1 (a) The first answer gains no marks as this is to do with the size of the organisation.

The second answer is about cost. This again gains no marks. This student has not read and understood the question.

The third answer is valid and gains two marks, as it is much easier to implement a network if the users have already used one.

The fourth answer is good and gains two marks.

(b) All the points the student has made here are correct and they have made reference to features of both systems so full marks here. **(8 marks out of 12)**

Student answer 2

1 (a) The performance required from the network will determine the power of the server that is needed to run a network.

How the system will be used. If the network will be used interactively by all users then the network will need to have a topology and hardware components designed for speed.

Whether the network needs to work with existing systems. A network may already be in place or there may be applications that need to work with the new network or additional network.

Security issues. For financial transactions a very secure network is needed.

(b) Peer-to-peer networks are much cheaper to set up as no expensive central server and no specialist network software are needed.

With a peer-to-peer network the data is not centrally stored, whereas with a client-server network all programs and data are stored centrally.

Client server networks make use of a powerful server at the heart of the system and this server makes the network much faster than most peer-to-peer networks.

With a client-server network, all the security and backup is centrally maintained by the network manager, which means that the process is more rigorous than if it were left to individuals.

Examiner's comment

1 (a) There are no marks for just mentioning the factor but up to two marks for a more detailed explanation. So, for example, if the student had simply said 'performance' they would not get a mark. For an explanation such as 'The performance required from the network' would get the mark.

Two marks each are given for the first three points but the last point only gains one mark because more detail is needed.

(b) Here the student has presented a good list of comparisons. Notice the way the student has actually compared the features. It is much better to do this than just produce a list of the features of each type of network, as with this there is the danger of repetition. There are more than four relevant points made here and the student has made reference to both systems, so full marks are given for this answer. **(11 marks out of 12)**

Examiner's answers

1 (a) Two marks for a complete explanation of each factor. There is no mark for just the factor on its own and the factors must not include either cost or the size of the organisation. Factors such as:

How the system will be used – whether a LAN or WAN will be needed (1) will reflect on how complex the network needs to be (1).

How the network will need to fit in with existing systems – for example, a network may be expanded or have to communicate with another network (1). The organisation may want the network to work with existing hardware or software (1).

What performance is needed from the network – this will determine the hardware needed and the way that it is connected (1).

A high performance server will be needed if heavy network traffic is anticipated (1).

Security issues – how secure the network needs to be (1). This is important if important financial or personal data is to be transferred (1). Methods are needed such as encryption in order to keep the data safe from hackers (1).

(b) One mark each for the following points to a maximum of four:

A client-server has a server which is a more powerful computer (1) whereas all the computers in a peer-to-peer network are of equal status (1).

Peer-to-peer networks are simpler than client-server networks (1) so usually a person such as a network manager is not needed to oversee the network (1).

Client-server networks use centralised storage of data and programs (1), whereas with a peer-to-peer network data is stored all over the peer computers (1).

There is centralised backup with client-server and this improves file security (1), whereas with peer-to-peer networks the backup of data is the responsibility of each user (1).

With client-server there is complete reliance on the server (1), whereas if one computer in a peer-to-peer network breaks down, it may not affect the use of the network (1).

Worked example 2

2 A company is installing a new network. The company has to decide between a ring and a star topology.
   (a) Explain what is meant by the term topology. (2 marks)
   (b) There will be eight computers in their network. Draw sketches to show how the computers will be arranged in a ring network and a star network. (2 marks)
   (c) Explain the relative advantages and disadvantages of a star and a ring network. (6 marks)

Student answer 1

2 (a) A topology is a diagram showing the network.
   (b) Ring network   Star network

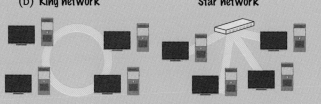

(c) One advantage of the star topology is that if one of the computers fails to work then the other computers can access data.
With the star topology, it is very easy to add extra computers, whereas with the ring network it is more difficult.
With a star topology you can change the communication lines between each computer and the central server. So, if one computer on the network is used for interactive enquiries, a high speed link to the server could be used.
One disadvantage of the star network is that more cable is needed and cable is expensive.

Examiner's comment

2 (a) This answer is not detailed enough as there is no mention that it shows how the computers/terminals or other devices in the network communicate with each other. No marks are given for this answer.

(b) The question clearly mentions that eight computers were being networked so the diagram should include eight computers. The diagrams did, however, show the correct topologies so one mark is awarded here.

(c) There are six marks awarded here, so there need to be six distinctly different points made. The first sentence gains one mark. The second sentence contains a comparison between the two networks and is worth two marks. The next two sentences are worth two marks as the second sentence adds further detail to the first sentence. The final sentence is worth one mark. **(7 marks out of 10)**

Student answer 2

2 (a) The term topology refers to the layout of connected devices on a network. It shows how the devices on the network communicate with each other.

(b) Ring topology

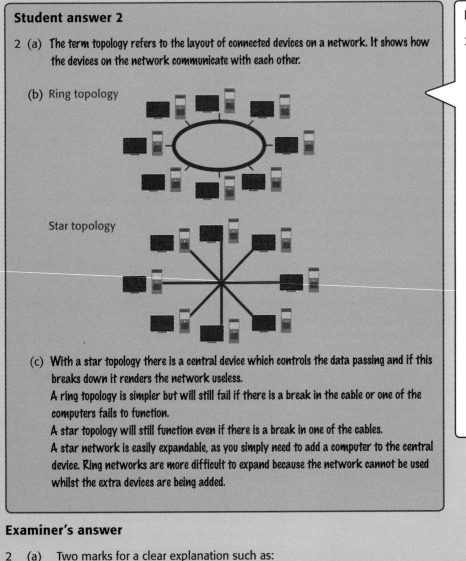

Star topology

(c) With a star topology there is a central device which controls the data passing and if this breaks down it renders the network useless.
A ring topology is simpler but will still fail if there is a break in the cable or one of the computers fails to function.
A star topology will still function even if there is a break in one of the cables.
A star network is easily expandable, as you simply need to add a computer to the central device. Ring networks are more difficult to expand because the network cannot be used whilst the extra devices are being added.

Examiner's comment

2 (a) This answer makes two correct points so is worth two marks.

(b) Both these diagrams showing each network topology are correct and the student was not penalised for not showing a computer/router/switch at the centre of the star network so two marks for this answer.

(c) In the first sentence they should have given the name of the central device which could be a computer/router/switch but this is not penalised here. One mark for this sentence.
There is one mark each for the other four sentences.
(9 marks out of 10)

Examiner's answer

2 (a) Two marks for a clear explanation such as:
A topology is a map of a network showing how the various devices are connected together. They show the way the devices communicate with each other.

(b) For two marks each topology has to be correct showing the correct number of computers.
Correct sketch of ring network showing computers connected in a circle.
Correct sketch of a star network showing the connections radiating out from a central point.

(c) One mark for each point for either topology.
Star networks:
Star networks need an extra hardware device/router/switch/computer at the centre.
If a star network central device fails, the whole network fails.
If a break in cables occurs the star network will still keep working for the other terminals.
With a star network you can use fast lines between terminals that need the increased speed.
Ring networks:
Ring networks are not as fault tolerant, as a break in one cable will cause the entire network to fail.
Cheaper to set up as cable lengths are less.
It is impossible to keep the network running whilst extra terminals are added.
All the computers have equal access to the network so no one computer can 'hog' the network.

Summary mind maps

Factors affecting the choice of a network

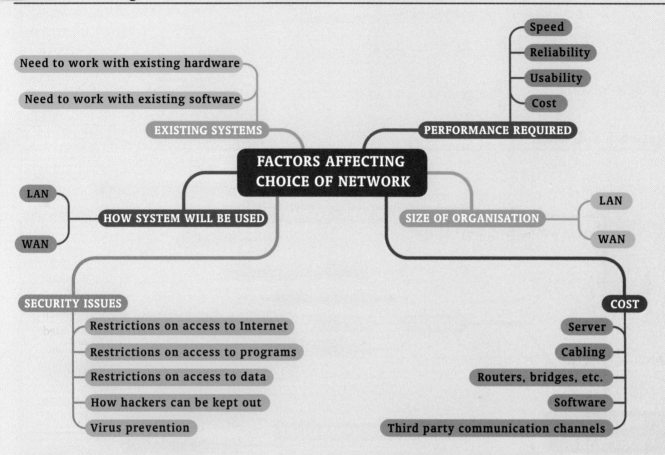

Need to work with existing hardware

Need to work with existing software

EXISTING SYSTEMS

PERFORMANCE REQUIRED
- Speed
- Reliability
- Usability
- Cost

FACTORS AFFECTING CHOICE OF NETWORK

HOW SYSTEM WILL BE USED
- LAN
- WAN

SIZE OF ORGANISATION
- LAN
- WAN

SECURITY ISSUES
- Restrictions on access to Internet
- Restrictions on access to programs
- Restrictions on access to data
- How hackers can be kept out
- Virus prevention

COST
- Server
- Cabling
- Routers, bridges, etc.
- Software
- Third party communication channels

The two types of network

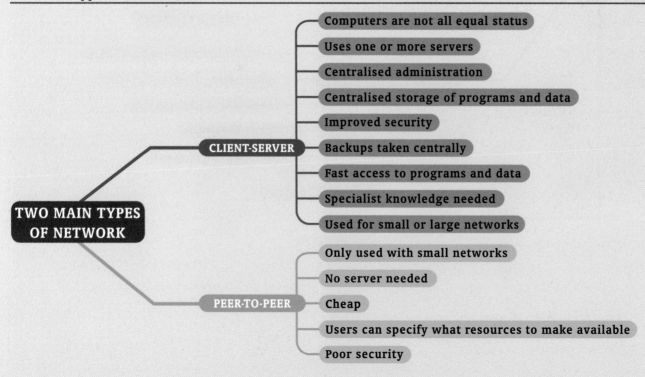

TWO MAIN TYPES OF NETWORK

CLIENT-SERVER
- Computers are not all equal status
- Uses one or more servers
- Centralised administration
- Centralised storage of programs and data
- Improved security
- Backups taken centrally
- Fast access to programs and data
- Specialist knowledge needed
- Used for small or large networks

PEER-TO-PEER
- Only used with small networks
- No server needed
- Cheap
- Users can specify what resources to make available
- Poor security

Network software

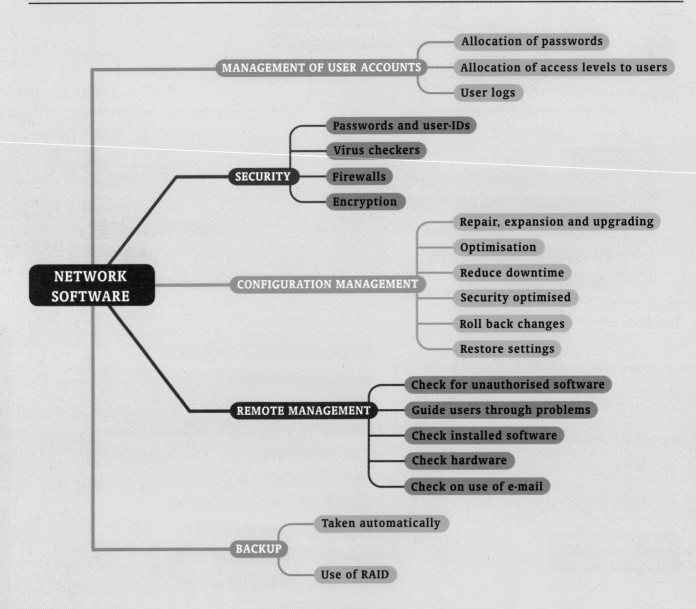

TOPIC 2: The Internet

Over the years the Internet has revolutionised the way we work and play. Internet access is seen as the key to economic development and it is a major source of income for companies.

In this topic you will look at aspects of the Internet, the methods of connection to the Internet and the moral, social and ethical issues associated with Internet use.

▼ The key concepts covered in this topic are:

▶ The impact of the Internet on business

▶ Connecting to the Internet

▶ Moral, social and ethical issues associated with the Internet

CONTENTS

Unit IT3 Use and Impact of ICT

The impact of the Internet on business

▼ **You will find out**

▶ About what the Internet is

▶ About file transfer protocol (FTP)

▶ About e-commerce

▶ About on-line databases

Introduction

There have been huge changes in the way businesses have been run following the introduction of the Internet. The Internet has allowed many new businesses to be started from scratch and many traditional businesses have had to react quickly to the challenges of doing business using the Internet.

In this section you will learn about those features of the Internet which provide benefits for business.

What is the Internet?

You should know about this from your AS work, but here is a definition you can use.

The Internet is a huge group of networks joined together. Each of these networks consists of lots of smaller networks. This means that the Internet consists of hardware.

File transfer protocol (FTP)

If you want to transfer files from one computer to another you can, of course, attach the file to an e-mail and send it as a file attachment. This method is slow and as storage on an ISP's server or other Internet server is limited, you could exceed your limit, which means the file transfer will be rejected.

FTP is used to transmit any type of file: computer programs, text files, graphics, etc., by a process which bunches the data into packages. A package of data is sent and when received, the receiving system checks the package to make sure that no errors have been introduced during transmission. A message is then sent back to the sender system to let it know that the package is OK and that it is ready to receive the next package of data.

When you transfer a music file by downloading it from the Internet onto your own computer, you are using FTP. FTP can be used to download a file from

a server using the Internet, as well as for uploading a file to a server. An example of uploading a file to a server would be putting a webpage or website on a server. FTP is used by companies to distribute information between businesses and other organisations such as their customers and suppliers.

FTP allows files to be transferred using the Internet

The main advantage with using FTP, rather than attaching files to e-mails for transfer, is that you are not limited by file size. FTP allows extremely large files to be transferred whereas with e-mail attachments there is a limit to the file size you can send.

E-commerce

Many people use e-commerce for the purchase of goods such as groceries, books, CDs, electrical goods, etc. In order for a company to implement an interactive on-line shopping service, there are a number of requirements.

Requirements needed to implement an interactive on-line shopping service

The main requirements for an on-line shopping service are:

- Trained staff to create and maintain the website – creating good e-commerce and updating the site with new products, new prices, new features, etc., requires technical expertise and design skills.
- An electronic catalogue/database of stock – the database of stock with a user interface that provides the user with information about products, prices, etc.
- Using the search facility the customer can go straight to the product they are interested in or they can just browse.
- Methods of secure payment/ shopping trolley – customers must be able to add goods to their trolley and then go to the on-line checkout to pay for them. Credit and debit card details need to be kept secure when transmitted over the Internet and encryption is used to ensure that hackers cannot access this information.

Requirements for an on-line shopping service

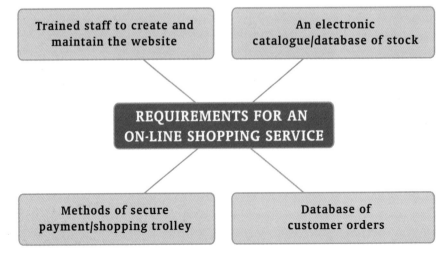

page **20**

- Database of customer orders – this database keeps details on what customers have ordered and is used in case goods need to be returned. It can also be used for repeat orders so the customer does not have to enter all their details in again, thus saving time. The database can also be used to help with the shop's marketing as they know what interests the customer.

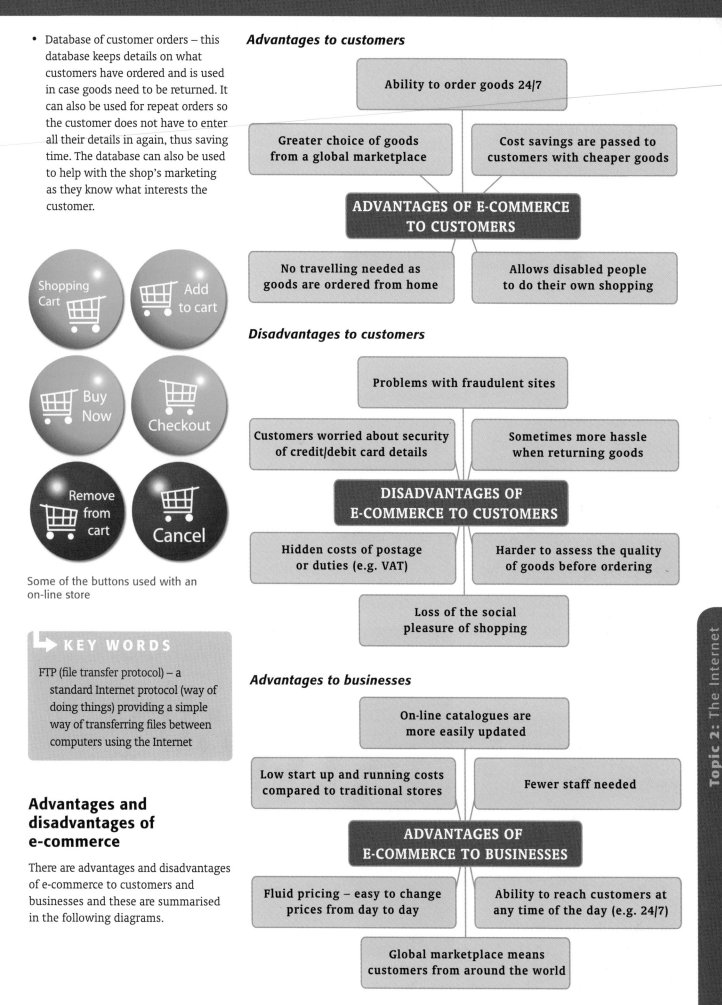

Some of the buttons used with an on-line store

KEY WORDS

FTP (file transfer protocol) – a standard Internet protocol (way of doing things) providing a simple way of transferring files between computers using the Internet

Advantages and disadvantages of e-commerce

There are advantages and disadvantages of e-commerce to customers and businesses and these are summarised in the following diagrams.

Advantages to customers

Ability to order goods 24/7

Greater choice of goods from a global marketplace

Cost savings are passed to customers with cheaper goods

ADVANTAGES OF E-COMMERCE TO CUSTOMERS

No travelling needed as goods are ordered from home

Allows disabled people to do their own shopping

Disadvantages to customers

Problems with fraudulent sites

Customers worried about security of credit/debit card details

Sometimes more hassle when returning goods

DISADVANTAGES OF E-COMMERCE TO CUSTOMERS

Hidden costs of postage or duties (e.g. VAT)

Harder to assess the quality of goods before ordering

Loss of the social pleasure of shopping

Advantages to businesses

On-line catalogues are more easily updated

Low start up and running costs compared to traditional stores

Fewer staff needed

ADVANTAGES OF E-COMMERCE TO BUSINESSES

Fluid pricing – easy to change prices from day to day

Ability to reach customers at any time of the day (e.g. 24/7)

Global marketplace means customers from around the world

The impact of the Internet on business
continued

Disadvantages to businesses

Network downtime can be very expensive

Increased competition from abroad offering cheaper goods

DISADVANTAGE OF E-COMMERCE TO BUSINESSES

Cost of delivery may make goods more expensive

Reliance on third party delivery companies who may be unreliable

On-line databases

A major advantage to a company using a network rather than a series of stand-alone computers is that the users are all able to access the same database, thus avoiding having to duplicate data. Because the data is constantly being modified, it will always be up-to-date.

Being able to interact with databases is therefore an important service provided by any network. E-commerce systems make use of on-line databases containing products, customer and order details. Electronic data interchange (EDI), where companies automatically exchange data, is used by large retailers for ordering goods automatically from their suppliers. This system performs ordering, checking and making payments, automatically without requiring any paperwork.

How to access on-line information

There are three main ways of finding your way around the Internet and these are:

1 Use the Uniform Resource Locator (URL): if you know the web

address (URL) of a site you can simply type it in. If you do not know the address of the sites of interest, then you can buy books (called directories) or buy one of the popular Internet magazines that contain them. Internet addresses are now as much a part of a company's identity as their phone or fax numbers and they nearly always feature in their advertisements.

2 Surf the Internet by following hyperlinks: you can surf the Internet, which means that you are using hyperlinks to move from one area of interest to another. These hypertext links are either in the form of text underlined or in a different colour on which you click to move to that site. In this way the users move from one site to another. If you are a website designer then you need to make sure that there are plenty of links to your site that will mean you are likely to attract a greater number of 'surfers'.

3 Use a search engine: you can use a special program, called a search engine, where you can enter certain key words or subject matter names and the program will search for those sites containing information containing these key words. Because of the huge extent of the material contained in the Internet, it can be quite difficult to know how to construct searches to narrow them down.

There are a variety of search engines in use and these include:

Google: http://www.google.com
Alta Vista: http://www.altavista.com
Yahoo: http://www.yahoo.com
Lycos: http://www.lycos.com

The URL is used to identify uniquely a webpage on the Internet

How a search engine works

Before a search engine can find information, it needs to store information about all the webpages stored on the Internet. There are hundreds of millions of webpages stored, so this is not an easy task but it is not done manually. Instead, a web browser called a web crawler (sometimes also called a web spider) automatically follows all the links it can find and then each webpage it comes across is analysed for content such as headings and sub-headings, key words, etc., to see how it should be indexed. This index is stored in a database. The data the web crawler finds about each webpage is added to this index.

When a search engine is used to perform a search using a number of key words, the search engine examines the index for these words and produces a list of the webpages which have the best match.

Usually as well as the title of the webpage some brief details about the content of the webpage are given. Many search engines rank the pages by relevance to the search condition with those with the greatest relevance being listed first.

Web crawler

A web crawler, also known as a web spider, is a program that automatically browses all webpages in a systematic manner. It does this to provide up-to-date data about webpages in order to produce an index which can be used by a search engine to enable fast searches.

How webpages are added to search engine lists

There are a number of ways by which webpages are added to a search engine list and it depends on the search engine being used. Generally a search engine will rank the webpages a particular search produces according to the following:

- the most relevant match to the search condition
- the most popular site
- the most authoritative site
- the ability of a company to pay for a higher ranking (not all search engines allow this).

You can search for images as well as text

Boolean searches

Don't be put off by the name. Boolean searches help you save time searching for information so they are worth knowing about. When you do a simple search you may be overwhelmed by all the information. Boolean searches help you narrow down a search.

AND

If you type in the search **USA AND flag** you will get all those documents that contain both words.

If you just type in **USA Flag** you will still get all those documents that contain both words. With most search engines you do not need to type the 'and' between the words.

AND means 'I want **only** documents that contain **both** words'.

OR

If you type in the search **USA OR flag** then you will get all the documents containing the word **USA**, all the documents containing the word **flag** and all those documents that contain both words.

OR means 'I want documents that contain either word. I don't care which word.'

NOT

Suppose you want to search for information about different pets but you can't stand cats. You can exclude cats like this: **Pets NOT cats**
If you wanted to search for information about pets in general but not information about cats, then you type in: **Pets NOT cats**

Searching for an exact match

If you want an exact match of words (i.e. the words side-by-side and in the same order), then put quotation marks around the words like this: '*Recipe for a chocolate chip cookie*'.

Searching for a quotation

If you know the exact wording of the quotation, you can type it into the search engine. To get the exact match you need to put quotation marks around the words like this: '*I have a dream*'.

Choosing the information to use

When you search for information you usually get too much of it. In deciding what information to use and what not to use, you need to ask the following questions:

- Is the information relevant for the purpose?
- Is the source of the information reliable?
- Is the information accurate (i.e., can it be checked)?
- Is the information unbiased?
- Is the information precise?
- Is the information appropriate for the intended audience?

> ### KEY WORDS
>
> URL (uniform resource locator) – the web address used to locate a webpage or website
>
> Search engine – software that can be used to search for information on the Internet

The impact of the Internet on business
continued

Distributed computing using the Internet

One main problem in collecting data is that there is so much of it to analyse. Analysing large amounts of data requires a lot of computer power and this power may not be available because of the cost.

In many cases this problem can be solved by using distributed computing using the Internet. Here, instead of using a huge expensive supercomputer to do the job, it could be done using a few less powerful computers connected together using the Internet but with each working on the same problem. In many cases computers just sit around not doing much for most of the time so why not use their processing power?

Some distributed systems ask home users to contribute some of their computing resources. For example, there is climate change research going on at the moment that requires a huge amount of data processing. Home users can contribute some of their wasted computer time to this project.

Distributed computing is a very useful tool for scientists who have huge amounts of data to analyse when trying to model systems such as the Earth's climate

Advantages of distributed computing

- reduces cost because an expensive powerful computer such as a supercomputer is not needed
- can pass work to computers anywhere in the world using the Internet
- improved performance as each computer can work on part of the data.

Disadvantage of distributed computing

- issues with the security of data spread out on so many different computers.

The SETI (Search for Extraterrestrial Intelligence) project

The purpose of the SETI project is to search for intelligent life outside the Earth and to do this a radio telescope like the one shown in the photo is used. Radio telescopes pick up radio signals from outer space. If the signals were confined to a narrow range of frequencies, then this would provide evidence of extraterrestrial life.

The problem the project has is that there is a lot of background noise which includes radio signals from TV stations, radar, satellites and from celestial sources. It is very difficult to analyse the data from radio telescopes and look for other signals that could indicate extraterrestrial life.

In order to search for the narrow-bandwidth signals lots of computing power is needed. At first supercomputers containing parallel processors were used to process the huge amount of data from the telescopes. Then someone came up with the idea of using a virtual supercomputer consisting of a huge number of Internet-connected home computers. The project was then named SETI@home and it has been running since 1999.

At the time of writing the SETI@home project uses 170,000 active volunteers around the world and uses 320,000 computers but even with this power they still need more!

Popular Power project: helping to develop flu vaccines

The Popular Power project is a non-profit making research project to help develop an influenza (flu) vaccine. The system made use of a computer model which modelled the human immune system and simulations were performed to see how different vaccines might perform. The trouble is that these viruses mutate, so a vaccine that works one year might not work the next year.

Since the project started thousands of home PCs have completed millions of tasks, which is like one very powerful computer spending hundreds of years on the problem.

The SETI Home project solved the problem of processing mounds of data by sharing the processing with home computers via the Internet

The Allen Telescope array is a series of 42 radio telescopes which collect signals from far-away galaxies and feed the data to the SETI project

EXAM TIP

Do not get distributed computing mixed up with distributed databases. In distributed computing the processing is shared across many different computers, whereas in distributed databases the data stored is spread across several servers mainly for the advantages of speed of access as well as improved security.

Performing simulations to find a vaccine to prevent flu is an important application of distributed processing using the Internet

Connecting to the Internet

▼ You will find out

▶ About cable access to the Internet

▶ About connection using a dialup modem

▶ About broadband

▶ About mobile access to the Internet

Introduction

There are a number of ways you can connect to the Internet: by cable or wirelessly. The method you use will affect the speed with which pages appear, files are downloaded, etc.

Cable access to the Internet

There are two ways of connecting to the Internet; dialup or broadband. In the UK we are ahead of the majority of countries in the world by having most people connected to the Internet by a fast broadband connection. For some people in this country and in many other countries, slow dialup modem connection to the Internet is the norm.

Dialup modem

Using a dialup modem to connect to the Internet is very slow and this limits its use. If you have used broadband and then use a dialup connection, you will notice it is frustratingly slow. In fact it limits your use of the Internet. Downloads that would have taken minutes can take the best part of an hour.

Dialup uses a modem which converts the digital signals into a series of sounds which are then passed along a telephone line. The sound signal is converted back to a digital signal, which the computer is able to understand, at the other end of the wire.

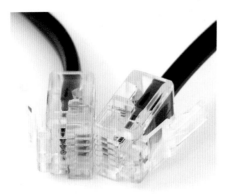

A telephone extension cable is used to connect the computer to the Internet using a dialup connection

Transferring data using a dialup modem is like transferring water along a narrow pipe with a tap on it. The narrowness of the pipe means that it is hard to get a lot of water through it. The tap means that to make the water flow you have to turn the tap on.

With broadband the pipe is much fatter, so lots of water can flow. The water flows all the time so you do not have to wait for the tap to be turned on.

Broadband

Broadband gives much faster access and transfer speeds to the Internet and allows you to watch on-line video, download files quickly, listen to on-line radio, watch TV programmes you have missed and so on. None of these would be possible without a fast broadband connection.

Advantages of broadband

The use of broadband has many advantages such as:

- Fast download times mean music and films and large multimedia files can be downloaded quickly.
- Does not tie up your phone line, so others can use the phone while you are on-line.

- Can listen to radio, watch full screen video, watch TV programmes, play on-line fast action games in almost real time.
- Search engines work much faster, saving you time when you are searching for information.
- No time wasted trying to connect to the Internet.
- Always on, so it is quick for programs such as virus checkers to update their files automatically.
- Web cams and videoconferencing can be used.
- Cheap phone calls can be made using the Internet.

Disadvantages of broadband

There are not many disadvantages of broadband but here are some:

- Expensive owing to a higher monthly subscription for the service.
- Broadband may not be available in the area or country where you are.

Broadband offers fast download times which are essential when downloading large files

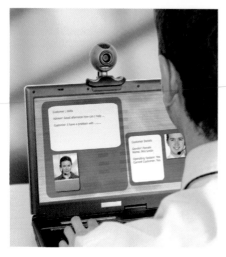

The use of web cams is only feasible with a broadband connection

Mobile access to the Internet

Many people have to travel around as part of their work, so they need to have mobile access to their e-mails and the Internet. There are many devices that offer mobile access to the Internet and these include:

- laptop computers
- PDAs
- mobile phones.

There are a number of advantages and disadvantages to mobile access to the Internet and these are covered in the following sections.

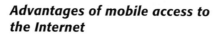

Advantages of mobile access to the Internet

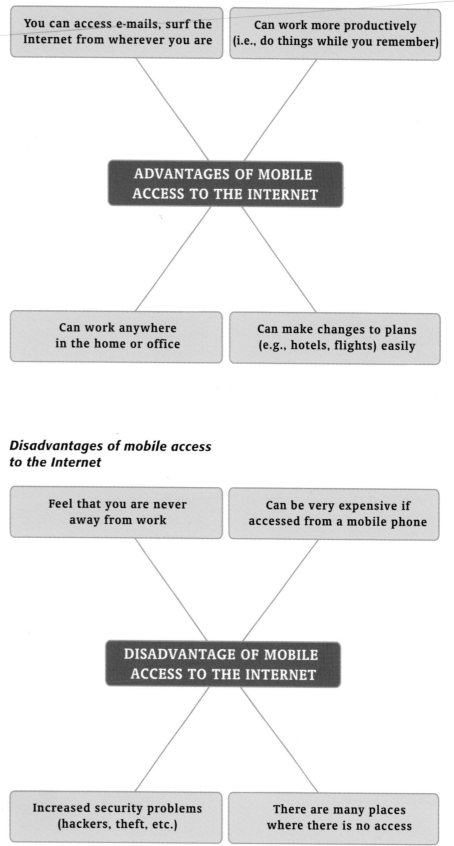

You can access e-mails, surf the Internet from wherever you are

Can work more productively (i.e., do things while you remember)

ADVANTAGES OF MOBILE ACCESS TO THE INTERNET

Can work anywhere in the home or office

Can make changes to plans (e.g., hotels, flights) easily

Disadvantages of mobile access to the Internet

Feel that you are never away from work

Can be very expensive if accessed from a mobile phone

DISADVANTAGE OF MOBILE ACCESS TO THE INTERNET

Increased security problems (hackers, theft, etc.)

There are many places where there is no access

Moral, social and ethical issues associated with the Internet

Introduction

The use of the Internet by individuals and organisations has raised a number of issues that need to be considered such as moral, social and ethical issues.

Moral issues

There are a number of moral issues associated with use of the Internet and these include:

- Deliberately setting up websites containing incorrect information – people may rely on and use this information thinking it is correct.
- Bullying – in chat rooms, by e-mail, in blogs, by text message is a problem especially for the young.
- Inappropriate websites – people are able to view inappropriate material such as pornography, racism, violent videos, how to make explosives, etc.
- Using e-mail to give bad news (e.g., redundancy, demotion, firing, etc.) when explaining face-to-face would have been better.
- Spreading rumours – it is easy to spread rumours using the Internet. You only have to tell a few people in a chat room and the rumour will soon spread. Normally, if someone started a rumour that was untrue and it caused another person distress, then the person starting the rumour could be sued. When rumours are started over the Internet it is difficult to identify the person responsible.

Ethical issues

Ethical issues are those issues which are not necessarily illegal but are dubious such as:

- Plagiarism – copying material without attributing or referencing the source of the information. This could also involve using websites which sell essays or coursework.
- Sending spam (i.e., the same advertising e-mail to millions of people) – people waste time deleting spam if the spam filter allows it through.
- Companies monitoring staff use of the Internet and e-mail. Some organisations will even read personal e-mails.
- Using someone's wireless Internet connection without permission. Sometimes it is possible to connect to the Internet using an open network. The net result of using the network is to slow the network down for legitimate users.
- Using photo editing software to distort reality – by using photo/ video editing software you can distort reality and you can no longer believe what you see in video, TV, newspapers, magazines and on websites.

Social issues

Social issues affect the way society functions and the Internet can be said to cause a number of problems such as:

- Privacy issues – social networking sites, e-commerce sites, Internet service provider records, e-mail monitoring at work, etc., all erode a user's privacy.
- Gambling addiction – gambling can cause many social problems and it is on the rise with the ease with which bets can be made using the Internet.
- Obesity – many activities in the past involved physical exercise which kept people healthy. Use of the Internet for long periods of time is not a healthy activity.
- Addiction to computer games – many children spend hours playing computer games and their social skills and schoolwork can suffer as a result.

Copyright 2005 by Randy Glasbergen.
www.glasbergen.com

"**We found someone overseas who can drink coffee and talk about sports all day for a fraction of what we're paying you.**"

- Widens the gaps between the haves and have nots – Internet access widens the gap between rich and poor countries and individuals.
- Organisations moving call centres abroad – because the wage bill is less and the same service can be provided cheaply using the Internet and Internet phone links.
- The growth of e-commerce may mean shops have to close, leaving some city centres looking desolate.

Ownership and control of the Internet

The Internet is for everybody and no-one actually owns it. There is little control over the content of the material on the Internet, although some governments have started to control what can be seen on it. There is also no control over the people who can access the material on the Internet. This means that unless special software is used, children can easily gain access to pornographic or violent images.

The lack of 'policing' of the Internet also means that the information is not checked to make sure that it is accurate. It is therefore up to the users of the Internet to check the material's accuracy. When you are using information off the Internet you need to be able to check the material for its suitability and accuracy.

The availability of offensive, illegal or unethical material on the Internet

There are a lot of pornographic images/videos on the Internet. There are laws covering the production and distribution of this material but as much of this material comes from other countries, where the material is perfectly legal, there is not much that can be done to stop it. The main worry adults have is that young children could accidentally access this material. There is special software that is able to filter out this material but it is hard to be completely sure.

What is really worrying is that paedophiles use the Internet for distributing pornographic pictures of young children and they also lure children into meetings with them after they have spoken to them in chat rooms. You therefore need to be extremely careful arranging any meetings with anyone that you have spoken to on-line.

Material does not have to be pornographic to be offensive. An image of a pack of hounds attacking a fox may not be offensive to the members of a hunt but it could be offensive to animal lovers. Whether material is offensive or not can depend on the person. There is, of course, material that almost everybody would find offensive.

Censorship

Many countries in the world are not democratic and the people in charge of these countries do not allow the free passage of information to and from these countries. They often control the media (newspapers, TV and radio stations) so that they only allow news which shows the government in a favourable light. Censorship of the Internet by government allows them more control on what their people can and cannot view.

Effects on communities

The Internet affects us all and communities benefit by the use of the Internet. Here are some of the positive ways communities are affected:

- Blogs and chats can be set up to allow communities to discuss local issues such as planning, problem gangs and other policing issues, community events, etc.
- Housebound members of the community are less isolated as people contact them to check everything is ok.
- Opportunities for employment can be advertised within the community on local websites.
- Local citizens advice websites can be set up to deal with the problems residents have.

Negative effects on communities include:

- Lack of social interaction – people spend time browsing the Internet, playing computer games and communicating with 'cyber' friends rather than spending time with people in the community.
- Local shops shutting – more orders for goods are placed using the Internet so local shops close.

Censorship means the practice of censoring. This involves checking content and removing some or all undesirable material (e.g., material government wants to keep secret, and violent or sexually explicit material)

Case studies and Activities

▶ Case study 1 pp. 24–25

How home computers can help scientists better understand the mysteries of the universe

There is a project at the University of Illinois in America that is using distributed computing across the Internet to better understand the universe. Because of the computing power and bandwidth requirements for this huge project, the project designers have asked home computer users for their help with this research.

The project is called Cosmology@Home and is similar to the SETI@Home project. When a home user runs Cosmology@Home on their home computer, it uses part of the computer's processing power, disk space and bandwidth to help with the project.

Basically the university has cosmological models that describe how the universe works and the task is to find which of these models best describes the huge amount of experimental data from particle physics experiments and astronomical measurements. The parameters in the models are changed to compare the theoretical predictions with what actually happens.

1 Explain what is meant by each of the following terms:
   (a) Distributed computing (2 marks)
   (b) Bandwidth (1 mark)
   (c) Computer model. (2 marks)
2 In this project, home computer users have been asked for their help.
   (a) Give one reason why it was not possible to run the model using the university's own computing facilities. (1 mark)

(b) State two computing resources a home computer gives to this project. (1 mark)
(c) Explain why the cosmology model requires so much computing power. (2 marks)
3 Compare and contrast the advantages and disadvantages in using either a dialup or broadband connection to access the Internet. (4 marks)
4 There are many scientific experiments going on which rely on distributed computing.

(a) Explain what distributed computing is and describe two reasons why it is used when analysing the results from large-scale scientific experiments. (4 marks)
(b) Describe one application for distributed computing. In your description you should make clear the reasons for using distributed computing and the advantages it brings. (4 marks)

▶ Case study 2 pp. 28–29

A problem caused by an Internet message board

Around 500 Internet yobs trashed a 14 year old's birthday party at a church hall.

A teenager was about to celebrate her 14th birthday with family and friends when around 500 drunken youths turned up and gate-crashed the party.

Unbeknown to the young girl, a message about the party turned up on an Internet party message board.

The young girl and her friends and family were distraught as people smashed bottles, vomited, and smashed doors. The police were called and five patrol cars were needed to help quell the drunken youths. The police arrested four of the youths for being drunk and disorderly.

1 The example in the case study shows the problems caused by the free passage of information on the Internet.
   (a) Explain what is meant by an Internet message board. (2 marks)

(b) Some message boards are moderated by the Internet service provider.
   Explain how this would have helped prevent this situation. (1 mark)

2 Free passage of information can create problems for society. Describe a different situation where problems for society have been created by the free passage of information using ICT systems such as the Internet. (3 marks)

▶ Case study 3 | pp. 28–29

Rwanda has its sights on becoming the ICT centre of Africa

Rwanda, a country in Africa, is trying to become the centre of IT in Africa. This is despite the fact that it is a very poor country compared to its near, more wealthy neighbours that have wealth due to oil, diamonds and copper.

The government in Rwanda wants to change from an agriculture-based economy to a knowledge-based economy. Two fibre optic rings circle the capital and another cable has been laid across the country.

Rwanda is one of the least-developed countries but its leaders see high-tech as the best way of trying to compete globally. Others, however, disagree and feel that the money should be spent more on necessities such as electricity for everybody in the country.

The future does look bright because nearly 70% of the population can read and they all speak the same language, which makes establishing a web presence easier.

Rwanda hopes to import cheap refurbished computers and since in some places there is little electricity, they intend to use low power computers with batteries that can be recharged using free solar power.

The aim is to have many of the computers in telecentres with broadband connections to the Internet. This would enable some Rwandans to find business opportunities, some to find jobs, and farmers to find out how to grow better crops. For the people who cannot read or write, ICT can be used to help them learn to read and write.

Some people inside the country think the whole idea is wrong, saying that you cannot build a school for a student to study at before you give them something to eat. Other people say that providing the infrastructure means the private sector will invest and this will benefit everyone.

1 Access the CIA website World Factbook using the following web address:
https://www.cia.gov/library/publications/the-world-factbook/index.html
Type in or select the country Rwanda. Use the information contained on the webpages to fill in the details in the column for Rwanda.
Now obtain the figures for the UK and fill in the other column.
Write a short paragraph about the differences you have spotted between a poorly developed country, Rwanda, and the much more developed and technologically advanced UK. (5 marks)

Question	Rwanda	UK
Population		
Life expectancy (male)		
Life expectancy (female)		
Literacy of whole population		
Gross domestic product (GDP) per capita (i.e. per person)		
Telephone (main lines)		
Telephone (mobile)		
Internet hosts (i.e. ISPs)		
Number of Internet users		

2 (a) Describe **three** ways in which the use of the Internet would help some of Rwanda's population. (3 marks)
  (b) Give **one** reason why not all the population may benefit by access to the Internet. (1 mark)
3 Do you think this investment in ICT is good for Rwanda? Give a brief reason for your answer. (2 marks)

▶ Case study 4 | pp. 28–29

Chinese Web filtering

In certain countries, such as China, the government uses a firewall that filters out access to sites that they do not allow, which are usually sites that criticise the government or present the country in an undesirable way. The firewall blocks banned subjects, certain Web addresses and certain words.

Many people are worried that if they try to use these words or websites the government could identify who they are and then take action against them.

1 Web filtering is often done in schools or by the parents of young children. Give two reasons why this is necessary. (2 marks)

2 (a) Give **one** reason why Web filtering is performed by the Chinese authorities. (2 marks)
  (b) Give the name of the device/software that is used to block access to certain content using the Internet. (1 mark)

Case studies and Activities *continued*

▶ Case study 5 | pp. 28–29

On-line essay banks fail students

Students too busy or lazy to write their own essays, assignments or coursework may turn to the Internet for help.

Students have always been adept at cutting and pasting material from websites to cobble essays together and then pass it off as their own work. Luckily many education institutions have special software which can spot plagiarism and this software searches the Internet for sentences the same as the ones used.

Some students get around this by paying someone to produce an original piece of work for them. Buying custom work like this is clearly cheating. Apart from the ethical issues, there is the problem that the quality of the work bought is quite poor and unlikely to get anything like the grade promised.

One student who bought as essay which got an 'F' grade said, 'It was such a waste of money – I am never going to do that again'.

1 Give **two** reasons why essay banks could be considered to be unethical. **(2 marks)**

2 Describe **one** way in which the use of essay banks could affect society as a whole. **(1 mark)**

3 Do you think that essay banks should be made illegal? Give a reason for your answer. **(2 marks)**

▶ Activity 1: The Internet and human rights

There is a website set up by an organisation called 'Human Rights Watch' and on this you will find details of all the human rights abuses around the world.

The web address of this site is: www.hrw.org. Take a look at the site to see the extent of the problem in other countries.

There is a site that looks at the rights and liberties people should enjoy when using the Internet. The site is: www.cyber-rights.org/

Use search conditions with various search engines to find other websites that cover human rights and the Internet. You could use a multiple search condition like this: 'human rights' AND 'Internet'. If you find any good sites, then write down their web addresses and include them in your work.

Write a short summary about the way some governments in countries around the world do not allow their citizens full access to Internet services.

▶ Activity 2: The SETI project

For this activity you are required to produce a short summary on the latest use of distributed computing for the SETI project. The website where you can find the information is at:
  http://setiathome.berkeley.edu/

▶ Activity 3: The climate model

For this activity you are required to write a short explanation on how distributed computing is used to help with climate research. The information you need for this paragraph can be found at the following website:
http://www.bbc.co.uk/sn/climateexperiment/theexperiment/distributedcomputing.shtml

Questions

1   A person is using a modem at present but because they spend a lot of time using the Internet they would like to be able to surf the Internet faster.
   (a) Explain what the term 'surf the Internet' means. (1 mark)
   (b) Explain why broadband would be better than using a modem. (2 marks)
   (c) Broadband offers 'video on demand'. Explain what this means. (2 marks)
   (d) Give the names of **two** things that can be done using broadband that would be difficult to do using a connection via a modem. (4 marks)
   (e) Why is bandwidth so important when you are transferring large files from place to place? (2 marks)

2   A company sets up a website to advertise its products and to allow customers to place on-line orders.
   (a) Describe **two** methods by which a customer could find the website using the Internet. (4 marks)
   (b) Once the customer has found the company's website they then have to find the products they are interested in. Outline **two** ways they could quickly find this information. (4 marks)

3   The Internet can be used by organisations for all sorts of purposes.
   Explain, by giving an example, how each of the following could be used by an organisation:
   (a) File transfer protocol (FTP) (2 marks)
   (b) On-line databases (2 marks)
   (c) E-commerce. (2 marks)

4   Discuss the various methods for connecting to the Internet. In your discussion you should discuss the methods and associated advantages and disadvantages. (4 marks)

5   It is possible to access information from on-line databases in a number of ways.
   Briefly describe how each of the following can be used to access information:
   (a) URLs (2 marks)
   (b) Boolean searches (2 marks)
   (c) Hyperlinks. (2 marks)

6   (a) In order for a company to implement an interactive on-line shopping service there are a number of requirements. State **three** requirements and for each one, describe why it is needed. (3 marks)
   (b) Discuss the advantages and disadvantages of e-commerce to
      (i) a customer
      (ii) the business. (4 marks)

7   (a) Explain the purpose of a search engine. (2 marks)
   (b) Explain how a search engine works and how webpages are added to search engine lists. (4 marks)

8   Discuss the advantages and disadvantages of mobile access to the Internet. (4 marks)

9   Many large research projects make use of distributed computing using the Internet.
   (a) Explain what is meant by distributed computing. (3 marks)
   (b) Describe an application you know about where distributed computing is used. Make sure that you state clearly why distributed processing was chosen in the application you are describing. (6 marks)

10 A newspaper article states 'there is no ownership or control of the Internet'.
   Produce a convincing argument either way, discussing, with suitable examples, whether you consider this statement to be true or false.
   (NB You can agree or disagree and you will be marked on the strength of your arguments.)
   (6 marks)

Exam support

Worked example 1

1 The use of the Internet causes major moral, social and ethical issues. Other than crime, outline **two** of the above issues giving **two** appropriate examples to help explain the issues. (8 marks)

Student answer 1

1   A social effect of use of the Internet is that stores are closing down on the high streets, owing to people choosing to buy goods over the Internet. Many cities will have lots of closed down shops such as travel agents, bookstores, etc. People will lose their jobs and local economies will suffer. Also there will be nothing to do on a Saturday because you cannot go to the shops.
There are lots of websites with incorrect information so young children will be given wrong information when they do projects. Young children will not be able to question whether information is correct or not and I think these sites should be banned.

Examiner's comment

1 The student should have looked at the marks allocated for this question. As there are 8 marks the student should have read the question carefully and given a more comprehensive answer.
They have to explain two issues from; social, ethical or moral. This student looks as though they have read the question to mean that they have to cover only two problems and not cover several problems for two issues. Again and again reading and understanding the question is essential to maximise marks, even if you can only answer part of the question.
The student's answer was OK for the parts they covered but they needed to write about some other problems so lack of coverage has limited their marks.
(4 marks out of 8)

Examiner's answer

1   The students should cover a range of the following:
Widening economic gap between haves and have-nots
Effects on communities of shops closing owing to e-commerce/Internet
Censorship of the Internet by foreign governments
Privacy issues (cameras, details recorded, invasion of government into everyday life, etc.)
Plagiarism (buying coursework, essay banks, copying straight from websites)
Addictions to chat rooms, gaming and gambling

Student answer 2

1   There are many ethical issues. For example, it is almost impossible for a person to have any privacy. There is more involvement by the state in everyday life. Identity cards, phone companies keeping call details, ISPs keeping e-mail details, cameras monitoring you as you walk down the street or use your car all erode privacy. Face recognition systems can identify you and even schools are using fingerprints to recognise pupils.
Another ethical issue is the spread of the call centre, where people often have to work for low pay and sometimes these call centres are moved abroad simply because they cost less to run. Should this be allowed when the jobs should be retained in this country?
Some students now use essay banks to copy bits of essays from and combine with bits of their own so as to get good marks which is not fair. Some children can buy GCSE coursework on-line from Internet auction sites.
One social issue is that the use of the Internet widens the gap between the haves and the have nots. People cannot shop online unless they have a credit or debit card and people with low incomes or poor credit history cannot get these. The haves can also take advantage of Internet special offers which people without the Internet do not have access to.

Examiner's comment

1 In this answer the student has explained the following problems: privacy, job losses to abroad, plagiarism and the widening gap between members of society.
The student has given examples where relevant and has constructed their answers well and has used accurate spelling, punctuation and grammar.
They have used the correct terminology in their answer.
(8 marks out of 8)

Lack of social interaction (e.g., have virtual friends rather than real friends)

Websites which deliberately set out to misinform or deceive

Problems with copyright issues/intellectual property

Inappropriate websites that promote terrorism, suicide, racial hatred

Using the Internet and social networking sites to bully others

Spreading rumours in blogs or in chat rooms

6–8 marks Candidates give a clear, coherent answer fully and accurately describing and explaining at least three issues giving relevant examples. They use appropriate terminology and accurate spelling, punctuation and grammar.

3–5 marks Candidates give explanations to a range of issues, but responses lack clarity or relevant examples. There are a few errors in spelling, punctuation and grammar.

0–2 marks Candidates simply list up to three issues or give a brief explanation of one or two issues. The response lacks clarity and there are significant errors in spelling, punctuation and grammar.

Worked example 2

2 A new completely on-line store is being created which offers designer goods cheaper than the high street stores.

   (a) The on-line store offers an interactive shopping experience for customers and a high level of customer service. Outline in detail four requirements, other than hardware, in order to successfully implement this system. **(4 marks)**

   (b) Give two advantages to the shop in on-line shopping. **(2 marks)**

   (c) Give two advantages to the customer in on-line shopping. **(2 marks)**

   (d) Describe two potential problems a customer might have when shopping on-line. **(2 marks)**

Student answer 1

2 (a) Website design software will be needed to both create the website and to keep the content up-to-date, add new pages, etc. Website design staff will be needed who have the technical knowledge and design skills to create a good website that will attract customers and who will keep the website up-to-date.

There must be a connection to the Internet.

   (b) They do not need premises

The shop makes more money

   (c) You can shop from home which means you do not have the expense of petrol or parking and you do not have to waste time looking for goods that you want to buy that the stores do not have in stock.

The customer can often save money as it is much easier to browse for the cheapest item or use one of the price comparison sites. Also, stores frequently have Internet only offers which are only available to on-line customers.

   (d) It is a lot of hassle buying clothes over the Internet as you cannot try them on and then if they don't fit you have to waste time queuing at the Post Office to send them back. Sometimes when you buy goods from abroad you think you are getting a bargain but then when they come into the country, customs add some duty on them which has to be paid before they are delivered. They can then end up costing you the same or more than buying them in this country.

Examiner's comment

2 (a) For each mark the student needs to describe in detail a requirement. The first two requirements have been explained in sufficient detail for a mark each. The third requirement is simply a statement of the requirement which lacks detail, so no marks for this.

There is no fourth requirement.

   (b) 'They do not need premises' is not strictly true. They still need premises but they do not need the size of premises nor do the premises have to be situated on the expensive high street. No marks for this.

'The shop makes more money' is too vague – the shop could make more money in lots of different ways. If the student had added 'by employing fewer staff than a traditional store' or 'by having smaller overheads', they would have got this mark.

   (c) The two advantages have been well described and are worth two marks.

   (d) These are two very good answers, so full marks here.

(6 marks out of 10)

Exam support *continued*

Student answer 2

2 (a) Software will be needed to create the website for the shop.
Suitably qualified people will be needed who have specialist knowledge of setting up websites.
A connection will be needed to the Internet which could be provided as a specialist Internet server or could be provided by another company such as BT or Virgin.

(b) People come to you so it is easier.
They can make more money than a shop.

(c) They do not have to leave the house so it is much less time consuming than traditional shopping.
Savings can be made as it is much easier to shop around on the Internet to get the best price.

(d) They may have trouble getting their money back if the goods are faulty.
They may not get the same customer service as they would do with a traditional shop.

Examiner's comment

2 (a) These are three suitable points and have been suitably described for one mark each.

(b) The student has not made it clear what the first point refers to, so no marks for this part of the answer. The second point is not necessarily true – many traditional stores are more profitable than on-line stores, so no marks for this.

(c) Two good points have been made here so two marks.

(d) The first point is not strictly true as the law protects the consumer for on-line and traditional stores.
The second point is given a mark although it is a little vague.

(6 marks out of 10)

Examiner's answer

2 (a) Four requirements (one mark each) such as:
An Internet service provider (ISP)
Maintaining a company website (experienced staff with website knowledge)
A catalogue of stock in the form of a database
Methods for secure payment (shopping trolley/basket, checkout, etc.)
A database of customer orders

(b) Two advantages (two marks each) such as:
Lower overheads than high street stores – no expensive high street premises, store detectives, etc.
Can reach customers in any part of the country or the world for a relatively small cost
Fewer employees need to be employed as many of the ICT systems are automatic
Can link the e-commerce system to other systems such as accounts, stock control, etc., to save on administration costs

(c) Two advantages (one mark each) such as:
People who live in isolated rural areas will now have access to those products only available in large cities
Disabled or elderly people can shop for goods without leaving their home
Delivery firms will do well owing to the increase in goods being sent direct to people's homes
Fewer trips to shops will be made thus reducing the congestion and pollution in towns and cities
Shopping will take less time and this will free people to do other things

(d) Two problems (one mark each) such as:
Bogus sites may be set up to obtain money from customers so it is hard for customers to tell if a site which they have not heard of before is genuine
Some Internet shopping sites are poor on customer service and it is not always easy to return or change goods
Shops in city centres may become empty owing to increased competition so staff can become unemployed
People often like to browse and meet others when shopping

Summary mind maps

The advantages of e-commerce to customers and businesses

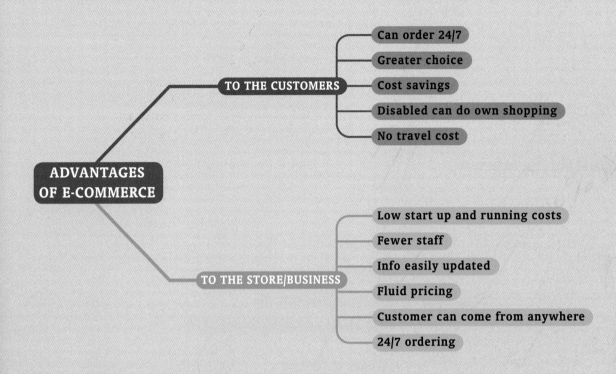

ADVANTAGES OF E-COMMERCE

TO THE CUSTOMERS
- Can order 24/7
- Greater choice
- Cost savings
- Disabled can do own shopping
- No travel cost

TO THE STORE/BUSINESS
- Low start up and running costs
- Fewer staff
- Info easily updated
- Fluid pricing
- Customer can come from anywhere
- 24/7 ordering

The disadvantages of e-commerce to customers and businesses

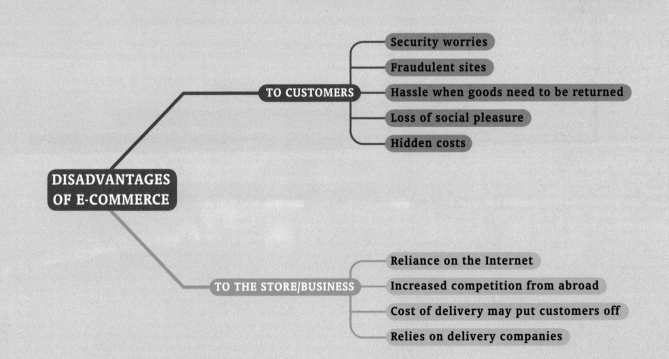

DISADVANTAGES OF E-COMMERCE

TO CUSTOMERS
- Security worries
- Fraudulent sites
- Hassle when goods need to be returned
- Loss of social pleasure
- Hidden costs

TO THE STORE/BUSINESS
- Reliance on the Internet
- Increased competition from abroad
- Cost of delivery may put customers off
- Relies on delivery companies

Ways of accessing the Internet

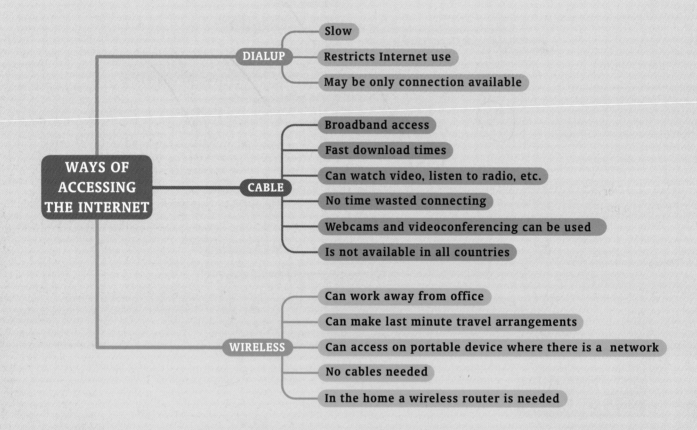

DIALUP
- Slow
- Restricts Internet use
- May be only connection available

WAYS OF ACCESSING THE INTERNET

CABLE
- Broadband access
- Fast download times
- Can watch video, listen to radio, etc.
- No time wasted connecting
- Webcams and videoconferencing can be used
- Is not available in all countries

WIRELESS
- Can work away from office
- Can make last minute travel arrangements
- Can access on portable device where there is a network
- No cables needed
- In the home a wireless router is needed

TOPIC 3: Human–computer interface

This topic follows on from Topic 9 of Unit 1 for the AS and looks in more detail at human–computer interfaces and the factors which should be taken into account in their design.

In order to use computers there must be an interface between the computer and human user and there are a number of different types of interface. Later on when you produce your project work you will have to design your own human–computer interfaces for others. It is important to realise that before a human–computer interface is designed it is essential to understand the needs of the people who will be using it. Often their needs are wide, as the interface will need to be used by people with widely different ICT skills and abilities. Sometimes the interface is to be used by a specific group of people such as children, engineers, doctors or people with a specific disability.

▼ The key concepts covered in this topic are:

▶ The factors to be taken into account when designing a good user interface

CONTENTS

Unit IT3 Use and impact of ICT

The factors to be taken into account when designing a good user interface

▼ **You will find out**

▶ About the factors to be taken into account when designing a good user interface

Introduction

Some hardware and software has been specially designed with a particular group of users in mind. However, the vast majority of ICT systems are used by a wide range of users. In this section you will look at what needs to be considered when creating a good user interface.

When creating a good user interface, there are a number of factors to consider and these include:

- consistency of signposting and pop-up information
- on-screen help
- layout appropriate to task
- differentiation in user expertise
- clear navigational structure
- use by disabled people.

Consistency of signposting and pop-up information

A good user interface will consist of consistent signposting and pop-up information.

What this means is that all the aids to navigation such as the Next and Previous buttons, pop-up menus, icons, etc., all look the same from screen to screen and all appear in the same position on the screen.

On-screen help

Everyone has been a beginner at using ICT systems at some time. It can be frustrating to know what you want to do but not be sure how to do it. This is where on-line help comes in.

All software packages should have an on-line help facility where users can get help supplied by the package, rather than have to look through manuals or user guides.

Provide users with on-line help

On-screen help for novice users

Some help screens can be very off-putting and frequently use unfamiliar terms in their explanations. Help screens should explain things simply and giving the user examples best does this.

Most users perform a variety of tasks using the software and are expert at some tasks whilst novice at others. Besides providing help should the user need it, the software should recognise and anticipate the users' goals and offer assistance to make the task easier. Microsoft Office uses Wizards that help you through some of the more complex tasks. This form of assistance allows the users to accomplish their tasks in as short a period as possible.

Layout appropriate to task

You would not have the same layout for a piece of software to be used by young children learning how to spell as you would have with a piece of CAD software used by an architect to design complex buildings. As these people are performing totally different tasks, they need a layout appropriate to the task.

The interface to teach children spelling should:

- have a minimum amount of text on the screen
- use bright colours to attract young children to the package

- have an uncluttered appearance
- involve minimal use of the keyboard
- use speech synthesis so they can hear words.

The interface for CAD should:

- be customisable – it should allow the user to customise the screen (e.g., include those items they use and get rid of any items they never use)
- minimise mouse movements – interface should have a layout that minimises the mouse movements
- keep working area as large as possible – include pull-down menus to keep the working area of the screen as large as possible
- use a large screen for complex interfaces – so that more of the diagram can be seen on the screen at one time
- use other input devices – such as graphics pads/tablets so that selections can be made from the tablet rather than the screen thus leaving the screen clearer for the actual plan
- design pull-down menus so that the selections used most frequently are situated at the top of the menu – this avoids the need to move down through the menu more than is necessary.

Differentiation in user expertise

Users can be divided into:

- novices – people who have never used the software before
- experienced – people who have used the software before but only know and use some of its features
- experts – people who have many years experience of the software and know and use all its facilities.

Each of these users will have different needs for the user interface. The novice user's priority will be ease of learning and easy access to help. The expert user will want to get the job done in the least possible time. Here are some ways the human–computer interface can be used to differentiate between users:

Provide short cuts for experts – experts often type at a high speed and will be able to memorise commands using a combination of keys and this will save them time over using the mouse and clicking on icons and pull-down menus. A novice user can use the mouse, so many packages provide an alternative interface.

Increased numbers of ways of performing the same operation – user interfaces offer more than one way to achieve the same result and the choice is left to the user. For example, a novice user may prefer to use a drop down menu or click on an icon in order to print out a file whereas the experienced user may find it faster to issue a command using a sequence of keys such as Ctrl+P.

Each level of user will have different needs

Clear navigational structure

It should be clear to the users how to accomplish certain tasks. So for a complex task the user can be guided through using a series of small steps. For example, the mail merge wizard in the word-processing package Word takes the user one step at a time through the process of creating a mail merge using their own data.

Many websites simply use hotspots without telling the user to click on them.

The user should never be left wondering what to do next.

Forward and back buttons should always be positioned at the same place on the screen.

Next buttons should be the same and positioned in the same place. If a user wants to flick quickly through a series of pages, it is annoying to have to position the mouse before clicking. It is much easier to keep the Next button in the same place so all the user has to do is click to take them to the next page.

Use by disabled people

People with special or particular needs need to use computers as do disabled people. ICT systems can present these people with many new opportunities and make their lives more fulfilling.

Users with a sensory impairment – the user may not be able to read the letters on the screen properly – use a font that is easy to read and make sure that the size of the font is large enough for these users to read.

If a person is blind, then ICT can help them by the use of a 'talking' computer where the words are spoken when typed in by the user, or output on the computer. Blind users can also use special Braille keyboards to enter data and they can use Braille printers to produce output in Braille with raised dots.

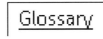

Explain difficult words or phrases

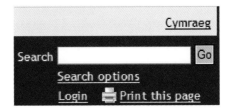

Offer different languages. This site can be translated into Welsh

Read Text

Allow a user to have the webpage read out loud to them – ideal for people with sight impairment

EXAM TIP

Try to remember the items in this list of factors by heart. Once you have done this, it is relatively easy to think up a couple of examples for each one when you are asked about them.

Users with a physical disability – this usually affects the user's mobility. For example, they may not be able to use their arms or hands or may be unable to walk. In some cases the disability is so severe that the person is almost paralysed.

People who are unable to write because of their disability can use voice-activated systems to put data into the computer.

Ways in which the accessibility of a website or other ICT system can be improved

Websites and other ICT systems are often designed to be used by the general public. This would include people of all ages, all nationalities, in different situations (at work, for leisure, etc.), with a range of disabilities, with different educational backgrounds and different ICT skills. This covers just about everyone.

Look at the following showing what can be done to make a website more accessible to users:

Use plain, simple language.

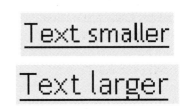

Allow a user to change the size of the text

Allow a user to change the colour of the text and background

Case study and Questions

▶ **Case study** pp. 40–41

Using a human–computer interface to unlock a person's potential

Stephen Hawking is probably the most famous physicist alive today, since he has appeared in many television programmes and has written many best-selling books on popular science including the famous *A Brief History of Time*. What is even more remarkable is that he has overcome a tremendous physical disability to do this. Stephen has a condition which is a form of motor neurone disease which is a progressive illness where you lose almost all neuromuscular control. This basically means you can become completely paralysed.

Stephen Hawking has a mind which is one of the best in the world, yet he cannot communicate with the outside world without the use of special equipment. Had all this equipment not been available, then he would have been unable to communicate with the outside world. Instead he has written many books, appeared all around the world and is a professor at Cambridge University.

Initially Stephen made use of a PC and a system called Equaliser. Stephen could operate this system by wiggling one of his fingers on a switch. There are a set of lines on the screen containing several words per line and a scanning system moves a highlighted bar over the words in turn and Stephen is then able to wait till it passes

over the word he wants before pressing the switch with his finger to make the selection.

Stephen lost his voice through his illness but he can speak electronically using a voice/speech synthesiser but the speech has an American accent!

As his illness has progressed he has had to adapt the human–computer interface to be able to cope with his increasing paralysis. Now he can only communicate by scrunching up his right cheek which operates an infra-red switch that is attached to his glasses. Using this switch he is able to talk, write notes and books, browse the Internet and send e-mail. The computer is attached to his wheelchair and allows wireless access to networks including the Internet.

The system also allows him to operate remote control doors in his home.

1 Explain the meaning of the term 'human–computer interface'. (2 marks)
2 Describe **two** requirements of the human–computer interface for Stephen Hawking. (2 marks)
3 Describe a different human–computer interface that can be used with a particular type of disability. You should make it clear in your description what the disability is and how the interface works. (4 marks)

▶ **Questions 1** pp. 40–41

1 When designing any ICT system, the human–computer interface is an important part of the system. Give the names of **four** factors that should be taken into account when designing a human–computer interface and for each factor describe why it is important. (8 marks)
2 Here are some of the things a user might find useful in a user interface.
   Explain briefly why each of these features is useful.
   (a) Easy reversal of actions. (1 mark)
   (b) The ability to go back to previous screens. (1 mark)
   (c) Using colours/flashing text to give warning messages. (1 mark)
   (d) Offering the user some feedback such as a sound of a click, or a picture of an egg timer. (1 mark)
   (e) Offer the user a choice in the way that commands are issued. (1 mark)

3 There are a number of factors which should be considered when designing a good user interface. You are designing a user interface for a self-running multimedia presentation.
   Describe how you would design each of the following factors to ensure ease of use of the presentation:
   (a) Clear navigational structure. (2 marks)
   (b) Layout appropriate to task. (2 marks)
   (c) On-screen help. (2 marks)
4 (a) Explain, by giving an example, how the needs of an expert user of software will often be different from those of a novice user. (3 marks)
   (b) Explain one way in which the needs of an expert user and a novice can be accommodated when designing the human–computer interface for a piece of software. (2 marks)

Exam support

Worked example 1

1 **When designing any ICT system, the human–computer interface is an important part of the system. Give the names of four factors that should be taken into account when designing a human–computer interface and for each factor describe why it is important. (8 marks)**

Student answer 1

1 The ability to adjust the size of the text. For example, in a PDF file you can adjust the size of the document by magnifying it so that people with poor eyesight will be able to see it.

The Next button or other buttons used to navigate should be in the same place on the screen so that users immediately know where they are on each screen.

On-screen help should be provided so that the users can type in a phrase or sentence and the software will do it for them.

The user should be able to adjust the colour combinations of text and background on the screen.

Examiner's comment

1 The factor and reason for the first point are correct. The second factor only gains one mark because the student has failed to state specifically why it is important. They should have stated what the importance is of having Next positioned at the same place on each screen.

The third factor only gets one mark for the mention of on-screen help. The reason is not a sensible one.

The final factor states what the factor is but fails to state why it is important. Maybe the student thought that the 'why' is obvious, but it still should be included to get the mark. **(5 marks out of 8)**

Student answer 2

1 The font size is important because the old and the very young need a large font, whilst other users can have a smaller font to enable more information to be seen on the page.

There should be a clear navigation structure so that the user can move forward and backward though the screens without wasting time.

The interface should be intuitive so that it is easy to use.

No bad colour choices for screen and background will make the screen easy to see, particularly for users with poor eyesight or who are colour blind, and in some packages or websites you can easily change the colour combinations.

Examiner's comment

1 There needs to be a full explanation of each factor and why it is important to gain the two marks for each factor. The first factor, the font size, has its relevance explained enough to gain two marks.

There are two explanations for the second factor, so two marks for this.

The third factor, although correct, has not been explained in enough detail so no marks are awarded here.

The final factor about the colour has been well explained and is worth two marks. **(6 marks out of 8)**

Examiner's answers

1 Just a statement of the factor gains no marks so students have to give further description of the factor and/or details of what makes the factor relevant to a good user interface for the two marks.

Any four of the following should be described in detail:

Font size – some users will want to see more on the screen so font size should be small (1) or young and old users with poor recognition or eyesight need a larger font (1).

On-screen help – important in case help is not available from other sources (1) as it is always available with the program (1).

Layout appropriate to task. Experts may prefer to type in commands rather than use a mouse (1). Less experienced users will prefer to use the mouse and GUI (1) as they do not have to learn commands.

Clear navigation structure. It should be clear for users how to get to the next step or screen (1) and navigational features (e.g., Next, Forward and Backward arrows) should be positioned in the same place (1).

Colour choice. Use combinations that allow contrast between text and background (1) and allow users to change the colours (1) so if they are colour blind, they can avoid the red/green combination (1).

Consistency of signposting and pop-up information. So that interface is intuitive (1) which makes the software easier to learn (1).

Worked example 2

2 Discuss using examples how a human–computer interface can be designed with disabled users in mind. (4 marks)

Student answer1

2 Users who cannot use their hands for typing could make use of speech recognition as a way of issuing commands and inputting information.
Partially sighted users could use interfaces where you can adjust the size of the items such as fonts on the screen and they will need to be able see the text on the background.

Examiner's comment

2 Only two good points are made here so only two marks for this. **(2 marks out of 4)**

Student answer 2

2 Users who cannot use a keyboard will use other input devices such as speech recognition, use of special input devices such as pipes you can blow into or special sensors that detect eye movement. The design of the interface should use plenty of contrast between text and background for users with poor eyesight. Combinations of colours should be considered so that users who are colour blind can use the interface.
In some websites you have a choice of combinations of colours. People with poor coordination can make use of larger mice with big buttons.

Examiner's comment

2 One mark each for the two specialist input devices for disabled users.
The information about contrast and using different combinations of colours gains two marks.
One mark is given for the information about people with poor coordination.
Note although five possible marks, this questions has a maximum of four. **(4 marks out of 4)**

Examiner's answers

2 One mark for each point to a maximum of 4 marks.
Use of speech recognition rather than keyboards for users who cannot use keyboard or mouse (1).
Use of specialist input devices such as those which use blow pipes or eye movements (1).
Ability to magnify areas of the screen to aid users with bad eyesight (1).
Ability to increase the font size to aid users with poor eyesight (1).
Use of correct colour schemes to help people who are colour blind (1).
Use visual messages rather than beeps or warning noises for users who are deaf (1).
Use a large mouse for people with poor coordination (1).
Use plenty of contrast between the text and the background to aid people with poor eyesight (1).

Summary mind maps

The factors to be taken into account when designing a good user interface

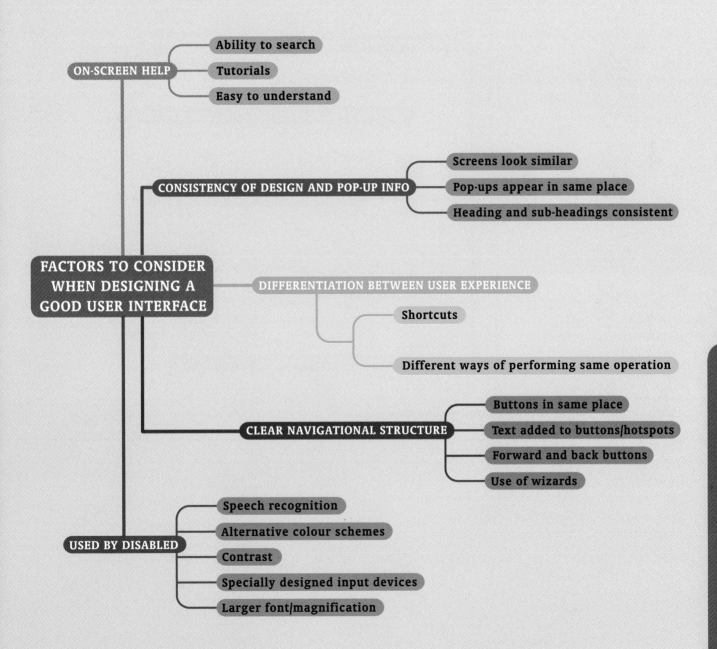

Ways in which the accessibility of a website or other ICT system can be improved

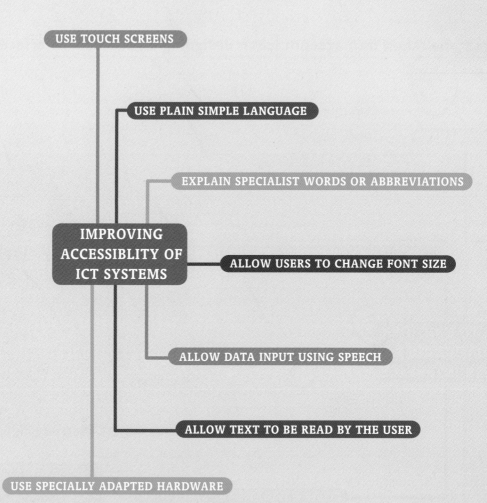

USE TOUCH SCREENS

USE PLAIN SIMPLE LANGUAGE

EXPLAIN SPECIALIST WORDS OR ABBREVIATIONS

IMPROVING ACCESSIBLITY OF ICT SYSTEMS

ALLOW USERS TO CHANGE FONT SIZE

ALLOW DATA INPUT USING SPEECH

ALLOW TEXT TO BE READ BY THE USER

USE SPECIALLY ADAPTED HARDWARE

For most people the only choice of workplace is either the office or the factory floor. Many people would prefer to live in a different part of the country, so it makes sense, if possible, for employers to satisfy this. If you talked to many employees of a company, you might find that many of them travelled long distances to work each day, especially if they are commuting to the centre of a large city such as London. Clearly it is wasteful all around for people to waste time getting to and from work. There is also the environmental aspect to consider. When cars are stationary in traffic jams they are producing exhaust fumes which clog up the atmosphere. Valuable resources such as petrol are being consumed.

Now, with the increased use of technology, it is possible for many workers, especially those employed to do administrative tasks, to work from home and therefore avoid these problems. The developments that have made this possible include the decrease in costs of communication and the increased use of networks including the Internet to share work.

▼ The key concepts covered in this topic are:

▶ Telecommuting

▶ Codes of conduct

CONTENTS

Unit IT3 Use and Impact of ICT

Telecommuting/teleworking

Introduction

In this topic you will learn about how many workers now use telecommuting/teleworking in their jobs and the advantages and disadvantages to themselves and the employers in doing this.

You will also look at an aspect of working with ICT which aims to cut down a number of problems that employees have when using ICT equipment. This aspect is called a code of conduct and this is a document given to employees which spells out what they can and can't do using ICT systems.

Telecommuting

Telecommuting means performing job-related tasks by using telecommunications to send and receive data to and from a central office without having to be physically present. It also means you can work at home rather than having to commute to an office each day.

With telecommuting, employees are given limited flexibility in working location and hours. This means telecommuters enjoy the flexibility of working that suits them but they must still get the work done.

The ICT developments which have enabled more people to work from home include:

- Internet access
- e-mail access
- mobile computing
- mobile phones
- data warehouses (where all the organisation's data is kept in a huge, single database)
- videoconferencing
- high speed broadband links.

Types of job and person to which telecommuting/ teleworking is suited

Not all jobs or people are suited to telecommuting/teleworking.

- Some jobs are ideally suited for working from home. Examples are programmers, website designers, accountants, data entry clerks, clerks who process insurance claims, etc.
- The employee must be trusted. If personal or sensitive data needs to be sent, the employee must keep this data safe and private.
- The employee must be self-motivated. There are plenty of distractions at home.
- The employee must have a place to work. They will need room in their house for the equipment needed.

Telecommuting and teleworking – is there a difference?

Yes there is a subtle difference but you will not be tested on it as the two words are often used to mean the same thing. Strictly speaking teleworking means using communications to save a journey. For example, you could use videoconferencing in an office to take part in a meeting with delegates from around the world.

You have not travelled and have used telecommunications instead, so this is teleworking.

You can now see that using ICT at home to do your work would also be teleworking as you are using telecommunications rather than travelling to work.

From now on and in the examination questions telecommuting and teleworking will be used interchangeably.

Hardware for teleworking

Hardware for teleworking would typically include the following:
- computer
- screen
- Internet connection (wireless router, cable router, etc.)
- microphone (used for videoconferencing)
- webcam (used for videoconferencing)
- internet phone (used for making cheap phone calls using the Internet)
- printer.

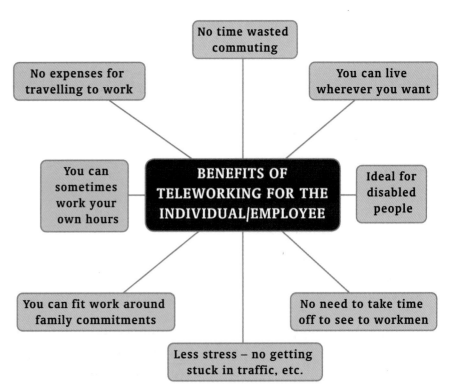

No time wasted commuting

No expenses for travelling to work

You can live wherever you want

You can sometimes work your own hours

BENEFITS OF TELEWORKING FOR THE INDIVIDUAL/EMPLOYEE

Ideal for disabled people

You can fit work around family commitments

No need to take time off to see to workmen

Less stress – no getting stuck in traffic, etc.

Working from home, called teleworking, is very popular with employees

The benefits of teleworking for the employee

Teleworking makes it easier for people to live and work where they choose, as it is possible for some staff to work from home. It reduces traffic congestion and carbon dioxide emissions and is therefore 'greener'. This has an environmental benefit since there is no commuting to work. Also it helps support rural areas where people normally have to move away to get work.

The benefits of teleworking to the employer

There are also benefits in teleworking to the employer and these are shown in the following diagram:

Smaller offices are needed

Fewer backup staff need to be employed (e.g. cleaners, caretakers)

Staff less likely to spend time off sick

BENEFITS OF TELEWORKING TO THE EMPLOYER

Less office furniture needed (e.g. desks, chairs)

Staff may be more amenable to working flexible hours

Reduced office overheads (electricity, gas, insurance, etc.)

The disadvantages of teleworking to the employee

There are some disadvantages in teleworking and they are summarised here:

Home costs such as heating, lighting increase

Employee may feel isolated

Some employers may pay teleworkers less as there is more competition for jobs

No workmates to go out with

DISADVANTAGES OF TELEWORKING TO THE EMPLOYEE

Boundary between home and work is lost

Loss of status for some staff – no plush offices, etc.

May not be a quiet place in the house to work

Other people in the house may keep disturbing you

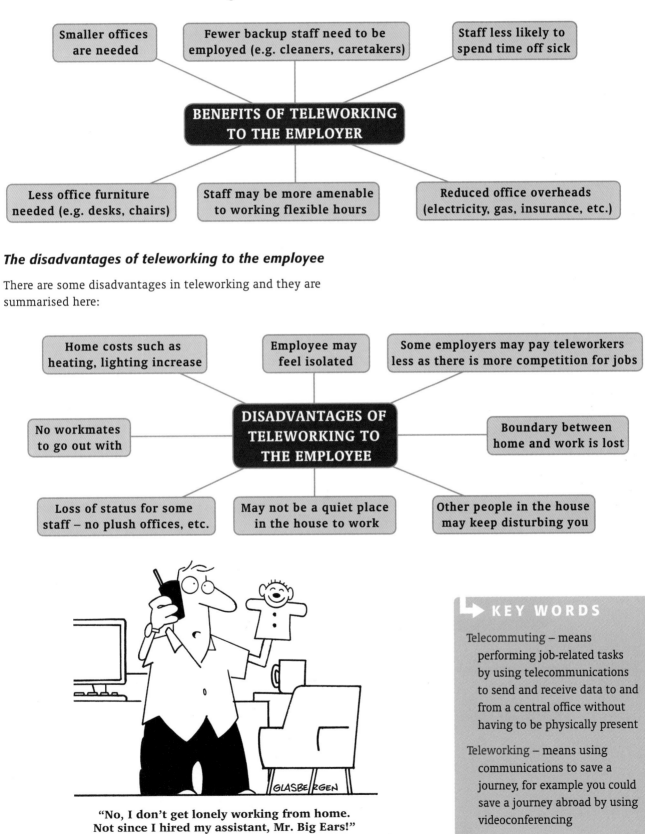

GLASBERGEN

"No, I don't get lonely working from home. Not since I hired my assistant, Mr. Big Ears!"

> **KEY WORDS**

Telecommuting – means performing job-related tasks by using telecommunications to send and receive data to and from a central office without having to be physically present

Teleworking – means using communications to save a journey, for example you could save a journey abroad by using videoconferencing

The disadvantages of teleworking to employers

Employers have less control of employees when they telework. There are a number of disadvantages and these are summarised in the following diagram:

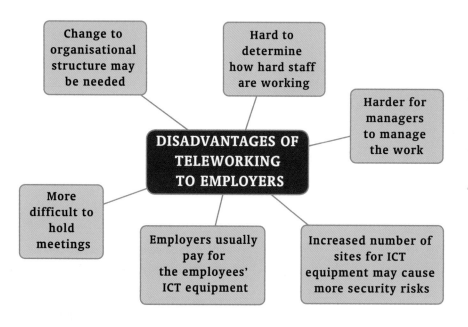

Change to organisational structure may be needed

Hard to determine how hard staff are working

Harder for managers to manage the work

DISADVANTAGES OF TELEWORKING TO EMPLOYERS

More difficult to hold meetings

Employers usually pay for the employees' ICT equipment

Increased number of sites for ICT equipment may cause more security risks

The benefits of teleworking to society

Society benefits by teleworking in the ways shown here:

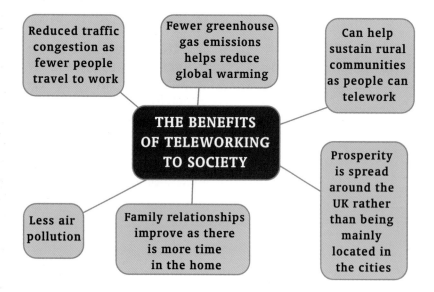

Reduced traffic congestion as fewer people travel to work

Fewer greenhouse gas emissions helps reduce global warming

Can help sustain rural communities as people can telework

THE BENEFITS OF TELEWORKING TO SOCIETY

Less air pollution

Family relationships improve as there is more time in the home

Prosperity is spread around the UK rather than being mainly located in the cities

Videoconferencing allows face-to-face meetings to be conducted without the participants being in the same room or even the same geographical area. In addition to sending the video and audio of the people taking part in the videoconference, videoconferencing can be used to share documents and presentations.

Because of the high bandwidth requirements for the video and audio, it is necessary to compress and decompress the signals in real time and this is done using a device or software called a codec (coder/decoder).

Videoconferencing systems consist of the following components:

Hardware

- High specification multimedia PC
- Video cameras or webcams – sometimes the cameras can be operated remotely so it is possible to zoom in on a particular speaker
- Microphones
- Screen (this can be a computer screen or it could be a large plasma display allowing many people to view the picture)
- Loudspeakers
- Sometimes the codec (to code/decode the signals) is hardware.

Software

- Sometimes the codec (to code/decode the signals) is software.

Data communications

A connection to a high speed digital network.

Face-to-face meeting being conducted over a wide geographical area

Benefits of using videoconferencing

There are many benefits in using videoconferencing and these can be classified into benefits for different groups of people.

Benefits to the employee

- Less stress as employees do not have to experience delays at airports, accidents, road works, etc.
- Improved family life as less time spent away from home staying in hotels.
- They do not have to put in long working hours travelling to and from meetings.

Benefits to the organisation

- Much cheaper as they do not have to spend money on travelling expenses, hotel rooms, meals, etc.
- Improved productivity of employees as they are not wasting time travelling.
- Meetings can be called at very short notice without too much planning.
- Short meetings can be conducted where it would not be feasible for people to travel long distances for such short meetings.

Benefits to society

- Fewer people flying to meetings will cut down on the number of flights needed and hence reduce the amount of carbon dioxide emitted helping to reduce global warming.
- Roads will not be clogged up with traffic and this will cause less stress and cut down on pollution.

Disadvantages/limitations of videoconferencing

- The cost of the equipment – specialist videoconferencing equipment is expensive.
- Poor image and sound quality – image quality is seldom as good as you would get with a TV, owing to the need to compress and decompress signals sent over the communication links.
- People can feel very self-conscious when using videoconferencing and may fail to come across well.
- Although documents and diagrams in digital form can be passed around, an actual product or component cannot be passed around.
- Lack of face-to-face contact may mean a discussion may not be as effective.

Uses of videoconferencing

- **Education** – some schools use videoconferencing for teaching A-levels where there are too few students to justify having a specialist teacher. One teacher can therefore be used to teach students in lots of different schools.
- **Medicine** – busy doctors can use teleconferencing to hold meetings about patients, and X-rays, ultrasound images, laboratory analyses can be passed digitally to the participants.
- **Business** – used extensively in business for conducting meetings at a distance.

Videoconferencing in hospitals

Videoconferencing is becoming quite popular in hospitals and has a number of uses such as:

- Providing a link between patient, doctor and interpreter for those patients who cannot speak English.
- Helping patients who live in rural locations who find it difficult to come to hospital. This is particularly important in rural locations where hospitals can be many hundreds of miles away.
- Training medical staff. Staff can learn from experts quickly without spending time attending courses in a remote location.
- Expert consultation with specialists who may live a long way from the patient and the doctors. Some patients have illnesses which are complex and the doctors in the hospital may not have experience in dealing with them and so need to get outside help.
- For regional meetings where staff would normally have to travel to a meeting venue.

Videoconferencing has now reached the stage where it is hard to tell who are the people in the room and who aren't!

KEY WORDS

Bandwidth – a measure of the amount of data that can be transferred using a data transfer medium

Topic 4: Working with ICT

page **51**

Codes of conduct

▼ You will find out

▶ About what a code of conduct is

▶ About the reasons for having a code of conduct

▶ About what a code of conduct would contain

Introduction

There are many laws applicable to the use of ICT including the Data Protection Act and the Computer Misuse Act and all employees must work within the law. In addition to obeying laws, when using ICT employees must act in a way that does not cause harm or annoyance to other users of ICT. By everyone agreeing to only use the ICT facilities in a certain way, they can get on with their work without hindrance.

In this section you will learn about why organisations have a code of conduct and what a typical code of conduct would consist of.

What is a code of conduct?

A code of conduct is an agreement made by an employee to obey the rules of the organisation and work within specified guidelines as regards use of ICT and the Internet.

Why have a code of conduct?

There are a large number of problems an employer has in allowing employees to use their ICT equipment. Without proper guidelines in the form of a document called a code of conduct, the employees will be able to do as they please and this can land the organisation with a series of problems, some of which could result in them being fined.

The answer is to have a code of conduct which clearly spells out to its employees the guidelines laid down by the organisation concerning the use of ICT and the Internet. Obeying the code of conduct is something that is laid down in contracts of employment. Should an employee decide not to obey the code of conduct, then they will be subject to a series of disciplinary procedures which can eventually include dismissal.

The rights of others should be respected

The potential problems

There are lots of problems when employees use ICT in the workplace and these include:

- Introduction of viruses – by downloading games, not scanning portable media, not keeping virus scanners up-to-date, etc.
- Misuse by employees of the ICT facilities, e.g. using telecommunications for own purposes (e.g., phone calls, e-mail, videoconferencing, etc.) and using printers for personal use.
- Distribution of material that is racially or sexually offensive – for example, sending offensive jokes by e-mail or text messages, circulating offensive images over the organisation's network, etc.
- Misuse of data for illicit purposes – for example, using e-mails and text messaging to bully someone at work or school/college.
- Inappropriate use of mobile phones – in restaurants, schools and on public transport.
- Blackmail, computer fraud or selling to other organisations.
- Violating terms of copyright or software agreements thus causing the company to face legal action from software suppliers or other affected organisations.

Employee code of conduct

An employee code of conduct consists of rules drawn up by the senior management or their advisors of an organisation that set out what an employee is/is not allowed to do in the course of their employment. It also details the sanctions which will be applied should the employee not obey the rules. Usually the code of conduct will be set out in the corporate information technology security policy but sometimes the code will be contained in a separate document which the employees have to read, agree to its contents and then sign.

What does a code of conduct contain?

An employee code of conduct would usually include the following.

Responsibilities

All members of organisations who use the IT facilities must act responsibly and each user should be responsible for the security and the integrity of the resources under their control.

Users must respect the rights of other users, respect the integrity of

You must be aware of laws relating to ICT

the physical facilities and controls and comply with all the pertinent licences and contractual agreements.

Since computers and networks can provide access to resources both inside and outside the organisation, such open access should be treated as a privilege and requires that all individual users act responsibly.

Users must act responsibly by ensuring that viruses are not introduced through failure to scan media, etc. They must also ensure that they are not negligent by leaving their computer logged in so others can access the data, not leaving laptops where they are easily stolen and so on.

Respecting rights of others

People who use ICT systems have rights that need to be respected. ICT systems such as e-mail, blogs and chat rooms can be misused by other people. For example, they may spread a false rumour about someone or use ICT to bully a person. Employees need to feel safe in the workplace, so all employees must respect each other.

Abiding by current legislation

There are many laws which cover the way ICT can be used. Current laws include The Data Protection Act 1998, The Computer Misuse Act 1990 and The Copyright, Designs and Patents Act 1988. Employees must act in accordance with these laws and failure to do so is serious and could result in dismissal and a criminal prosecution by the police.

Adverts for goods on the Internet have to abide by legislation called the Trades Descriptions Act. Financial services such as loans, mortgages and insurance have to obey rules set out in the Financial Services Act.

Complying with licensing agreements

When you buy a piece of software you do not own it and are not completely free to do what you want with it. When you buy a piece of software you are buying a licence to use it. When organisations purchase software to use over a network, they are purchasing a licence for a certain number of computers to use the software simultaneously. It is important that employees do not run more versions of the software than the software licence allows.

Authorisation

Access to the organisation's information resources, without the proper authorisation from the security manager, the unauthorised use of the organisation's facilities, and intentional corruption or misuse of information resources will usually be a violation of the code of conduct.

Security policy

The security policy could include the following:

- non-disclosure of passwords
- non-disclosure of company data to any third party
- to ensure that printouts of company data are not left lying around
- to make sure that any unwanted documents are disposed of with care

- users and system administrators must guard against abuses that disrupt or threaten the viability of all systems.

Data access permissions

Employees should not access data or files unless their permissions allow it. This means, for example, people should only access those files which are essential for the performance of their job.

Security

Employees must take the security of hardware, software and data seriously and obey certain rules that will make any loss of these resources less likely. Here are some rules which can be put into a code of conduct to improve security:

- Rules about not revealing passwords to others and regular changing of passwords.
- Rules concerning the personal use of e-mail.
- Rules concerning the use of the Internet (e.g., employees may not access social networking sites or chat rooms or auction sites during working hours).
- Rules concerning data transfer. Many organisations will not allow the downloading of any material off the Internet onto the company's computers. Downloading of large files such as music files or videos can use valuable bandwidth and make the Internet slower for others in the organisation to use legitimately.

"Information security is a major priority at this company. We've done a lot of stupid things we'd like to keep secret."

Penalties for misuse

The code of conduct for employees will only be taken seriously if there are penalties for misuse. These penalties will need to be applied according to the seriousness of the breach. Penalties for misuse involve:

- informal warnings – given verbally and not recorded on file
- written warnings – more formal and recorded on file
- dismissal
- prosecution.

Alleged violations of the employee code of conduct will normally be investigated further and should there be any substance to the investigation, then further action will be taken. In some instances this could include criminal or civil action.

Informal warnings

Minor infringements of the policy could be unintentional. For example, passwords that are badly chosen, excessive disk space consumption owing to bad file housekeeping, etc. These unintentional breaches of the code of conduct are best dealt with informally by the user's line manager.

Written warnings

More serious infringements need to be dealt with in a more formal manner in case further action needs to be taken in the future. Such infringements would typically include sharing accounts or passwords, leaving documents laying around on your desk, etc. Serious infringements are usually dealt with formally by issuing a written warning for the first infringement and possibly dismissal for the second. Serious infringements are likely to include the following:

- unauthorised use of terminals
- attempts to steal data or passwords
- unauthorised use of or copying of software
- repeated minor infringements.

Dismissal

Very serious infringements may result in dismissal of an employee as a last resort or where employees have not taken notice of a number of written warnings. Actions of the employee which cause embarrassment to the organisation or could result in the company being prosecuted often lead to dismissal.

Prosecution

For the very serious infringements, there could be immediate dismissal and if the actions the employee took were illegal then the police could be called in and a criminal prosecution could result. Although many organisations would shy away from the police being called in from a publicity point of view, the seriousness of the offence, particularly if the employee's actions had caused a serious loss to the organisation, may mean that there is no other choice.

Infringements of this kind would include theft of software or data, fraud, infringement of the Data Protection Act, downloading pornography off the Internet, etc.

The difference between legal and moral issues with respect to codes of conduct

A legal issue is an issue which is serious and against the law. If the issue is illegal then the police or other authority can bring about a prosecution which can lead to a fine or even imprisonment.

A moral issue is an issue which, although most people would consider wrong, is not actually illegal.

Disinformation

Disinformation is false information intended to deceive or mislead. Disinformation can be a moral or a legal issue as the examples here show.

Disinformation as a moral issue:

- A computer contractor (e.g., website designer, programmer, network engineer, etc.) offering to take on a contract when they do not know enough about the field.
- A systems analyst advising a client to buy a certain make of hardware because they will get a free holiday if the deal goes through.
- A computer salesperson in a store advising a client to buy a certain make of computer with associated hardware because the commission they will get is higher rather than it being the best computer to meet their needs.
- Not fully informing potential customers or clients of all the available facts concerning products or services (e.g., the imminent introduction of new models or improved services or imminent special offers).

Disinformation as a legal issue:

- An estate agent putting false information about a house on their website in contradiction of the Properties Act which covers what estate agents cannot do.
- A salesperson selling software claiming the software will do things it cannot do, which is against the Trades Descriptions Act.
- A hospital not supplying a patient with information about their illness to cover up a mistake that has been made in the medical diagnosis. Refusing to supply the correct personal information is in breach of the Data Protection Act.

The most serious infringements can result in dismissal

Privacy

Privacy is about people being able to keep information about their life private. The law protects personal data being misused but there are some things which are not illegal but against most people's morals.

Privacy as a moral issue:

- Companies buying lists of information off each other in order to cold call people to try to sell them goods or services.
- Companies monitoring their staff's use of e-mail or the Internet with a view to detecting misuse or just out of curiosity.

Privacy as a legal issue:

- Selling personal details of people who have not given their permission for the details to be transferred in contravention of the Data Protection Act.
- Not notifying the Information Commissioner that the organisation is processing personal data. Notification is a requirement of the Data Protection Act.

Did you know that all the searches you perform and e-mails you send are recorded by your ISP?

Employment patterns

The introduction of ICT has led to a change in employment patterns as fewer people work from 9 to 5 Monday to Friday.

Legal issues

More likelihood of contracting certain illnesses – there is some risk associated with working with ICT equipment such as RSI, back ache and stress. Organisations have a legal obligation to protect the employees against these risks by the use of the correct equipment (proper lighting, adjustable chairs, wrist rests, etc.) or correct working practices (changes in activity, regular breaks, etc.).

Organisations will protect themselves from possible legal action by employees by training the employees to use ICT equipment safely and forcing them to adopt safe working practices by incorporating it into their code of conduct.

Moral issues

There are a number of moral issues raised by changes in employment patterns:

- Employees feel spied on – the use of computers to monitor performance, bosses looking at personal e-mails and time spent on the Internet mean that many employees feel threatened.
- Employers taking advantage of a person's personal circumstances – some employers take advantage of a person's situation (e.g., mother with young children, carers, disabled, etc.) to offer them work at home using ICT for lower pay.
- Part-time work – with the use of ICT many more people work part-time. Part-time work offers employers more flexibility but the employees do not always have the same rights as full-time workers.

Equity

Equity is about fairness. For example, rich countries can take advantage of the latest ICT developments, whereas poorer countries have to make do with older equipment.

Within countries the population can be divided into information poor (lack of computer and Internet knowledge and access) and information rich (fast broadband access with good ICT knowledge). Information-rich people can take advantage of cheap loans, cheap holidays, etc., but information-poor people do not have access to this information.

Intellectual property rights

It is right that people who develop new software, hardware, communication methods, etc., should be rewarded for their work. It is not right that this work be copied by others. Many organisations will state in their code of conduct that any work produced during working hours belongs to them.

With ICT, fewer people need to commute to work

Questions and Activities

▶ Questions 1 pp. 48–55

1 (a) Explain the meaning of the term telework. (2 marks)

(b) Give **two** advantages to the employee of teleworking. (2 marks)

(c) Give the name of a job that is suitable for teleworking and give a reason why this job is particularly suited for teleworking. (2 marks)

2 (a) Give the names of **four** ICT developments that have allowed staff who are normally office based to work from home. (2 marks)

(b) Working from home using ICT equipment is not appropriate for every type of job. Give the names of **two** jobs that would be appropriate for working from home, giving reasons for each of your choices. (4 marks)

3 (a) Explain the difference between the terms telecommuting and teleworking. (2 marks)

(b) Videoconferencing is a popular application of ICT in hospitals. Describe **two** uses in hospitals for videoconferencing. (4 marks)

4 A company is thinking of allowing some of their employees to work from home.
Allowing telecommuting gives advantages to the employee as well as the employer.

(a) Discuss the ICT hardware needed for employees to telecommute. For each piece of hardware you describe you should explain why it is needed. (4 marks)

(b) Explain **two** advantages to the employee of telecommuting. (2 marks)

(c) Explain **two** advantages to the employer of telecommuting. (2 marks)

(d) Losing out on the social side is one of the disadvantages to the employee of telecommuting. Explain **two** different disadvantages to the employee in telecommuting. (2 marks)

5 Unfortunately some employees misuse an organisation's ICT facilities.

(a) Describe **three** ways in which an employee can misuse ICT facilities. (3 marks)

(b) Many organisations have a code of conduct to deter their employees from misusing the ICT facilities.

(i) Describe what a code of conduct is and describe **three** things it would contain. (5 marks)

(ii) Explain how employers enforce the code of conduct. (2 marks)

▶ Activity 1: Code of conduct

Here are some examples of the misuse of IT facilities which are included as part of the employee code of conduct for an organisation. Your task is to decide on the level of the infringement from minor, serious to very serious and then to decide on an appropriate action for the organisation to take.

1 Using the organisation's network to gain unauthorised access to other computer systems.
2 Knowingly or carelessly performing an act that will interfere with the normal operation of computers, terminals, peripherals or networks.
3 Attempting to circumvent data protection schemes or uncover security loopholes.
4 Violating the terms of software licensing agreements or copyright laws.
5 Using electronic mail to harass other people.
6 Moving large files across the network during peak use periods thus slowing the network down considerably for other users.
7 Posting information on the Internet that may be slanderous or defamatory in nature.
8 Displaying sexually explicit, graphically disturbing or sexually harassing images on the organisation's computer systems.
9 Bringing games disks into the company and running them on their machines.
10 Using the organisation's IT facilities for doing private work for which payment is made.
11 Extracting data from a database that violates the data protection laws.
12 Not changing their password regularly enough.
13 A terminal left with personal data displayed on it without the user being at the terminal.
14 Not virus scanning data disks before being used in the organisation.
15 Copying software owned by and licensed to the organisation and then re-selling it at car boot sales.

Exam support

Worked example 1

1 **Many companies (multinational companies) have offices in many different parts of the world. This makes it hard for staff to feel they all belong to the same organisation.**

(a) **Explain how the organisation can use ICT to enable staff working in different places around the globe to communicate effectively. (8 marks)**

(b) **There are a number of problems in communicating using ICT.**
Describe three disadvantages of using ICT for communicating. (6 marks)

Student answer 1

1 (a) They can use text messaging as texts are cheaper than phone calls made abroad. It also means they can read them at a time to suit. They can send e-mails. E-mails are good because they are stored automatically and they can arrive almost instantly. Replies can be written quickly and you do not have to waste time explaining what you are replying to.
You can use chat rooms where you can meet and chat to your colleagues in a chat room if you get lonely.

(b) If the equipment breaks down then you cannot communicate.
People like to chat face to face. It is harder to tell if someone is lying or how they feel about what you are saying by simply looking at their face.
E-mail is no good for bringing bad news – no-one wants to be sacked from a job by e-mail as this should be done personally.

Examiner's comment

1 Eight marks are available for part (a) so there need to be eight relevant facts.
Text messaging, although an important communication method, is only suitable for short messages and is not a method by which people in organisations communicate, so no marks for this answer.
The answer about e-mail makes three relevant points so three marks here.
Most companies would not want staff discussing organisation business in a chat room, especially if it were open to the public. No marks here.
Students should be referring to business methods of communication and not the way they communicate on a personal level with their friends. **(3 marks out of 8)**
Part (b) has six marks available so there need to be six valid points.
There are two answers here – each with a statement and further explanation which are both correct so four marks here. **(4 marks out of 6)**

Student answer 2

1 (a) Staff can use e-mail to communicate with colleagues. This is faster than ordinary mail which can take weeks to arrive in some countries.
Replies are easy to make because you only have to click on reply and type your message to the original e-mail.
You do not have to wait for the post or queue for stamps, etc.
The organisation could set up a blog which allows all staff to post their comments. This allows people to air problems or grievances they have.
The company managers could choose to do something about them or not.
Staff can use videoconferencing to organise virtual meetings where everyone can see each other and they can pass around electronic documents and watch presentations. No time is wasted travelling to meetings, and the costs are much lower as the management do not have to pay for travel, meals, hotel costs, etc.

(b) People sometimes like a change away from the office and they like to socialise with others. Videoconferencing takes this away.
It is hard for people to act naturally in a videoconferencing situation and many people like proper face-to-face contact.
E-mail is useful for quick communication but it can appear quite abrupt.
People may not feel it is a good idea to post up material on blogs and message boards as they feel the comments could be easily traced back to them

Examiner's comment

1 Part (a) has been well answered and includes all relevant points and is clearly expressed. There are eight separate points here which are correct for this answer, so full marks for this section. **(8 marks out of 8)**
Part (b) is also a very good answer where five valid points are made. **(5 marks out of 6)**

Examiner's answers

1 (a) One mark for a statement of a suitable communication method that must be appropriate for a business. Then one mark for each explanation about how the communication method can be used.
E-mail to be used to communicate with colleagues (1). Provides fast communication as there is no wait for post (1). Cheap method as e-mails are almost free (1). Good because original e-mail and reply can be kept together so no time wasted searching for original e-mail (1). Can attach files and other documents to e-mails for comments (1). Videoconferencing can be used for virtual meetings (1). It saves employees having to travel to a real meeting (1). Saves the company money by not having to pay for venue, travel costs, hotel costs, meals, etc. (1). Meetings can be called at short notice on an ad hoc basis (1). Forums/blogs/message boards allow staff to communicate with each other (1). They can set up discussions and ask others for comments (1).

   (b) One mark for the disadvantage and one mark for an explanation of the consequences that the disadvantage would have.
Lack of face-to-face contact (1). It is important to see people's faces and read their body language (1). Relies on technology which may not always be reliable (e.g., satellite links) (1). Equipment may break down and cause no communications at all (1). Sometimes more sensitive when giving bad news to communicate in person (1). Sometimes e-mails are too brief and can cause misunderstandings (1).

Worked example 2

2 'The growth of communication systems has resulted in an increasing number of people working from home, often referred to as telecommuting.'
Discuss, with the aid of suitable examples, the advantages and disadvantages to employees and organisations of such methods of working. **(8 marks)**

Student answer 1

2 Mothers with young children or carers who look after elderly relatives can benefit by telecommuting as they have flexible working times. They do not have to commute to work so can be in the house to look after people. Telecommuting is ideal for disabled workers because they do not have the trouble of getting to work on public transport.
It is, however, very difficult to motivate yourself in your own home.
There are benefits to organisations as well. They do not need as big offices as people are using part of their own house. You do not have to buy computer equipment as employees can use their own computers. Also you do not have to buy software as they will already have it.

Examiner's comment

2 The advantages to the employee are well described with suitable examples being given. There are three valid advantages and one disadvantage given to the employees.
The answer to the benefits to the organisation is weaker. The point about smaller offices is valid but there are no other parts to this answer worthy of marks. Employers will nearly always supply hardware and software so that they can control the security of the organisation's data. **(5 marks out of 8)**

Student answer 2

2 Advantages to the employee include being able to fit your personal life around work such as being able to work into the evening if you have young children.

In addition, you do not have to live in cities and can live a better life in the country. There is no expensive commuting either by train or by car so the money saved can be used for enjoyment.

Disadvantages to the employee include the feeling of being more isolated as there are no workmates to chat to and go out with. The employee may find it hard to separate their work life from their home life and this may cause friction with partners. They will need some space to do the work and this may not always be available. They will need to be well motivated as they will not have a boss standing over them checking up on them all the time.

Benefits to the employer include not having to have such a large office, with the resulting cost savings in rental, heating, lighting and cleaning. They can also recruit staff from a much wider area, which means they are likely to get better more motivated employees. Workers who telecommute are likely to be more loyal and stay with the company longer.

Disadvantages to the employer include not being in control of the security of the data. It is hard to know who is looking at the personal data that might be stored. Also, it is harder to manage these employees who are in remote locations.

Examiner's comment

2 This is an excellent answer. Notice the way the student has sectioned the advantages and disadvantages off into different paragraphs. There are a large number of valid points raised here and no incorrect points and the student has expressed themselves well. This answer is worth full marks. **(8 marks out of 8)**

Examiner's answers

2 Candidates should include points similar to the following in their answers:

Benefits to the employees:

Flexible working hours – as long as the job gets done

Can fit in with caring for young children, disabled relatives, elderly, etc.

Not restricted to where in the country you can live

No time spent travelling to work so can spend more time on leisure or with family

No cost travelling to work

Disadvantages to employees:

Have to be motivated to cope with distractions at home

Need space in order to work

Do not get the same social aspect as when working with others

Increased home bills such as heating, lighting, insurance, etc.

Benefits to the organisation:

Smaller offices needed so reduced costs

Can choose employees from a wider area with suitable skills

Fewer backup staff need to be employed (e.g., cleaners, security staff, etc.)

Staff are more amenable to working unsocial hours if needed

Staff are less likely to spend time off sick

Disadvantages to the employer:

Harder for managers to manage the work

Hard to determine how hard staff are working

Security issues of having company data on computers away from the office

Changes to the structure of the organisation may be needed

Need to supply the equipment for home workers which can be expensive

6–8 marks Candidates give a clear, coherent answer fully and accurately describing one advantage and disadvantage to the employees and one advantage and disadvantage to the organisation. Accurate spelling, punctuation and grammar is used.

3–5 marks Candidates give answers but they lack clarity or relevant examples. There are a few errors in punctuation and grammar.

0–2 marks Candidates do not discuss and simply list three advantages/disadvantages or give brief explanation of only one or two advantages/disadvantages. The response lacks clarity and there are significant errors in spelling, punctuation and grammar.

Code of conduct

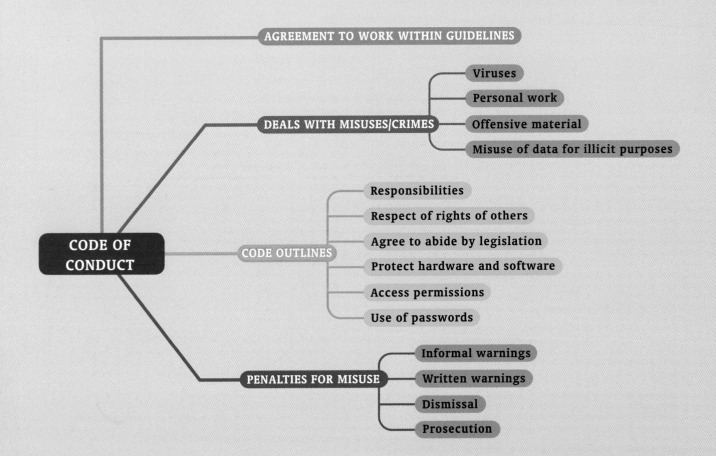

AGREEMENT TO WORK WITHIN GUIDELINES

CODE OF CONDUCT

DEALS WITH MISUSES/CRIMES
- Viruses
- Personal work
- Offensive material
- Misuse of data for illicit purposes

CODE OUTLINES
- Responsibilities
- Respect of rights of others
- Agree to abide by legislation
- Protect hardware and software
- Access permissions
- Use of passwords

PENALTIES FOR MISUSE
- Informal warnings
- Written warnings
- Dismissal
- Prosecution

All good companies maintain strict security of their ICT resources in order to protect their competitive advantage, ensure that their image is not subject to bad publicity and to protect personal data from being disclosed. It is essential that organisations protect their ICT systems in a cost-effective manner with appropriate levels of security. ICT systems are vulnerable to two classes of threats, accidental and deliberate.

Accidental threats would include such things as human error, fire, failure of equipment, natural disasters (floods, earthquakes, etc.) and deliberate threats would include fraud, sabotage, vandalism, arson, espionage, etc. These threats can come from within the organisation or from outside.

To deal with these threats, all organisations should have an ICT security policy that should be produced by, and have the backing of, the senior management and directors. The ICT security policy is a document containing all aspects of security within an organisation and it contains conditions and rules that need to be obeyed by all the staff.

In this topic you will learn about the threats to ICT systems and how these threats can be prevented or minimised and also about how data can be recovered if the original data is lost. You will also look at the components of an ICT security policy.

▼ The key concepts covered in this topic are:

▶ Threats to ICT systems, consequences and the need for backup procedures

▶ The factors to take into account when designing security policies

▶ Operational procedures for preventing misuse

▶ Prevention of accidental misuse

▶ Prevention of deliberate crimes or misuse

▶ Factors determining how much a company spends to develop control, minimising risk

CONTENTS

Unit IT3 Use and Impact of ICT

Potential threats and consequences, and backup procedures

▼ You will find out

▶ About the threats to ICT systems from natural disasters

▶ About the threats to ICT systems from faulty hardware and software

▶ About the threats from fire

▶ About the threats from loss of power supply

Introduction

A threat to an ICT system such as fire, theft, deliberate damage, power loss, etc., is a source of danger.

The potential threats to ICT systems are many and some are more likely to happen compared to others. The amount of damage done can also vary from a slight inconvenience (e.g., having to remove a virus) to the complete loss of hardware, software and data.

Any user of ICT systems needs to be aware of the threats, because only then can measures be taken to minimise the damage should the threat turn into reality.

Threats to ICT systems can cause the loss of data which causes loss of money in terms of:

- legal action
- lost business
- lack of confidence by customers or members of the public
- lost computer time
- the need for staff to spend time sorting problems out.

Where do the threats come from?

There are a huge number of threats to computer systems. Here is a list of the main threats but you may be able to think of some more:

- viruses
- worms
- adware
- spam
- sabotage, deliberate abuse by staff
- fire
- natural disasters
- terrorism
- Trojans
- spyware
- hacking
- accidental abuse by staff
- theft
- faulty hardware or software

Threats from natural disasters

In Britain we do not generally suffer from natural disasters like a lot of other countries, but with climate change this may change. Some natural disasters and their consequences are shown below.

⇨ KEY WORDS

Hacker – a person who tries to or succeeds in breaking into a secure computer system

Hacking – the process of trying to break into a secure computer system

UPS (uninterruptible power supply) – a backup power supply (generator and battery) which will keep the computer running should the mains power supply fail

EXAM TIP

Hacking is normally considered more of an external than an internal threat. Make sure when you are describing hacking that you mention how the Internet can be used with a home computer to gain access to an organisation's data.

Earthquakes – loss of power, loss of communication lines, damage to ICT systems caused by building collapse, etc.

Lightning strikes – lightning strikes can cause momentary losses of power which can cause data loss. Lightning can also cause more serious damage with the complete loss of hardware, software and data

Floods – water damage to hardware, software and data, loss of power or communication lines

Tidal waves – usually these occur after earthquakes, when they are called tsunamis

Volcanoes – fire and smoke damage, destruction of buildings

Gales – loss of power lines, destruction of communication equipment, etc.

Threats from faulty hardware or software

Like any electrical device, computers can and do go wrong. The trouble is that although hardware can be repaired or replaced, it is not easy to replace programs and data, especially if no backup copies have been kept.

Faulty hardware – computer hardware is fairly reliable but can and does break down and you have to be prepared for this. The main problem would be caused by the hard drive becoming damaged, rendering the data and the programs unusable.

Faulty software – software, especially bespoke software and sometimes packaged software, can contain errors (or bugs as they are called) and these can cause damage or loss of data.

Threats from fire

Fire is a serious threat in any workplace and loss of ICT systems can occur, so precautions need to be taken to minimise the threat such as:

- no smoking in any computer rooms
- power sockets should not be overloaded
- wiring should be checked regularly for safety
- bins should be emptied regularly
- do not leave large quantities of paper lying around
- fire alarms/smoke detectors in all rooms
- install a sprinkler system
- use fireproof safes to store media containing programs and data
- remove backup copies off-site.

Computer or hardware theft

Computer theft involves a thief stealing the computer or other hardware. If a computer is stolen then the hardware, software and data will be lost. A firm may be in contravention of the Data Protection Act 1998 if it can be proved that they did not have adequate security to prevent the loss of any personal data stored.

Computer theft is common, particularly with laptops. Laptops are particularly vulnerable to theft because they are:

- small, light and easily concealed
- often used in public places (cafes, on a train, at an airport, etc.)
- put into car boots
- very desirable and easy to sell by thieves.

Hacking

Hacking involves attempting to or actually breaking into a secure computer system. Usually a hacker (i.e., the person who does the hacking) is a proficient programmer and has the technical knowledge to be able to exploit the weaknesses in a security system. Once a hacker has gained access to an ICT system they may:

- do nothing and be content that they have managed to gain access
- gain access to sensitive or personal data
- use personal data to commit blackmail
- cause damage to data
- deliberately alter data to commit fraud.

The spread of viruses

Connection of an organisation's computers to the Internet increases the risk of viruses being spread to the internal network. The latest virus scanning and removal software should be installed on all computers.

Denial of service attacks

A denial of service attack is an attack on a secure system of an organisation so that the organisation is deprived of some of their resources. For example, a denial of service attack on an on-line bookshop could mean that the bookshop's network is so overwhelmed with requests that there is a temporary loss of network connectivity. This means that if you tried to place an order for a book, while the attack was taking place, you would not be able to. As well as inconveniencing customers, there is usually a loss of business, owing to customers not being able to place orders.

Problems with power

Power loss can occur for all sorts of reasons. It can be the result of natural disasters, extreme weather and/or simply from a workman cutting through a cable whilst doing road repairs.

Power loss

A standby power system will keep the power supplied and the computers running until the mains power is restored. Standby power will usually consist of either stored power (for short losses of power) or a combination of stored power and a generator. Stored power consists of banks of batteries. Generator power is generated using diesel or petrol.

Because there is a slight delay between losing the power and starting the generator, batteries are also needed to provide power during this interval.

Standby power is sometimes referred to as a UPS (uninterruptible power supply).

Changes in the power supply

Power fluctuations, sometimes called spikes and surges, occur more often than complete power loss. You notice these when your lights start to flicker. Power fluctuations can cause problems with computers and can be a cause of data loss.

Consequences of losing data

The main consequences of losing data are:

- Loss of business and income – losing details of customers and their orders will mean the company will not know that a customer has placed an order and they will not know whether an order has been paid for.
- Loss of reputation – organisations will not look good if they cannot look after data properly. There have been many recent news stories about government departments losing personal data.
- Legal action – there is a requirement under the Data Protection Act 1998 for organisations to keep personal data safe. Organisations who fail to do this will face prosecution.

The factors to take into account when designing security policies

Introduction

There are many things that can be done in order to eliminate or reduce the threats to ICT systems and in this section you will be looking at what factors need to be taken into account when designing a security policy.

Physical security

Physical security involves protecting hardware and software using physical rather than software methods. The two main purposes of providing physical security are:

- to restrict access to the computer equipment
- to restrict access to the storage medium.

To restrict access to the computer equipment it is often advisable, as a first stage, to make sure that access to the building or room is restricted. If access is gained, then some way of preventing theft of the computers is needed.

Prevention of misuse

There are two methods used to help prevent misuse of ICT systems:

- physical methods
- logical (software) methods.

Logical methods use the software to control access to programs and data stored on the ICT system. Physical methods do not use software but instead use things such as locks, security guards, cables to secure computers to desks, etc.

Physical methods

- Controlling access to the room – by using keypads on the doors where a code needs to be entered, or the use of special magnetic cards to open doors or the use of biometric methods such as fingerprint or iris recognition.
- Controlling access to the building – by the use of uniformed security guards who will challenge visitors, log people in and out of the building and ensure access to rooms is controlled, etc.

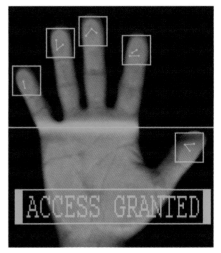

Controlling access to the room

Use locks on computers

Physical and logical methods are used to protect ICT systems

Lock computers away at night

Use of devices to prevent removable media being inserted

Use security cameras

Use of fireproof safe

- Use locks on computers – to prevent them from being switched on.
- Locking the computers away at night or securing them under steel covers – prevents access or theft.
- Use of security cameras in computer rooms – makes computers less likely to be stolen or abused.
- Securing computers to desks using strong metal cables – prevents theft.
- Use of devices to prevent removable media being inserted – for example you can get devices that do not allow CD/DVD drives or USB ports to be accessed, thus preventing unauthorised copying of data.
- Use of fireproof safe for the storage of data on portable storage media.

Software security (also called logical security)

If people do gain unauthorised access to the room containing the computers, there needs to be a second line of defence to prevent them gaining access to the software or data. This is achieved by using software security.

Software security usually involves:

- using log-ins and passwords to restrict access to the computer
- using levels of access to certain programs, files and data.

Audit trails for detection

Many transactions occur using ICT systems without any paperwork being generated, which may seem to make it quite difficult to trace transactions. Luckily all ICT systems provide audit trails where it is possible to track all the details of a particular transaction.

For example, for a sales processing system it could be checked that a customer made an order, the money for the order was paid and that the goods were dispatched and received by the customer. Any irregularities in the process could be identified by the audit trail and investigated. Audit trails provide records which can be used to track the transactions. Audits are performed at regular intervals and they act as a deterrent, since staff realise that someone is checking things.

Audit trails allow a record to be kept of:

- who has made changes to data
- when the data was changed
- what changes were made.

Continuous investigation of irregularities

One way of picking up on misuse of credit/debit cards is to query any transactions that are out of the ordinary for that customer.

Irregularities in places – sometimes credit card payments for large amounts abroad are rejected by the credit card company. The credit card company ask the purchaser to contact them so they can ask them a series of questions to verify that they are the genuine card holder and that the transaction is genuine.

Irregularities in amounts – a high value transaction on a credit card may set the alarm bells ringing, particularly if the person has never made a high value transaction before. Before allowing the transaction to go ahead, the bank will ask the customer to contact them so they can check that the transaction is genuine and that no-one is using their identity illegally.

System access – establishing procedures for accessing data such as log-in procedures, firewalls

System access controls

System access controls ensure that access to ICT systems containing the organisation's data, programs and information is controlled in some way, so that only authorised access is allowed. System access is controlled using the following methods.

Log-in procedures

A user-ID/username is a name or number used to identify a user of a network. Once the network knows who is using the network, it can allocate resources such as storage area and access to certain files.

Passwords are strings of characters kept secret by the user and are used to access the ICT system. The password makes sure that the person who gives the user-ID/username is the person they say they are.

It is never a good idea to write your password down.

Access rights

Access rights restrict a user's access to only those files they need in order to perform their job. Their rights are initially allocated to them by the network manager and when they log on by giving their user-ID and password, these rights are allocated by the computer.

A user can have a number of different levels of access to files including:

- Read only – a user can only read the contents of the file. They cannot alter or delete the data.
- Read/write – a user can read the data held in the file and can alter the data.
- Append – they can add new records but they will be unable to alter or delete existing records.
- No access – they cannot open the file so cannot do anything to it.

> **EXAM TIP**
>
> If you are asked about levels of permitted access, when you mention the different levels of access, it is always best to give an example of the different types of staff who would be given each level of access.

'Sorry about the odour. I have all my passwords tattooed between my toes.'

> **KEY WORDS**
>
> Password – a series of characters chosen by the user that are used to check the identity of the user when they require access to an ICT system
>
> User-ID – a name or number that is used to identify a certain user of the network or system
>
> Firewall – a piece of software, hardware or both that is able to protect a network from hackers

Firewalls

A firewall is either hardware and/or software that works in a network to prevent communication that is not allowed from one network to another. Suppose an internal network (called an intranet) is connected to the Internet. The intranet will be protected with high security but the Internet is a very low security network. A firewall basically controls the data traffic between the two networks and it looks at each packet of data to see if there is anything about the data that breaches the security policy. If it does then the packet of data will not be allowed into the intranet.

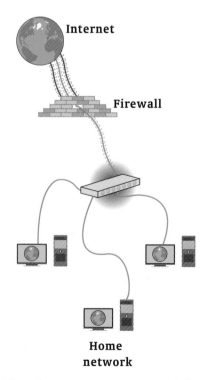

Firewalls are used to prevent spread of viruses and also to prevent unauthorised access (i.e., hacking)

Firewalls are also used to control what outside resources users have access to on the intranet.

Norton Personal Firewall can be used to protect your computer from unauthorised access whilst connected to the Internet. This particular firewall is software.

Firewalls can be:

- hardware
- software
- a combination of hardware and software.

Personnel administration

Prevention of misuse by staff is an important aspect of a security policy. Staff should be administered correctly in order for them to realise that if they do misuse the ICT facilities, it will be discovered and they will be disciplined. Personnel administration would include:

- Training – means staff are less likely to disobey the code of conduct, less likely to make mistakes with data, less likely to lose work, etc.
- Fitting the employee to the task – ensuring that the employee knowledge and skills match the task they have to complete.

- Ensuring that staff are controlled – managers should ensure staff are working safely and are ensuring the privacy and security of the data they are using.

Operational procedures including disaster recovery planning and dealing with threats from viruses

Organisations should put operational procedures in place as part of their security policy in order to minimise the various threats to ICT systems. Here are some examples of operational procedures:

- Each user can be given a code of practice that outlines things that they must do when accessing information.
- Access to operational data and programs by development staff, such as programmers and systems analysts, is desirable to prevent the opportunity of alteration to commit fraud.
- Rotation of staff duties is also used to prevent fraud, since it is less likely that two people would be like minded and also one could discover the fraud committed by the other.

- Procedures can be introduced which will deal with disaster recovery so everyone knows what to do if some or all of the ICT facilities are lost.
- Procedures should be put in place to reduce the likelihood of a virus attack, such as not allowing staff to download games, music, etc., and not inserting removable media into the computer.

Staff code of conduct and responsibilities

When employees use ICT facilities, they have a variety of computing and legal responsibilities. Since when at work, an organisation is often responsible for the acts of its employees, it is important that all staff members are aware of what these responsibilities are. Even though the organisation did not know about the acts of some of their employees in breaking the law, it could still be held liable. This happens if it was proved that it had not taken sufficient steps to prevent the illegal activity.

Most organisations have a code of conduct which sets out clearly what staff can and cannot do using the ICT facilities. Codes of conduct were covered in Topic 4.

Disciplinary procedures

Staff only take notice if there are serious repercussions in cases of misuse of ICT systems. Training needs to take place so that all staff are aware of the problems that misuses cause and also the consequences should they be caught.

'Somebody broke into your computer, but it looks like the work of an inexperienced hacker.'

Operational procedures for preventing misuse

Introduction

There are administrative procedures that organisations can put in place that will minimise or prevent the threats posed by employees. These procedures involve actions from the screening of employees to setting up a disaster recovery programme.

Screening potential employees

Choosing staff carefully can prevent problems in the future. ICT staff are in a position of trust and can present a number of threats if they are not chosen carefully.

Taking up references and thoroughly screening staff working in ICT is essential.

Routines for distributing updated virus information and virus scanning procedures

Viruses

Malicious damage can arise from inside or outside the organisation and can vary from a disgruntled employee altering a program so that it does not work properly or printing an insulting message on all the invoices when the employee has left the company, to a person deliberately introducing a virus.

Viruses pose the main threat under the heading malicious damage. A virus is a program that replicates (i.e., copies) itself automatically and usually carries with it some payload which causes damage.

Once a computer or media has a virus copied onto it, it is said to be infected. Most viruses are designed to do something apart from copying themselves. For example, they can:

- display annoying messages on the screen
- delete programs or data
- use up resources, making your computer run more slowly.

One of the main problems is that viruses are being created all the time and that when you get a virus infection it is not always clear what a new virus will do to the ICT system.

Apart from the dangerous payload many viruses carry, one of the problems with viruses is the amount of time that needs to be spent sorting out the problems that they create.

All computers should be equipped with a virus checker, which is a program that is able to detect and delete these viruses. These virus checkers need to be updated regularly, as new viruses are continually being developed and would not always be detected by older versions of virus checkers.

Ways by which viruses can be spread

Viruses can be spread by:

- external e-mail
- internal e-mail
- the organisation's intranet (an intranet is an internal network that makes use of Internet technology)
- shared disks
- clicking on banner advertisements on the Internet
- downloads from sites such as games sites.

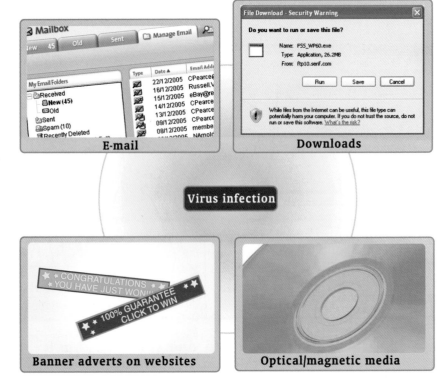

E-mail

Downloads

Virus infection

Banner adverts on websites

Optical/magnetic media

How to prevent viruses

The best way to avoid viruses altogether is to use virus checking software and adopt procedures that will make virus infection less likely.

Here are some steps that can be taken to prevent viruses entering an ICT system:

- install virus checking software
- do not open e-mails from unknown sources
- keep virus checking software up-to-date – configure the virus checking software so that updates are installed automatically
- have a clear acceptable use policy for all staff who use computers
- train staff to be aware of the problems and what they can do to help
- do not allow programs such as games, video or movies to be downloaded onto the organisation's ICT systems
- do not open file attachments to e-mails unless they are from a trusted source
- if possible, avoid users being able to use their own removable media (floppy disks, removable magnetic drives).

Virus scanning procedures

Virus scanning procedures need to be in place and would typically include:

- Frequency of virus scanning – how often complete/partial scans take place.
- Time at which hard drives are scanned for viruses – usually when the computers are not being used for other purposes, as virus scanning slows the computers down.
- How portable media should be scanned before use.
- Methods by which virus scanning software is updated (e.g., updated automatically using the Internet).

Define procedures for downloading from the Internet, use of portable storage media, personal backup procedures

Users will want to download data from the Internet in the form of statistical data, photographs, updates to programs, presentations, etc., so there need to be procedures that will allow this. The problem is preventing users from downloading copyright material such as programs, music and films. Training and the use of a code of conduct can deter some users.

Procedures for downloading files from the Internet include:

- Always choose the option to 'Save this program to disk', saving it to a temporary folder away from your main network. Run then scan this file and if clean, re-file in the desired folder on your system.
- Do not install any software downloaded off the Internet onto your computer or company networks as these may contain viruses and could be illegal.
- Be aware of the risk of overloading your computer by storing too many large downloaded files. Please ensure that you keep the downloaded files for no longer than necessary.

Users will often want to store their own data on portable media or in a way that they can work on the files at home. Procedures need to be in place for allowing users to back up their own data.

Procedures for backing up data include:

- The types of storage media allowed for the taking of backups.
- The frequency at which backups should be taken.
- Where backups are to be stored (e.g., fireproof safe, outside the building, etc.).
- Procedures for the use of portable media attached to the computer via the USB port (e.g., whether the media needs scanning first, what data can be transferred, etc.).
- Procedures for the transfer of personal information. Many organisations may not allow it to be

downloaded onto laptops, portable storage media or transferred as a file attachment to an e-mail. Some organisations will not allow it to be transferred outside the building.

Establish security rights for updating webpages

If you have a website, you would not want others (e.g., hackers and disgruntled employees) making embarrassing changes to your website.

Websites need to have security so that only authorised staff can make changes and these rights are assigned according to user-IDs and passwords. These security rights offer certain staff access to change webpages.

Establish a disaster recovery programme

All organisations should consider what they would do if they lost their entire ICT facility (hardware and software). Organisations would still have the data as most data is transferred off-site should a disaster happen. This is extreme as not many organisations will experience this, although most organisations will experience loss of some part of their ICT facilities.

The disaster recovery programme is a series of steps that would be taken should some or all of its facilities be lost. The idea of the disaster recovery program is to minimise the loss of business and get things back on track as soon as possible.

Set up auditing procedures (audit trails) to detect misuse

When tasks are completed using ICT there are usually no paper records to check. This means you cannot follow the bits of paper to work out what has happened.

Instead the computer software keeps a record of the changes made and who made them. By looking at audit trails it is possible to determine whether any fraudulent activity has taken place and to identify the individual or individuals responsible.

Prevention of accidental misuse

▼ You will find out

► About backup and recovery procedures

► About standard backup to floppy disk

► About RAID systems

► About grandfather, father, son systems

► About backing up program files

Introduction

No matter what methods you put in place to protect hardware, software and data there is always a chance of loss through accidental misuse. Hardware is easily bought again, so it is the software and especially the data which needs protection. Methods need to be put in place to recover programs and data, should they be corrupted or lost.

Backup and recovery procedures

The importance of backup

Backup means keeping copies of software and data so that the data can be recovered should there be a total loss of the ICT system.

The data an organisation holds is a very valuable commodity and is usually worth more than the cost of the hardware and software added together. Think how a business would be able to operate without the following:

- customer database
- supplier database
- product database
- records of all correspondence, price lists, quotes, etc.
- accounts information.

Couple the loss of all this data with the fact that there could be no hardware or software to use and you have a real problem.

It does take effort to back up data, but the latest backup products will do this automatically and without anyone thinking about it.

A recent study has shown that of the companies that lose their data in a disaster:

- 29% are out of business within two years, and
- nearly 43% never open their doors after the disaster.

Backup procedures

Backup involves the creation of data and programs so that if the data or programs are damaged or lost they can be recreated from the backup copies.

Backup procedures are those actions a person or organisation can take to ensure that regular backup copies are taken. Backups should be taken regularly and on a routine basis and the backup copies should be away from the computer system and preferable off-site.

Where to keep backup copies

It is always best to keep backup copies off-site but this is sometimes inconvenient.

Keeping backup copies in a fireproof safe

You could keep backup copies in a fireproof safe. In most cases this will protect them from theft and the damage caused by a small fire. However, they are only fireproof for a certain period of time – usually two hours.

Ensure a fireproof safe is used for backups

Keeping backup copies off-site

Backup copies need to be kept off-site if possible. This is because if a building was completely destroyed, then the likelihood is that all the data, software and hardware would be destroyed. Although complete destruction of buildings is rare, it does happen – the terrorist attack on the Twin Towers is an example.

The attack on the Twin Towers caused the complete loss of two entire buildings.

One method of keeping backup copies off-site is to use removable storage media. Removable magnetic hard drives, pen/flash drives, zip drives and memory cards are all quite portable and can be used for backups.

Procedures for backup

Backups should be taken seriously. Here are some essential pieces of advice:

- use a different tape or disk each day and have a system for rotating them
- make one person responsible for the taking of backups
- keep backups safe (i.e., in a fireproof safe) and preferably off-site
- rehearse backup recovery procedures – you need to be sure it is possible and you know how to recover data.

On-line backup services

There are a number of organisations that provide a service where you can back up your essential files on-line using the Internet. This is a good service and you pay for the service according to the amount of data stored using the service.

The advantage with these services is that once you tell the system which data you want backing up, you simply forget about it and your data is backed up in the background while you are not actively using the computer. Additionally, the backup data is stored on the server of the backup provider – so the backup is not kept on the same site as the original data. To prevent security problems, all the data is encrypted before being sent over the Internet and only the person who owns the data can actually access it.

The main disadvantage of on-line storage is trusting your data to another organisation who could possibly go out of business.

For more information on on-line backup look at the following website: http://www.datadepositbox.com

There is also a nice demonstration of the software and its facilities available at: http://www.datadepositbox.com/demo-citytv.asp

Scheduling backups

The main requirement for backups is that they should be easy to take. In many cases backups can be taken automatically and this is achieved by scheduling a time for the backups to start. In most cases, whilst the backups are taken, the ICT system will slow down. Network users will notice this loss of speed, so it is best to take backups when the computer is not being used. In a lot of situations this can be achieved at night but there are many ICT systems that are in use 24 hours a day so the taking of backups has to be scheduled to the least busy periods.

Backups can be:

- taken manually
- scheduled to be taken automatically.

Backup storage devices and media

There is a huge range of backup devices and media that can be used for taking backup copies. The choice of backup device/media depends on:

- storage capacity needed
- portability of device/media (i.e., weight and size)
- speed of data transfer (the speed with which data can be written to or read from the device/media)
- speed of access (the time it takes for the device to find a specific piece of stored data)
- ability to be connected to different computers or other devices such as printers, cameras, etc.

Magnetic tape

Magnetic tape is an ideal backup medium – it is cheap and has a high storage capacity. Magnetic tapes are removable media which means they can be exchanged with any compatible drive.

Large organisations use tape libraries for their backup. These use lots of tapes and some even use robotic arms to load the tapes into the drives.

Media used for backups

Summary of where to back up

Name of backup	Cost of backup	Storage capacity	Speed	Comments
3.5" floppy	Cheap	1.44 MB	slow	Very small storage capacity and not all computers have a drive to read them. Outdated now.
Flash/pen drives	Cheap	Up to 4 GB and rising	moderate	Very popular portable media. Has replaced the 3.5" floppy.
CD-RW	Free comes with the computer	Up to 700 MB	moderate	Good backup media for PCs containing a small amount of data.
DVD-RW	Free as usually built in	Up to 4.7 GB	moderate	Greater storage capacity means that it is more suitable for backup of data on a home PC.
Hard drive (Fixed)	Free as built in	160 to 250 GB and increasing all the time	fast	Huge amount of storage and some of the capacity could be used for backup but it would be on the same drive.
Hard drive (external or removable)	Moderate	Up to 500 GB and growing	fast	Great for fast backup. Needs to be disconnected and stored in a fireproof safe or stored off-site.
Magnetic tape drive	Expensive	Huge up to 8 TB	fast	Good option where large amounts of data need to be backed up. Some tape systems have removable tapes.
ZIP-drive	Cheap	Up to 750 MB and growing	slow	Disks can be removed and secured. Like a fatter removable floppy disk.
Internet backup	Cheap	Unlimited storage	slow	Charged according to amount of data stored. Has advantage that data is stored off-site.

Magnetic disk

The simplest form of magnetic disk backup simply takes the contents of one magnetic disk and copies it onto a different magnetic disk.

Magnetic disk

Optical media

This includes media such as CD-R, CD-RW, DVD-RW, etc. The main problem with optical storage for backup is that the transfer rate (i.e., the rate at which data is read to or copied from the media) is low, which means taking backups takes longer.

Pen/flash drives

These are very popular as they are small and portable and are ideal for backing up small amounts of work. They are easily lost or stolen.

Pen drive

RAID systems – mirror discs (redundant array of inexpensive discs)

Many network systems use a RAID (redundant array of inexpensive disks) system for the backup of data. Basically they use a series of magnetic disks on which to store the data. There are different RAID systems and in one type the system will automatically take over if the original data is damaged or destroyed, ensuring the continuity of service.

Clustering

To improve network security a technique called clustering is used. Here file servers and storage devices are networked together so that the dependence on one file server and one storage device is eliminated.

The grandfather, father, son system (the ancestral file system)

In some large ICT systems, which have large storage needs, two types of files are kept: master files and transaction files. The master file is the most complete version of a file and if it were lost or damaged then the whole system would be rendered useless. Transaction files are used to hold details of all the transactions (i.e., bits of business) since the master file was last updated. The transaction file is used to update the master file with the changes periodically (e.g., each night, every week, etc.).

There is always the chance that data held on either a disk or tape master file may be destroyed, for example by an inexperienced user, a power failure, fire or even theft.

For most companies, the loss of vital data could prove disastrous. However, using the grandfather-father-son principle it is possible to recreate the master file if it is lost.

The principle works like this. Basically three generations of files are kept. The oldest master file is called the grandfather file and is kept with its transaction file. These two files are used to produce a new master file called the father file that, with its transaction file, is used to create the most up-to-date file, called the son file. The process is repeated and the son becomes the father and the father becomes the grandfather and so on. Only three generations are needed and the other files may be re-used. Usually this system, called the ancestral file system, is used for tapes, although it may also be used for disks.

Backing up program files

In many cases programs, if lost, can usually be recovered easily as the original disks can be used to load the files back onto the system. Increasing numbers of programs are downloaded from the Internet, so if the originals are damaged or lost, then the software producers will allow them to be downloaded again.

Many companies develop their own software or spend a considerable time customising existing programs so they work better for their organisation. In this case the programs need to be backed up originally and at any time new changes are made.

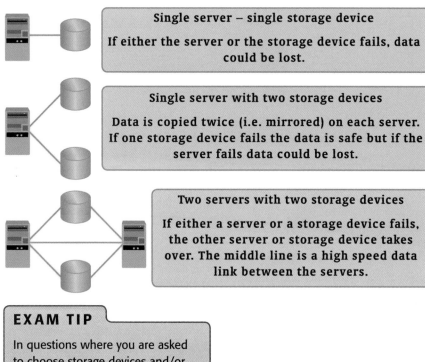

Single server – single storage device

If either the server or the storage device fails, data could be lost.

Single server with two storage devices

Data is copied twice (i.e. mirrored) on each server. If one storage device fails the data is safe but if the server fails data could be lost.

Two servers with two storage devices

If either a server or a storage device fails, the other server or storage device takes over. The middle line is a high speed data link between the servers.

EXAM TIP

In questions where you are asked to choose storage devices and/or storage media, always look to see if it mentions how much data is being backed up. This will determine the device and media. Many students put that you could back up a large amount of data on a floppy disk – clearly you can't. Floppy disks should no longer be mentioned as their storage capacity is too small for most uses.

Prevention of deliberate crimes or misuse

Introduction

ICT systems must be protected against people who wish to misuse them or deliberately damage them. Such people can include hackers, virus writers, disgruntled employees, fraudsters, blackmailers and thieves.

You also have to put in place methods to prevent misuse by employees, such as viewing personal information which is not necessary for their job, practical jokes, leaving computers containing data logged on whilst away from the computer and so on.

This section looks at the methods organisations use to help prevent deliberate crimes or misuse.

Methods for controlling access to computer rooms

Access restrictions

To prevent theft and illegal access to ICT systems, access to computer rooms can be restricted by the use of keypads. Access to rooms and computers can also be restricted using hardware which involves biometric testing. Biometric testing involves face recognition, voice recognition or fingerprint recognition. The advantage of this form of access is that there are no passwords or combination codes to remember.

Face recognition systems can restrict access to both rooms and computers. They can even be used to monitor the time that the users are at their workstation.

Methods of securing integrity of transmitted data

Encryption

Encryption scrambles data as it is passed along communication lines or wirelessly so that even if it is intercepted, it makes no sense to the interceptor. Encryption is also a feature of the latest operating systems, where the data stored on the hard drive is automatically encrypted so that if the computer is stolen or the data copied, it cannot be understood.

Copyright 2002 by Randy Glasbergen.
www.glasbergen.com

'Encryption software is expensive...so we just rearranged all the letters on your keyboard.'

How encryption works

Encryption works in the following way. Suppose Jayne in London wants to send a secure e-mail to Jack in Paris. When Jayne has typed in her e-mail she presses the 'encrypt' option on the mailer software. The software verifies with her who she wants to send the e-mail to. She chooses Jack's name from the list presented and all the people on this list are people for whom Jayne has a public key and can send encrypted messages to. The encryption software then automatically mixes and re-mixes every binary bit of the message with every bit in Jack's public key. The result is a binary mix of data that may be unscrambled only by the same software but using Jack's private key. When Jack receives the e-mail in Paris, he needs to select the 'decrypt' option and the software then asks him for a password that he types in and this decrypts his private key. The private key is a very long number and a large number of calculations are then performed which unscrambles the binary mess to give the message from Jayne. If the message was intercepted, hackers would be unable to see the message because they do not have the private key that is used to perform the calculations needed to unscramble the message.

Proxy servers

A proxy server is a server which can be hardware or software that takes requests from users for access to other servers and either forwards them onto the other servers or denies access to the servers. Proxy servers can be used to limit or block access to certain web addresses (URLs) or web services such as instant messaging and chat rooms.

Proxy servers are used by schools to make sure that pupils can only access certain information and it keeps them out of sites with dubious content and stops them wasting time in chat rooms or social networking sites when they should be doing other work.

Many organisations use proxy servers to provide content filtering and to ensure that their employees adhere to their acceptable use policy.

Methods to define security status and access rights for users

There are a number of methods used to define security status and access rights for users and these include:

- use of a hierarchy of passwords
- allocation of network resources to users based on user-IDS and passwords
- allocation of access rights to users based on their job or seniority (e.g., read only, append only, create new records only, etc.).

Methods for physical protection of hardware and software

There are many different ways in which hardware and software can be physically protected and these include:

- access to computer rooms restricted
- keyboard locks
- locks to computers which make use of biometric methods (retinal scanning, fingerprinting, face recognition)
- attaching cables to each computer so that you cannot remove any of them
- locks on drives to prevent removable media being inserted to prevent data or software being copied
- firewalls to protect networks from unauthorised access from hackers
- computers being locked away at the end of the day

- original copies of software stored in a fireproof safe
- backup copies of software taken regularly and stored in a fireproof safe or off-site.

Security of document filing systems

It is really no good having excellent IT security if the results of processing in the form of printouts are left on top of someone's desk for everyone to see and possibly photocopy. As well as physical and logical security we need to consider document security. Also, users must protect documents stored on their laptop computers and these are more likely to be stolen as they are used in public places and put in cars.
It is important that any printouts or reports are locked away when not being used and they are shredded before being put in the wastepaper basket.

"Oh, it was just like any other day at work.
Except for the part where I sneezed
by the paper shredder."

Risk management: costs and control

▼ You will find out

▶ About identifying potential risks

▶ About determining the likelihood of risks occurring

▶ About the short- and long-term consequences of the threat

▶ About how well equipped the company is to deal with the threat

Introduction

There are lots of threats to ICT systems, so organisations need to work out what the risks are, how likely they are to occur, the likely consequences should they occur, what can be done to minimise the risk and whether this can be done at reasonable cost.

Risk analysis is an important part of running ICT systems in organisations as many of them rely completely on their ICT system. In this section you will learn about risk analysis and how an organisation is able to assess how much money should be spent on the minimisation of risk.

Risk analysis

The main purpose of risk analysis is to make everyone in the organisation aware of the security threats to the hardware, software and data held. They need to be made aware of the consequences of any loss for a short or a sustained period, such as the immediate financial loss and the long-term loss caused by lack of confidence by customers, the bad publicity in the press and the inability to provide customer service.

In order to perform a risk analysis, it will be necessary to consider the following:

- Placing a value on each of the components of a successful information system which would include:
  - hardware
  - software
  - documentation
  - people
  - communications channels
  - data.
- Identifying the risks to the above and the likelihood of their occurrence.

Most organisations have a corporate information technology security review which looks at the computer-processed information with a view to identifying the risks of unavailability, errors and omissions, abuse, unauthorised disclosure and to determining their potential implications. Each risk will need to be examined from the point of view of the security and the loss assessed and its likely occurrence. The aim is to identify those systems crucial to the organisation and to look at the possible short- or long-term loss of such systems.

Here are just some of the many consequences of system loss:

- cashflow problems as invoices are sent out late
- bad business decisions through lack of management information
- loss of goodwill to customers and suppliers
- production delays caused by not having the correct stock available
- late delivery of orders causing customers to go elsewhere
- stock shortage or overstocking caused by lack of suitable stock control.

Identify potential risks

If ICT systems are to be protected, then the risks need to be identified. Here is a list of the risks to most ICT systems:

- viruses
- fire
- natural damage (floods, earthquakes, lightning, volcanoes, etc.)
- hacking (tapping into communication lines)
- systems failure owing to machine malfunction
- fraud
- power failure
- sabotage
- theft (hardware, software and data)
- blackmail
- espionage
- terrorist bomb attacks
- chemical spillage
- gas leaks
- vandalism
- spilling a drink over the computer equipment
- failure of the telecommunication links
- problems with data cables in networks
- malfunctioning hubs and routers, etc.
- software failure
- systems software containing bugs causing the computer to crash
- hard drive damage/loss
- strikes.

Likelihood of risk occurring

Some things are almost certain to happen sooner or later, such as a power cut, but others such as an explosion are much less likely, but all the threats need to be taken into account. Senior management have to decide the likelihood of the risk occurring and how the risk can be minimised at reasonable cost, and what levels of risk are acceptable to the organisation.

▷ KEY WORDS

Risk analysis – the process of assessing the likelihood of certain events happening and estimating the cost of the damage they could cause and what can be done at reasonable cost to eliminate or minimise the risk

Disaster recovery programme – a plan that restores ICT facilities in as short a time as possible in order to minimise the loss caused by the complete or partial loss of an organisation's ICT facilities

Short- and long-term consequences of threat

Short-term consequences of loss of data include:

- Resources (e.g., staff, equipment, etc.) need to be directed towards recovering data.
- The organisation may have to pay compensation to people who have been adversely affected by lost data.
- Financial loss due to loss of business through not being able to take orders.
- Embarrassment if details are reported in the press.
- Possible prosecution if the loss of personal data is due to lax security and a case can be brought under the Data Protection Act.

Long-term consequences of threat include:

- Loss of integrity means people do not want to deal with the organisation.
- Financial loss through loss in orders may result in the business going bankrupt.
- High cost in having to replace lost hardware, software and data.

How well equipped is the company to deal with threat?

Organisations need to continually ask how well they could deal with a threat should it occur. Threats and organisations change over the years, so this needs to be reviewed periodically.

The disaster recovery programme

The purpose of the disaster recovery programme is to ensure the availability of essential resources (staff, buildings, power, etc.) and computer equipment should a disaster occur. The plan will usually cover the following:

- the total or partial loss of computing equipment
- the loss of essential services such as electricity, heating or air conditioning

- the loss of certain key employees (e.g., losing all the qualified network staff in one go due to them choosing to form their own facilities organisation)
- the loss of maintenance or support services
- the loss of data or software
- the complete or partial loss of telecommunications equipment or services
- the complete or partial loss of the premises housing the IT equipment.

Explosions are much less likely to happen

▶ Activity: Creating a disaster recovery programme

There are many threats to ICT systems and the damage they might cause can be minimised by having a disaster recovery programme.

You have been put in charge of the ICT facilities in your school/college. These facilities cover both the school/college teaching networks and also the administration networks, which contain important details such as data about staff and students and details of all the financial transactions.

You have been asked to create a disaster recovery programme for your school or college. By reading the notes on disaster recover programmes in this topic and by conducting your own research using the Internet you should have a good understanding of the topic.

Produce the disaster recovery programme for your school or college. Ensure that your disaster recovery programme includes the following:

- How the school/college could cope with the loss of ICT hardware and software.
- How the school/college could recover any lost data.
- How the school/college could cope with the loss of certain key ICT staff.
- How the school/college could cope with the loss of telecommunication equipment and services.

Gales often bring down power or telecommunication lines

Case studies

▶ **Case study 1**   p. 74

Microsoft Vista making taking backups easier

Microsoft Windows Vista is the latest operating system by Microsoft.

Microsoft Vista is the latest version of an operating system which makes use of the latest technology available. A new more up-to-date operating system was needed because of the demands placed on home and business users as they use video, music, gaming and other multimedia demands on a day-to-day basis.

The software contains many new security features designed to keep data and files safe. In particular there are new controls which make sure that users cannot make changes that make their system vulnerable.

Even if a computer is stolen, one new feature called BitLocker technology encrypts the hard drive and renders it useless to someone else. This means that they cannot access the data and programs on the hard drive. This is particularly useful as more and more people use laptops in public places such as planes, trains, cafes, etc.

In Windows Vista backing up data is made much easier.

Other features of Vista include an easy to use Wizard which takes you though the steps of taking backups. It is easy to specify what files you want backing up, the device used to store the backup and the time to start the backup.

Read the above article carefully and then answer the following questions. You may need to do some research in order to answer these questions. Use books and on-line glossaries to help you. Good luck!

1 Vista is an operating system.
   (a) Write a brief description of the purpose of an operating system. (4 marks)
   (b) Describe **two** tasks an operating system would perform. (2 marks)
   (c) Microsoft Vista is an example of an operating system. Give the brand names of **two** other operating systems. (2 marks)

2 In the passage it says that 'there are new controls which make sure that users cannot make changes that make their system vulnerable'. By giving an example, describe a change which could be made to the operating system that will make the ICT system more vulnerable. (2 marks)

3 Vista uses a Wizard to help users back up their data.
   (a) Describe what is meant by the term Wizard. (1 mark)
   (b) Explain why a Wizard is a helpful feature for a user. (2 marks)

4 When an ICT system is used in a business, the data stored is often much more valuable than the hardware or software.
   (a) State, by giving an example, why the above statement can often be true. (2 marks)

   (b) Explain **two** ways in which data can be lost from a computer. (2 marks)
   (c) Backups are taken so that files can be restored if lost or damaged. Give the names of **two** types of storage media that are appropriate for backup copies. (2 marks)

5 (a) Explain the meaning of the term encrypt. (3 marks)
   (b) Explain how encryption of data on the hard drive of the computer renders it useless to a thief who steals the computer. (2 marks)

6 Backups can be scheduled to take place at any time of the day. State, giving a reason, the time of day when backups are best taken. (2 marks)

Good planning keeps flooded businesses afloat

During the serious floods in June 2007 many businesses had their offices flooded. Some of the businesses were well covered and had plans in place to relocate staff to a disaster recovery centre where staff could use the ICT systems and their backup data to get their business up and running again.

Some firms had their computer systems flooded and completely destroyed. Others had problems with the electricity supply owing to water seeping into cables.

One member of the business community said that smaller less organised companies may not survive this, but larger companies will pull through because they have plans in place to keep their business running.

1 Describe **two** plans an organisation could put in place to keep a business running even though the ICT facilities in an office cannot be used and the data stored on the computers has been lost. **(6 marks)**

2 It is best to keep backup data off-site.
  (a) Give **one** reason why backup data should be kept off-site. **(1 mark)**
  (b) Describe **one** method for keeping backup data off-site. **(2 marks)**

The police getting into trouble

One oil company ran a promotion to encourage drivers to buy their brand of petrol at their service stations in preference to others. To this end, the company placed a list of car registration numbers at each petrol station and if you were the owner of one of these numbers then you won a prize of £1000. Some police officers visited the garage and noticed the list of numbers and realised that they could use this list of numbers to type them into the Police National Computer (PNC) where they could obtain the addresses of their owners. They did this and then rang up the people on the list and said that if the owner were to give them a sum of money, then they would tell them how they could get £1000. Naturally, most people agreed. Eventually the officers involved were found out and severely reprimanded. Following an investigation, abuses of the PNC were found to be widespread with many private companies paying to receive information that it contained. Clearly these abuses had to stop and now in order to interrogate the database, the police officers have to identify themselves and the reason why they require the information. In addition to this, an audit can be performed where a particular search on the PNC is investigated to make sure that it was necessary and that it was a legitimate use of the system.

1 Large networks such as the Police National Computer are used by thousands of users every day.
  (a) Explain how user-IDs and passwords can be used to restrict access to only certain staff. **(2 marks)**
  (b) The Police National Computer has a series of access rights for those people authorised to use it. Explain what is meant by 'access rights' and give an example of how they might be used with this system. **(4 marks)**
  (c) Audit software is used with the Police National Computer. Explain why this software is useful and how it might prevent the type of breach in security explained in the case study. **(2 marks)**

2 Abuse of network resources is a problem for all organisations that use a network.
  (a) Other than unauthorised access to personal data, describe **four** ways a network can be abused. **(4 marks)**
  (b) Explain **two** things the Police could do in order to prevent misuse of the PNC's facilities by its own staff. **(2 marks)**

▶ Case study 4 | pp. 76–77

A terrorist attack

On a Saturday in June 1996 the police received a coded warning that a bomb had been planted at the Arndale Centre, which is Manchester's premier shopping area. Just over an hour after a speedy evacuation of the Centre and the surrounding area, the bomb exploded, injuring over two hundred people and destroying a large part of the Centre and ripping apart many of the business premises surrounding it. The bomb, which was the largest bomb explosion in peacetime Britain, caused extensive damage to the offices of the Royal and Sun Alliance insurance company where some staff were injured.

As these offices housed the company's mainframe computer, it was initially feared that the day-to-day operations of the company would be severely affected. The staff in the Liverpool office, which contained terminals that were networked to the mainframe, found that there was still some life in the system, even though there was extensive damage to the building the computer was housed in. There was some optimism that the system could be recovered, but to prevent the likelihood of gas explosions from the ruptured gas mains, the fire brigade cut off the electrical power. Effectively most of the hardware had been irreparably damaged during the explosion. However, like most sensible companies, this one had a contingency plan and it involved having a contract with a specialist data recovery company who had similar hardware and copies of software being used by Royal and Sun Alliance. Because they needed staff who understood the Insurance business to operate the computer, the Royal's staff were transported to the offices of the recovery company and they set to work recovering the data from the backup media which was kept off-site. By Monday morning all the data had been recovered and a temporary switchboard had been set up and not a single day's trading was lost.

1 The Royal and Sun Alliance insurance company has an ICT security policy. As part of this policy they performed a risk analysis and also established a disaster recovery programme.
   (a) Explain what is involved in risk analysis. (2 marks)
   (b) Describe the techniques used in the disaster recovery programme to recover the data used by the ICT systems. (6 marks)

2 Backup and recovery procedures are an essential part of ensuring the security of ICT systems.
   (a) Explain the difference between backup procedures and recovery procedures. (2 marks)
   (b) Give **three** things that must be considered when choosing a backup procedure. (3 marks)
   (c) Explain why recovery procedures are essential if an organisation such as this insurance company wants to ensure the security of its data. (2 marks)

Questions and Activities

▶ Questions 1 | **pp. 62–73**

1 What can organisations do in order to minimise the damage caused by:
  (a) a power cut (2 marks)
  (b) a virus attack (2 marks)
  (c) an inexperienced operator wiping the magnetic media by mistake (2 marks)
  (d) the deliberate alteration of important data by hackers (2 marks)
  (e) the key members of staff leaving with all the organisation's IT expertise and knowledge (2 marks)
  (f) A loss of the communication lines in a WAN (2 marks)
  (g) The loss of access to the organisation's premises owing to a fire in a nearby building (2 marks)
  (h) The deliberate destruction of company programs by a disgruntled employee. (2 marks)

2 An ICT manager is worried about the misuse of the ICT facilities by certain members of staff.
  (a) Give the names of **three** types of misuse of data. (3 marks)
  (b) Explain how the misuses you have identified in part (a) can be detected. (3 marks)
  (c) Most organisations make use of an 'ICT security policy'. Describe the advantages in having such a policy. (3 marks)

3 Some ICT applications use software which maintains an audit trail.
  Name **one** such application and state why this facility is necessary. (4 marks)

4 'ICT systems are mission critical; the consequences of failure could prove disastrous.'
  Discuss this statement, including in your discussion:
  • the potential threats to the system
  • the concept of risk analysis
  • the corporate consequences of system failure

  • the factors which should be considered when designing the 'disaster recovery programme' to enable a recovery from disaster. (8 marks)

5 The threats to ICT systems are many.
  (a) State **five** threats to an ICT system and for each one explain how the risk of occurrence can be reduced. (5 marks)
  (b) The threats you have mentioned in part (a) can have a number of consequences to an organisation should they occur.
  Describe **three** such consequences to an organisation. (3 marks)

6 Part of an ICT security policy will be concerned with backup and recovery procedures.
  (a) Discuss the methods used by organisations to back up their programs and data. (6 marks)
  (b) Explain how an organisation can ensure that the original data can be recovered should loss of hardware, software and data occur. (4 marks)

7 Most organisations make use of a staff code of conduct in order to minimise the risk from their own staff.
  (a) Describe **two** problems caused by the misuse of ICT systems by staff. (2 marks)
  (b) Describe how having a code of conduct can help reduce the incidence of both deliberate and accidental misuse by staff. (3 marks)

8 All ICT organisations should have an ICT security policy.
  (a) Discuss the factors which need to be taken into account when designing an ICT security policy in order to deal with the following:
    (i) accidental misuse
    (ii) deliberate misuse. (4 marks)
  (b) Explain what is meant by risk analysis and give an example of how an organisation would go about producing one. (4 marks)

Questions and Activities *continued*

▶ **Questions 2** pp. 74–77

1 Fire is a major threat to any ICT system.
  State **three** things that can be done to minimise the risk to an ICT system from fire. (3 marks)

2 The people who work in an organisation can be responsible for loss or damage to the organisation's data. This can be done maliciously or accidentally. Organisations take regular backups to recover data damaged or lost but they also try to prevent employees from causing loss or damage to data.
  (a) Describe **two** measures that could be incorporated into the hardware which could prevent loss or damage to data. (4 marks)
  (b) Describe two software measures that could be used to prevent the loss or damage to data. (4 marks)
  (c) Describe **two** procedures the organisation could adopt to prevent the loss or damage to data. (4 marks)

2 Access to network resources is often managed using passwords and different levels of permitted access for users.
  (a) Explain what is meant by a password. (2 marks)
  (b) Explain the meaning of the term 'levels of permitted access for users'. (2 marks)

3 There are many potential threats to ICT systems, so a number of security measures are put in place. Describe, by giving a relevant example, what each of these types of security involve.
  (a) Physical security (1 mark)
  (b) Personnel security (1 mark)
  (c) Software/logical security (1 mark)
  (d) Communications security (1 mark)
  (e) Document security. (1 mark)

▶ Activity 1: Producing a presentation on backup

You have been asked to give a presentation using presentation software on the importance of backup and the different types of backup available.

The firm you are presenting the information to has a very haphazard approach to backup at the moment and you will have to make a convincing argument that the time and effort in taking backups is absolutely essential.

The presentation is to last five minutes and during this time you will need to cover the following:
  • The types of threat to data.
  • The consequences to the organisation of losing their data.
  • The need for regular taking of backups.
  • The need for someone to be given overall responsibility for the taking of backups.
  • The types of backup systems that are available.
Here is what you know about the organisation's procedures on backups at the moment:
  • Someone has to remember to undertake the backup and if necessary take the backup off-site.
  • Often the backup copies are not removed off-site.
  • Everyone thinks it is someone else's job to take the backup.
  • Backups are never tested so no-one knows whether the data could be recovered from them.

▶ Activity 2: Preparing an ICT security policy for a school or college

Using your knowledge of this topic, produce an ICT security policy for a school or college. This policy should cover the use of the ICT systems by the administrative staff as well as the use of the ICT facilities by teachers/lecturers and also students/pupils.

When producing this document you should bear the following in mind:
  • Colleges and schools hold a lot of personal data (student records, personnel records, medical details, examinations results, references, etc.).
  • All schools and colleges are connected to the Internet and this brings a variety of security problems that you will need to deal with.
  • You will need to decide who will enforce the rules you will have to make regarding the use of IT equipment.
  • Many students like to play games on the school's/college's systems when they should be working.
  • Because so many students bring work on flash drives into the school/college there is a serious problem with viruses.

Remember the intended audience of your document. Not everyone will understand the technical terms used and they might not be as familiar with computers as you think.

Exam support

Worked example 1

1 All organisations should have an ICT security policy. You have been asked to produce an ICT security policy for a business.

Discuss the methods that could be adopted by the business to prevent (a) accidental misuse and (b) deliberate misuse of the ICT equipment.

In your answers to part (a) you should make reference to backup and recovery procedures and in your answers to part (b) you should consider methods for securing transmitted data. **(8 marks)**

Student answer 1

1 (a) No matter how hard you try, accidents happen, so it is best to consider ways of recovering the ICT systems should the misuse cause damage. You could train the users so that they do not delete files accidentally or copy over a new file with an older version.

Backups of data should be taken on removable media (CD-RW, magnetic tapes, portable hard drives) and then these should be kept off-site. If the data is destroyed then it can be recovered.

(b) Users should log off if they are away from their desks to ensure other people cannot use the computer to gain access to files they are not allowed to view. Key locks can be used to prevent unauthorised access to networks.

User-IDs and passwords provide control over access to files and levels of file access determine what files a user can see and also the file operations they can do (e.g., append, create new records, read only, etc.). When financial details are sent over networks, the data can be encrypted so that even if it is intercepted it could not be understood.

Examiner's comment

1 (a) The student needed to realise that this question is about items that should be in the ICT security policy. They do make the important point that accidental misuse is hard to protect against and it is best to consider how to recover lost data.

The part about training gains a mark as do the two points regarding taking of backup copies (one for mentioning typical media used and one for the removal off-site).

The student could have mentioned about the frequency of taking backups and how the backup should be tested to make sure that the original data can be recovered. **(3 marks out of 4)**

(b) The student has made some good points here and has gained full marks for this section. **(4 marks out of 4)**
(Total 7 marks out of 8)

Student answer 2

1 (a) Accidental misuse means making mistakes by erasing data, losing work, damaging computers, forgetting to take backups, spilling coffee over your computer and so on. It is hard to stop these happening, so staff have to be careful.

(b) Downloading programs illegally can lead to the firm being prosecuted, so the business should have a staff code of conduct which forbids it.

Leaving personal data on your computer while you go for lunch is bad, as others can see it and they could access other personal information using the computers.

When data is transmitted it needs to be made safe from hackers. It is hard to protect radio signals in wireless systems. The only way you can do it is with encoding.

Examiner's comment

1 (a) In this answer, the student has not properly read the question as they have produced an answer which talks about accidental misuse in a general way. They needed to tailor their answer to what should be included in the ICT security policy to deal with accidental misuses. No marks can be awarded for this section. **(0 marks out of 4)**

(b) The mention of the staff code of conduct gains one mark.

The section about leaving personal data on the screen does not gain a mark as they have failed to mention that employees should log off.

The last answer mentions 'encoding' when the student actually means 'encryption' so no marks for this answer. **(1 mark out of 4)**
(Total 1 mark out of 8)

Examiner's answer

1 (a) One mark each to a maximum of four for four points such as:

Need to back up data onto removable media or transfer data to another computer

Remove to another location off-site

Have a schedule by which backups are taken

Test the backup procedure by checking that data can be recovered using the backups

(b) One mark each to a maximum of four for four points such as:

Do not keep computers logged on when away from them/automatically log off computers after a period of inactivity

Use user-IDs and password protection to authenticate users

Use encryption to ensure that hackers cannot intercept data transmitted

Set up audit procedures to detect deliberate abuse.

Worked example 2

2 A student is working on some ICT project work at school using the school's computers. They want to continue working on the project at home on their laptop computer.

(a) Describe a suitable backup procedure that they could use. **(4 marks)**

(b) The threats to laptop computers are often greater than those to desktop computers. Give **one** reason why. **(1 mark)**

Student answer 1

2 (a) Store the work on a disk and keep the disk in a safe place.

(b) Laptop computers are lighter and so are easily concealed/ stolen.

Examiner's comment

2 In part (a) there is no mention of the type of disk nor is there any mention that the disk is to be removed from the computer, so no mark.

They do mention to keep the disk in a safe place but they have not said this should be away from the computer. It is still worth a mark.

The student needed to look at the marks allocated. Four marks usually means 4 valid points or perhaps 3 with an extra mark for the clarity of the explanation.

For part (b): laptop computers are lighter is a fact. But although it is obvious, the student has not been specific about the relevance of this. **(1 mark out of 5)**

Student answer 2

2 (a) Send an e-mail to their home e-mail address and browse
for and attach the file or files they are working on to the
e-mail. This means that the data will be sent off-site which
is best for security and they can download the file or files
when at home. There is the advantage in that there is no
media to lose, such as pen drives, CD-RW, etc. They can also
access the file on any computer connected to the Internet.

(b) Laptops are portable and if you carry one along the road in
a case then it is obvious you have one in the case and you
could be attacked and the laptop stolen.

Examiner's comment

2 (a) Here the student has written four sentences and
each one is relevant to the question and adds
more information about the backup method
chosen and the procedures that are adopted.
Full marks for this part of the question.

(b) Here the student has identified the threat which
is theft, and has given a reason why this is more
likely with a laptop. Full marks for this part of
the question. **(5 marks out of 5)**

Examiner's answers

2 (a) One mark up to a maximum of four for each of the
following points:
- Take a copy of the folder/files.
- Store the copy onto removable media such as magnetic floppy disk,
external magnetic hard disk, store on the server if students can access the
server from the Internet.
- Attach the file to an e-mail and send the e-mail to your home/school
e-mail account.
- Store the data on a removable pen/flash drive.
- Store the copy onto an optical disk such as DVD-RW, CD-RW.
- Files should be copied on a regular basis (e.g., at the end of a session).
- Copies need to be stored in a safe place away from the computer.
- It is essential that the backup copies are tested to make sure that the files
can be recovered.

(b) One reason for one mark such as:
- Laptops are smaller and so are easier to steal.
- Laptops are often used in public areas, so they are more likely to be stolen.
- Wireless links to networks in public places may introduce viruses.
- Laptops are more likely to be damaged (e.g., dropped, exposed to water,
etc.).

Worked example 3

3 **All organisations should have a backup procedure so that their data can be recovered if it were lost due to a security breach. Give five items along with reasons that would need to be considered when deciding on backup procedures. (10 marks)**

Student answer 1

3 Firewalls to prevent users hacking into the company's ICT systems.

Training to make sure that the users don't make mistakes and accidentally delete data.

The type of storage device such as pen drive or removable magnetic disk used to put the backup copy on.

Where to put the backup copy. It is best to store it away from the original data such as off-site.

How much data there is to store – if there is a large amount of data it would be best to store using magnetic tape as this has a very high storage capacity.

Examiner's comment

3 The first two answers the student has given show that the student has seen the word 'security breach' in the question and started to write about that. It is very common for students to answer the question they would like to have been asked. No marks for either of these two answers.

The next three answers are good. The student has now started to answer the question! **(6 marks out of 10)**

Student answer 2

3 How often to take backups. For example, with an on-line system where the data is changing by the minute, the backups need to be taken all the time. Other systems may only need backups once a day.

Where to keep the backups – off the premises is best, in case the backups are destroyed at the same time as the original data.

What medium to use to store the backups. This depends on how much data there is and how often it changes. Pen drives are good for small amounts and magnetic tape is good for backing up large amounts of data.

What type of backup to take – for example, there are incremental backups which only back up data that has changed since last backup.

Who takes the backup? It is best to give one person responsibility for taking backups.

Examiner's comment

3 This is a very good answer, and deserves full marks. **(10 marks out of 10)**

Examiner's answers

3 One mark for the name of the item and one mark for further expansion/explanation.

The type of backup that should be taken (1) such as full, incremental or differential (1).

How often the backups should be taken (1) such as continuously, every hour, every day (1), etc.

The backup medium/devices used (1) such as magnetic tape/disk (1), etc.

Where the backup is to be held/stored (1) – off-site, in fireproof safe, transferred using the Internet (1), etc.

Who should be responsible for the taking and storage of backups (1) – so that backups are treated as a high priority (1).

It is important when answering this sort of question to think how the marks may be allocated. The examiner will have a list of points which need to be made and you need to anticipate what these might be. Do not waste time writing sentences that do not add anything to the answer or are a repeat of information stated in the question.

Summary mind maps

Potential threats to ICT systems

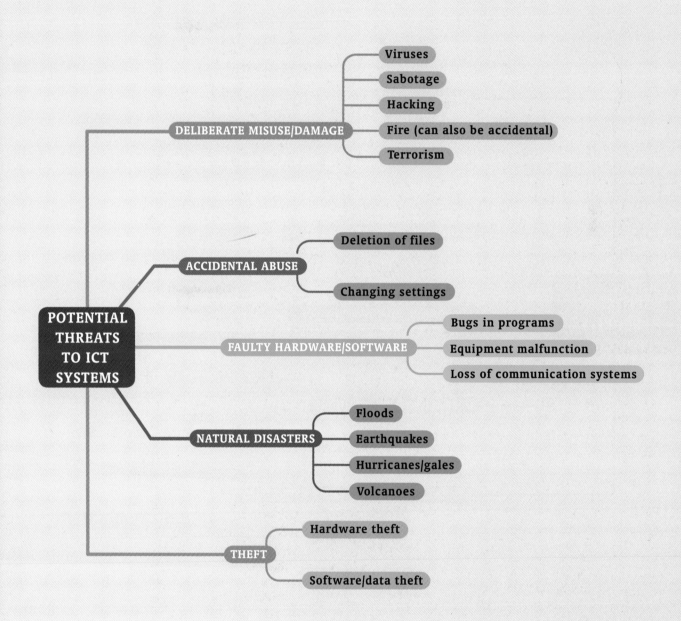

Summary mind maps *continued*

Factors when designing security policies

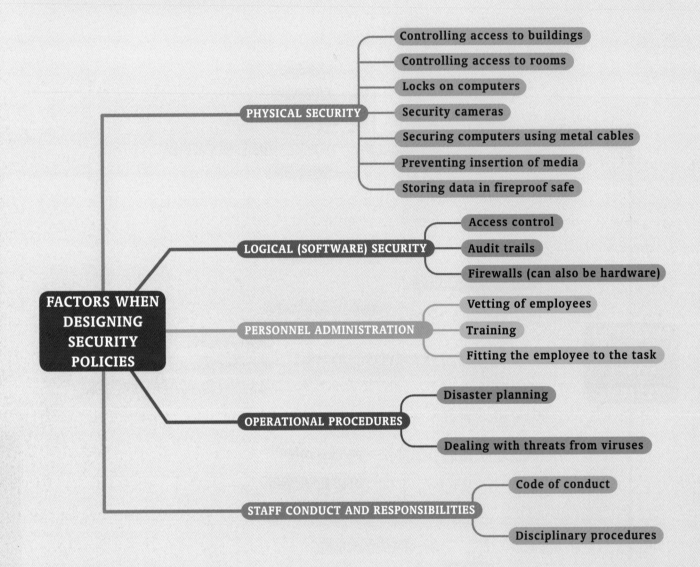

TOPIC 6: Database systems

All organisations have to manage the data they hold and the usual way of doing this is to use a database created using database software. Database software allows data to be entered and stored in a structured way that aids its retrieval. Databases can be flat file, which are of very limited use, or relational, which are more flexible but require specialist knowledge to set up.

In this topic you will learn about the features of relational databases which make them a powerful way of storing and extracting data. You will learn about the components of relational databases and how data may be put into a relational database in the most efficient way.

▼ The key concepts covered in this topic are:

▶ Databases

▶ Distributed databases

CONTENTS

Unit IT3 Use and Impact of ICT

Databases

Introduction

You came across the terms flat file and relational database in Topic 11 of the AS course. Some of this material has been repeated here so that you have a full and comprehensive treatment of the topic. In this section you will learn about why relational databases offer many advantages over flat files and you will also learn about the organisation of relational databases.

Flat files

The simplest storage system is the flat file. Flat files contain only one table of data which limits their use to simple data storage and retrieval systems. With a flat file, the applications software would access the set of data held in the table. This would mean, for example, the payroll system would access the file containing all the employees and their pay details. A human resources system would access a different file containing details about employees such as personal details, qualifications, posts held and pay. As you can imagine there is quite a lot of duplication across these two files as in flat-file systems there is not the facility to share files.

The problems of the flat file

It is possible to store all the data in the one table. For example, a tool hire company could store the details of customers, tools and rentals in the one table like this:

Each piece of application software accesses its own store of data; there is no sharing of data with a flat-file approach and this will lead to a number of problems

Payroll Dept ⟷ PAYROLL APPLICATIONS PROGRAM ⟷ Payroll data

HR Dept ⟷ HUMAN RESOURCES APPLICATIONS PROGRAM ⟷ HR data

There are a number of problems with this:

- There is no record of a tool unless it is hired out.
- Even if a customer has hired a tool in the past, their details (Customer No, Forename, Surname, etc.) still need to be re-entered and this wastes time. If you look at the first two rows of the table you can see that it contains some identical data.
- The tool details need to be entered as each customer hires it and this again wastes time.

- There are problems with data integrity. Inconsistencies in the data can arise when, for example, the customer changes their address, as some of the old records (i.e. rows in the table) will contain the old details.

There is a much more efficient way of organising this data and that is by storing the data in not one table but three and linking them together using relationships to form a relational database.

Customer No	Forename	Surname	First Line Address	Postcode	Tel No	Tool ID	Tool Description	Hire Price	Date hired	Date due back
1200	Steve	Smith	1 Dacre Street	L91 6TY	243 6782	0002	Steam stripper	£9.50	14/08/08	15/08/08
1200	Steve	Smith	1 Dacre Street	L91 6TY	243 6782	0002	Steam stripper	£9.50	19/08/08	21/08/08
1201	Jenny	Chung	12 Morris Street	L43 1WW	782 8722	0003	Carpet cleaner	£43.00	14/08/08	19/08/08
1202	Raymond	Chandler	8 Fell Street	L21 6TT	920 1111	0001	Pressure washer	£15.00	13/08/08	14/08/08
1203	John	Jacobs	99 Teesdale Rd	L44 7TU	976 6121	0004	Floor sander	£67.00	13/08/08	17/08/08
1203	John	Jacobs	99 Teesdale Rd	L44 7TU	976 6121	0001	Pressure washer	£15.00	17/08/08	20/08/08

Sample flat-file table

Flat files and relational databases

The differences between flat files and relational databases were covered at AS level but here is a reminder of the features.

Features of flat files:

- can be created using spreadsheet or database software
- all the data is held in a single table
- they can suffer from data redundancy (i.e., unnecessary duplication of data)
- only useful with simple applications
- very simple to set up.

Features of relational databases:

- data is held in two or more tables
- there are links between the tables
- data from any of the tables can be extracted
- greater knowledge is needed to set them up.

Relational databases

The basic component of any relational database is the table, which is a collection of data arranged in rows and columns. Relational databases contain many tables with each table containing related data. The tables are linked together which means that data in any of the tables can be combined to give the user meaningful information in the form of reports.

For example, in the tool hire company, each tool can be given a unique number (called Tool_ID) and its other details (tool description, hire price) in one table like this:

Tool ID	Tool Description	Hire Price
0001	Pressure washer	£15.00
0002	Steam stripper	£9.50
0003	Carpet cleaner	£43.00
0004	Floor sander	£67.00

Tool table

Another table could list the customers, who are each given a unique customer number, along with other information such as name, address and telephone number like this:

Customer No	Forename	Surname	First Line Address	Postcode	Tel No
1200	Steve	Smith	1 Dacre Street	L91 6TY	243 6782
1201	Jenny	Chung	12 Morris Street	L43 1WW	782 8722
1202	Raymond	Chandler	8 Fell Street	L21 6TT	920 1111
1203	John	Jacobs	99 Teesdale Rd	L44 7TU	976 6121

Customer table

A further table, called rentals, can be used to record which customer has which tool, using the appropriate tool ID and customer numbers. The rental table would also include the date the tool was hired and the date it was due back so the hire store knows when the tool is overdue.

Tool ID	Customer No	Date hired	Date due back
0001	1202	13/08/08	14/08/08
0004	1203	13/08/08	17/08/08
0003	1201	14/08/08	19/08/08
0002	1200	14/08/08	15/08/08
0002	1200	19/08/08	21/08/08
0001	1203	17/08/08	20/08/08

The Rentals table contains fields (Tool ID and Customer No) that appear in the other tables

In a relational database the tables are linked by having a matching field in both tables. For example, Tool ID appears in both the Tools table and the Rentals table and it is this field that supplies the link. There is also a link using Customer No between the Rentals table and the Customer table. The ability to link (or relate) tables is an important feature of relational databases.

Relational database organisation

By using a relational approach, you can avoid some of the data problems associated with other approaches such as the flat file. Relational database organisation deals with the following issues:

- data consistency
- data redundancy
- data integrity
- data independence.

Data consistency

In some organisations, the same data can be found in different files. This is wasteful because the data may need to be input twice and also if the data is changed in one of the files, then it must also be changed in the other file to ensure consistency. If this is not done, then you can get the situation where the data depends on the file you are using. The use of more than one file to hold the data is a problem when there is no central pool of data and the data in such databases soon becomes inconsistent.

Data redundancy

The whole point of producing a central pool of data is that once created, this data can be subsequently shared between a number of applications. The main advantage in this approach is that data need not be duplicated. If the data is kept separately, then any change to one piece of data needs to be altered in any of the other places it is kept. If this is not done, then the data is no longer consistent. For example, the marketing department may keep a database of customers as will the accounts department. If the customer notifies the marketing department that they have changed their address, as well as altering their database accordingly, they will also need to contact the accounts department to tell them to change their records as well.

Databases *continued*

The problem is that in a larger company, the people in the marketing department may not know which other departments also keep the names and addresses of customers, so the system breaks down. Clearly a single customer database to be used by all the departments has the advantages of not having to type and store the same data unnecessarily and also not having to make several alterations to all the occurrences of the data.

Most organisations now keep the data separate to the applications used to process the data and this means that if the applications software is changed, then the data can be kept on its own so that it can be used with another application.

Using a centrally stored pool of data in a database does reduce most of the duplication but it is impossible to eliminate duplication completely. Data which is repeated unnecessarily is called redundant data.

Data integrity

Data integrity means the correctness of the data. As soon as some of the data contained in the database is discovered to be inaccurate, the users start to lose faith in all the data in the database. There are a number of steps that can be taken to ensure the integrity of the data and these include the following.

Making sure that errors do not occur during the transcription of the data

In some systems, someone has to fill in a form and the details from the form are then entered into the computer. The filling in of the form is called transcription, and the mistakes that occur during this process are called transcription errors. Transcription errors are hard to eliminate but careful checks by the management and thorough training of the staff who do the transcribing can reduce their occurrence.

Using verification methods

When source documents such as invoices, application forms, orders, etc., are used, the data is read off them and then typed into the computer. Verification methods are methods that ensure that the data being typed in is identical to that on the source document. This check will compare what they have typed in against what was on the original document. In other words, they will be proof reading what they have typed.

Using validation methods

Although verification checks that no errors have been introduced during the typing, the data on the source document may have been incorrect to start with. Validation is performed by the database and it checks the correctness of the data by the use of data type checks, range checks, etc.

Ensuring that there are procedures in place for regular updating

Databases need to be regularly maintained. This maintenance will involve continual updating of the information it contains. For example, in a school or college, a form will need to be filled in every year so that the pupils/students can inform the school/college about any changes to their details.

Making sure that there are no errors in operating procedures

The wrong file could be used to update a master file, resulting in the wrong details being stored.

Data independence

Data independence means that it is possible to change the data without changing the applications which process it. Using the DBMS (database management system) the structure of the database can be changed without affecting the existing programs

provided that new fields are not created. This is because the data and the applications which use it are separate and then interact with each other via the DBMS.

Data independence means that new applications can be developed to access the data and if completely new systems are used then the existing data can still be used.

The use of primary keys, foreign keys and links

The main building blocks of any relational database are the tables. Each table contains fields and there are a number of special fields called primary keys and foreign keys.

Primary keys

A primary key is a field that is used to uniquely define a particular record or line/row in a table. It is unlikely that any text field could be unique so primary keys are nearly always numeric fields.

If you made a field such as surname a primary key, then as you were typing in data and you tried to enter a surname that had already been entered in a different record, the database would not accept it. It is necessary to make sure that a number uniquely defines the record. Such primary keys include membership number, product number, employee number, catalogue number, part number, account number, etc. If a primary key has not been defined, then most databases will create one automatically. For example, the relational database software Microsoft Access uses a primary key called an AutoNumber, and this gives each record a number based on the order the record was entered into the database. The first record being entered will be given the counter value 1 and the next 2 and so on.

Links

When two or more tables contain the same field, they can be linked. This means that although the data is stored in different tables, it can be combined together in various ways. Links between tables are often called relationships and they are one of the main features of relational databases.

Foreign keys

A foreign key is a field of one table which is also the primary key of another. Foreign keys are used to establish relationships between tables.

Database normalisation

Normalisation is a mathematical technique for analysing data and is a staged process which improves the database design at each stage. At this level we need to look at normalisation as a three-stage process called 1st normal form, 2nd normal form and finally, 3rd normal form.

Normalisation:

- Minimises the duplication of data – you do not need to enter data any more times than is necessary.
- Eliminates the redundancy of data – avoids the unnecessary repetition of the same data.
- Ensures that data integrity is maintained – it makes sure that the data is error free and that there are not different versions of the data, depending on whether it has been updated or not.
- Allows the flexible extraction of information from the database.

Restructuring data into normalised form

During the analysis for a new hospital system the following information was found.

Each ward in the hospital will have its own name and a unique reference number. The number of beds in each ward also needs to be recorded along with its name and reference number. Each ward has a complement of nurses who are given unique staff numbers which are recorded along with their names. Each nurse works in only one ward.

Inpatients are given a patient number when they arrive and this is recorded with each patient's name, address, telephone number and date of birth. When admitted to one of the wards, each patient is assigned to one consultant who is responsible for their medical care. Consultants have their own unique staff numbers recorded with their names and specialisms.

Suppose we decide that we can put all of the details in a single table and that this table is called PATIENT then we can list the following fields:

PATIENT
Ward_number
Ward_name
Number_of_beds
Nurse_name
Nurse_staff_number
Patient_number
Patient_name
Patient_address
Patient_tel_no
Patient_DOB
Consultant_number
Consultant_name
Consultant_specialism

The above represents the data in its un-normalised form.

To go from un-normalised form (UNF) to first normal form (1NF)

The collection of data is in first normal form if it contains no repeating data item groups. We therefore need to remove the repeating groups from the above list and put them in their own list. By examining the list we can see that the field patient-number does not have associated with it exactly one (Nurse-staff-number, Nurse-name) since many nurses working on the same ward will look after the patient. This makes this group of fields a repeating

group and therefore to go to first normal form we need to remove this group and place it under its own table and give this table a name that reflects what it holds. PATIENT-NURSES is a suitable name in this case. To obtain the details of a particular patient's nurses, one needs to know the Patient-number as well as the Nurse-staff-number. Both of these fields need to be the primary key since they are both needed for identification purposes.

We now have the following:

PATIENT (Patient-number, Patient-name, Patient-address, Patient-tel-no, Patient-DOB, Ward-number, Ward-name, Consultant-number, Consultant-name, Consultant-specialism)

PATIENT-NURSES (Patient-number, Nurse-staff-number, Nurse-name)

To go from first normal form (1NF) to second normal form (2NF)

Here we look at the tables with two keys to see if each of the fields in this table depends on both keys or just one. If a field depends on just one of the keys then it should be removed with its key and grouped in a new table.

In our example we need to look at the entity PATIENT-NURSES because this table contains two keys (remember the primary keys are underlined) and check that the other fields which aren't underlined depend on both of the keys (i.e. the underlined ones). The only non-key field we have is Nurse-name, which although it depends on Nurse-staff-number, does not depend on Patient-number. We need to take this and put it with a copy of its key into a new table which we will call NURSE. On doing this, the data is now said to be in second normal form (2NF).

PATIENT (Patient-number, Patient-name, Patient-address, Patient-tel-no, Patient-DOB, Ward-number, Ward-name, Consultant-number, Consultant-name, Consultant-specialism)

PATIENT-NURSES (Patient-number, Nurse-staff-number)

NURSE (Nurse-staff-number, Nurse-name)

Databases *continued*

To go from second normal form (2NF) to third normal form (3NF)

To go to third normal form it is necessary to look at the fields in each of the tables to see if any of the fields are mutually dependent and if they are, they need to be moved to a separate table. When moving the fields it is necessary to leave one of the fields in the original table to use as the key for the newly created table.

For example, in looking at the tables and fields in second normal form, we can see that Consultant-name and Consultant-specialism are mutually dependent on Consultant-number. We now move this group to a new table called CONSULTANT and leave the field Consultant-number behind to provide a link between the tables.

In addition, Ward-name is mutually dependent on Ward-number so these can be removed and placed in a new table. Again Ward-number is also left in the original table to provide the link for the relationship.

The data is now in the following third normal form.

PATIENT (<u>Patient-number</u>, Patient-name, Patient-address, Patient-Tel-no, Patient-DOB, Ward-number, Consultant-number)

PATIENT-NURSE (<u>Patient-number</u>, <u>Nurse-staff-number</u>)

NURSE (<u>Nurse-staff-number</u>, Nurse-name)

CONSULTANT (<u>Consultant-number</u>, Consultant-name, Consultant-specialism)

WARD (<u>Ward-number</u>, Ward-name)

The fields are now in third normal form and are said to be fully normalised.

The advantages of different users having different views of data

Although the data held in a database is the same data no matter who uses it, the data can be presented differently to different users. For example, managers would need an overall view rather than a detailed view, whereas a member of staff dealing with customer accounts would need the detail of who owes what.

The main advantages of different users having different views of data are:

- Administrators will need a detailed view of the data.
- Managers can have an overall view that is not obscured by a mass of detail.
- Data can be presented graphically to make trends over time easier to spot.

Database security

In a flat-file approach, all the data for a particular application is held together

and this means that a person could access either all of the data or none of it. With a relational database, it is possible to only allow access to certain elements of the data. This means that you can give different levels of access to different people depending on what they need in their job.

How security is improved in a relational database

There are a number of ways a relational database has improved security compared to a flat file and these are:

- The data is stored separately to the programs used to access it.
- There is a hierarchy of passwords allowing people to access only that information necessary for them to perform their job.
- It is possible to restrict access to only part of a program which only uses some of the data.

Data warehousing

Can you imagine a system which will store all the details of every item you have bought from a certain supermarket over the last ten years? If you use a store loyalty card then all the

Large numbers of servers and storage devices are needed for a data warehouse for a large organisation

items bought and the way you paid for them can be linked to you.

Because of the huge amount of data involved, a very large database, called a data warehouse, is used to store the data. A data warehouse is used to store all an organisation's historical data and it is used by management information systems to extract information that will help managers make decisions.

The data warehouse is a corporate resource which everyone in the organisation can use provided they have access rights.

Examples of how a data warehouse might be used include:

- Finding out the day of the week on which a particular store sold the greatest number of a certain product in 2006.
- How employee absence due to sickness varied over the last year between the Newcastle branch and the Manchester branch.

Data mining

Once the data has been stored in a data warehouse it then needs to be 'mined' to discover:

- patterns in the data
- associations in the data (e.g., people who read the *Times* newspaper are more likely to drink red wine)
- trends over time (e.g., a person is buying more healthy food and is drinking less alcohol).

By 'drilling down' into the mass of data, data mining allows users to understand the data more by discovering meaningful patterns in the data. Looking for meaningful patterns in a huge mass of data is possible with the use of data mining software which presents the results in the form of tables and graphs.

Data mining can produce information such as:

- lists of customers likely to buy a certain product (based on what they have bought before)
- comparisons with competitors
- useful 'what if' results from modelling exercises
- predictions for future sales

- analysis of best sites for shops
- sales patterns
- customer buying patterns
- who is most likely to change their credit card
- those customers who are most loyal to the company/product.

Applications of data mining

Data mining is used for many applications as you see here:

- Helping in the fight against terrorism – since 9/11 the US government has been analysing people's travel, spending and communications habits using data mining, in order to spot patterns of abnormal behaviour that could lead it to terrorists.
- Fighting shoplifting in the clothes retailer Jaeger – using data mining with information about transactions and position of the clothes in the stores, they found that most of the clothes stolen were situated near doors despite them usually being security tagged. By spending more on CCTV and cooperating with the police, they managed to gain prosecutions and recover the stolen goods.
- Identification of customer needs – Virgin Media, who supply broadband, telephone and cable TV packages, use data mining to segment and target customers most likely to buy new services or upgrade those services they already have.

Database management system (DBMS)

Database management systems (DBMSs) are applications packages based around the need to hold a collection of centralised and structured data for further manipulation in various ways. All database management systems allow the user to set up their own databases and most packages are fairly flexible as to how this is done. Database management systems keep the data separately from the programs and this means that when programs are developed, they are independent of how the data is stored. Database management systems:

- allow the database to be defined
- allow users to query the database
- allow data to be appended (added), deleted and edited
- allow the user to modify the structure of the database
- provide adequate security for the data held
- allow the user to import and export data.

The figure below shows the older method of storing data where the data for each application is stored separately and the applications programs can be used to access the data. The trouble occurs when the same data needs to be used by different applications.

The flat-file approach keeps the data for each application separate

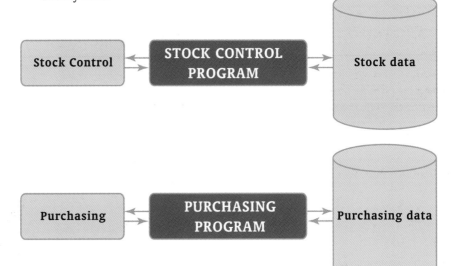

Databases *continued*

It means that each application will need to be updated when changes are made otherwise data about the same thing in different applications will no longer be consistent.

This figure shows the relational database management system approach, where all the data is held in one place and all the applications can have access to it. We will now look at the advantages of the relational database management system.

Advantages in using a DBMS

- It makes people think about the data being stored, and stores it in a logical and structured way.
- Data independence – data can be kept separate to the applications using it. This is useful if the database program

or other application programs are changed, then it is no longer necessary to re-input the data, although you usually have to convert the data using a special program.

- Avoids data redundancy. Data is only entered once and stored once no matter how many applications use it.
- Because the data is held centrally, it is a corporate resource to be used by all departments rather than belonging to one or more departments.
- Data integrity is maintained. An update of the data in one place ensures that the data is up-to-date in all the other applications that use the data.
- Increased security. Centralised access is easily established and this means that the security is

improved over when the data was fragmented around the system.

- Data definitions are standardised. Before database management systems, it was common to find different applications using different names for the same item of data. With the data dictionary provided with most DBMS, this problem is eliminated because everyone uses the same names and definitions that have been established by the data dictionary.

Disadvantages in using a DBMS

- Learning how to use a DBMS can be difficult and take some time. DBMS are quite complex and need a lot of knowledge about analysis and design before they can be successfully implemented.

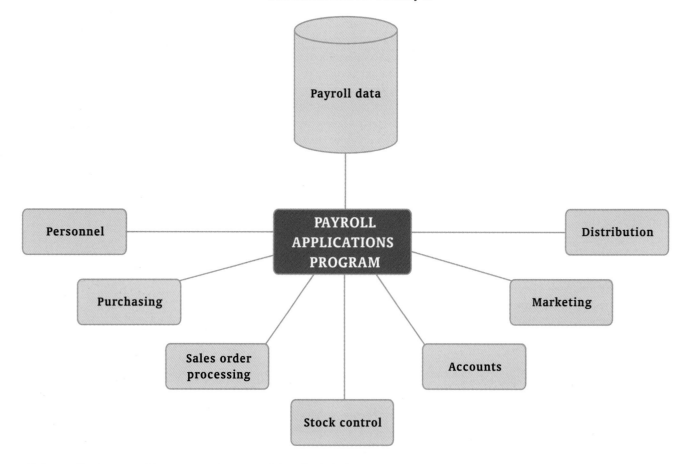

All the applications are able to access the store of data through the DBMS

- Costs for the development of a DBMS can be very high.
- The whole data is stored in a central location and this means that it is more vulnerable than when the data is distributed around the system. A centralised system needs good security and a disaster recovery plan, which should be tested.

Queries

Queries are requests, written in a special language, for specific information, posed to databases. For instance, from a database containing names and addresses, you may want to obtain a list of all those entries with the surname 'Jones', or details of accounts where outstanding credit exceeds the credit limit. Database management software allows users to design specific queries.

Query languages

Different databases have different methods of performing queries to access information.

There are a number of query languages available but the most common is Structured Query Language (SQL). Like all computer languages you do need to remember a list of instructions and how to use them in order to use SQL. Luckily there is another way called Query by Example (QBE), where a user is able to construct sorts, searches and queries by simply clicking on fields and criteria. This ultimately changes into SQL but the user does not have to know any SQL commands to use QBE.

SQL

SQL consists of a small number of commands that the user can combine in order to extract particular details from a database. It is now the industry standard language for the extraction of information from databases.

In SQL, the SELECT command is used to query the database and this command is constructed in the following way:

SELECT field list
FROM table
WHERE condition

The field list is used to list the fields we want to retrieve, while the table list indicates in which table the listed fields can be found. The condition is a Boolean expression used to identify those records to be retrieved.

Example 1

It is necessary to extract the names of all employees earning over £30,000 per year in the production department of a company. The employees' details are stored in a table called PERSONNEL.

The SQL instruction to do this is as follows:

SELECT Surname
FROM PERSONNEL
WHERE Department = 'Production' AND Salary > 30000

Example 2

Suppose we want to extract a list of the names and addresses of employees who work in the production or marketing departments from the PERSONNEL table. We could use the following SQL statement:

SELECT Surname, Street, Town, Postcode
FROM PERSONNEL
WHERE Department = 'Production' OR 'Marketing'

Example 3

Suppose you wanted to add an extra five days' holidays for those workers who work in the production or marketing departments, you could perform what is called an action query. Using an action query you can update certain fields without having to go through them all and alter certain ones manually.

UPDATE Personnel
SET No_of_days_holiday = No_of_days_holiday + 5
WHERE Department = 'Production' OR 'Marketing'

Using SQL you can:

- combine data from any of the tables in the database
- select which fields to use
- specify search criteria
- select which fields to put into the report
- specify orderings or groupings
- give the query a name and save it so it can be re-used
- save the results of the query.

Data dictionary

A data dictionary is a central store of information about data such as meanings, relationships to other data, origin, usage and format. A data dictionary is important, particularly for staff who are developing new applications to use the data held in a database. It allows the different staff to work consistently and to understand how the data has been set up.

When a data dictionary is produced for a database it will typically contain:

- details of tables
- field names
- field types
- field length
- validation used on the field.

Data dictionaries are used to describe the properties of the fields in a database. The data dictionary holds data about data and can be made to appear as a table either on paper or on the computer screen.

The data dictionary does not have to be completed manually. Many database management systems (DBMS) are able to produce a data dictionary automatically once the database has been produced.

Distributed databases

▼ You will find out

▶ About how data is stored in a distributed database

▶ About the advantages in using a distributed database

▶ About the disadvantages in using a distributed database

Introduction

Many organisations do not store all their data in the one storage location. Instead the data is spread out in various locations over a network but to a user it appears no different to the data being stored in one place. In this section you will look at the advantages of using this type of database, called a distributed database.

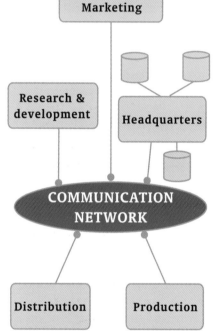

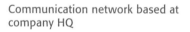

Communication network based at company HQ

In this network all the data is stored on the server located at the company's headquarters. This means that data created at the sites is passed along the communication lines to the central database at headquarters. The problem is that if there is a break in communication or a failure at one of the sites, then the data cannot be processed and the data could be corrupted. In addition to this, as all the network traffic has to go through to the headquarters, this is a network bottleneck and this can slow access to the data.

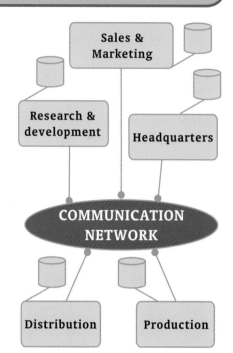

Communication network based on distributed database

The diagram above shows a distributed database. Here the data is distributed across several servers at different sites. The data can be stored locally, which means that the data created at the site is stored at the site, which means that access speeds are higher. There is still access to other data stored on any of the other servers and this will be faster as there is less network traffic. To a user of the database it appears that all the data is in one place and the database functions the same as if all the data were located together.

Advantages of using distributed databases

The advantages of using distributed databases include:

- Does not rely on the storage of data in a single location, so there is less risk of all the data stored being inaccessible.
- There is improved performance of the database – queries run faster and complex data mining is completed in less time.

- Applications can continue to function if the local server experiences a failure, but other servers with replicated data remain accessible.
- Applications may normally access a local database rather than a remote server to minimise network traffic and achieve maximum performance.

Disadvantages of using distributed databases

The disadvantages of using distributed databases include:

- They are more complex and therefore cost more to install and maintain.
- There is an increased security risk because files are transferred across networks.
- If one of the servers fails, then it can have an effect on the database and staff may not be able to access some of the data.
- The system relies on data communications, so if a communication line fails, then the data may not be able to be accessed.
- As large numbers of staff access the database, there is a chance that you could get inconsistencies in the data.

▶ KEY WORDS

Distributed database – a single database that is under the control of a database management system (DBMS) where the storage devices are not all attached to a common processor. Instead the data is stored in storage devices attached to multiple computers usually located across a network

Case studies

▶ Case study 1 | pp. 94–95

The use of data mining by banks

In order to remain competitive, banks need to offer their customers the right product, at the right price at the right time and obviously to make a profit in the process. Many banks now use data mining to achieve this.

Using artificial intelligence and data mining, banks can uncover complex patterns or models in data that will help them solve business problems such as direct marketing, evaluation of credit risk and fraud detection.

A spokesperson for one of the banks said: 'There has been a switch from a focus on products to customers and looking at their households and how we can help them.'

By using the huge store of transactional data stored in a data warehouse for its 6 million customers, one bank has data mined all the transactions for all these customers and come up with a profitability figure for each customer. Doing this gives the banks a better idea of how they can improve their service to customers and increase the bank's profit as a result.

1 The following terms are used in the case study. Give a brief definition for each:
   (a) Data mining (1 mark)
   (b) Data warehouse (1 mark)
   (c) Transactional data. (1 mark)

2 Data mining can identify patterns in data. Explain, by giving an example, what this statement means. (2 marks)

3 Describe **one** advantage that data mining offers a bank. (2 marks)

4 Other than its use in banking, briefly describe another example of data mining. (2 marks)

▶ Case study 2 | pp. 94–95

The data explosion

In the modern business world, growth, mergers, acquisitions and new ICT systems running alongside older systems has meant there are huge quantities of data held on different systems in different departments and in different geographical locations. It has been estimated that by 2012 the amount of data stored will have increased 30 times compared with 2008.

The challenge for businesses is to be able to use this data for profitability analysis, generating reports in order to comply with certain laws, analysing sales and marketing campaigns and predicting buying trends.

Data warehouses are used to store transactional data and lots of other data from other systems and the data warehouse is usually a separate system in order not to slow down operational systems. This means that the systems used to perform all the transactions in the business are not the same as in the data warehouse.

Managers need information quickly in order to make timely decisions, and the data warehouse along with data mining tools allow them to drill down into this mass of data to collect certain facts about the business.

1 Explain what is meant by a data warehouse and give the name of **one** system which is used to supply the data warehouse with its data. (4 marks)

2 A data warehouse is a central pool of information for the whole company and it can be accessed by anyone with suitable permission.
   (a) Not all staff are able to access all of the information held in the data warehouse.

Describe **two** ways in which access to all the information is prevented. (2 marks)
   (b) Data mining is used to drill down into the mass of data. Explain what is meant by data mining and, by giving an example, describe how it is useful to a business. (4 marks)

Questions and Activities

Questions 1 pp. 90–94

1 A patient database used by a hospital contains two tables. The structure of these two tables is shown below.

Patients	Consultants
Patient Number	Consultant Number
Surname	Consultant Name
Forename	
Date of Birth	
Street	
Town	
Postcode	
Contact Phone Number	
Home Phone Number	
Consultant Number	

(a) Why is it better to store the data in two separate tables, rather than keeping it all in one table? **(2 marks)**

(b) Why is Date of Birth rather than age stored in the Patients table? **(1 mark)**

(c) Which field would be the primary key:
   (i) In the Patients table?
   (ii) In the Consultants table? **(2 marks)**

2 Organisations hold lots of data in relational databases with a Database Management System (DBMS).

(a) Explain what is meant by a relational database and explain the main components of one. **(2 marks)**

(b) Explain what is meant by a Database Management System (DBMS). **(4 marks)**

3 The manager of a tool hire company wishes to use a relational database management system (RDBMS) to help keep track of the business. The database stores the data in three tables, namely: TOOLS, CUSTOMERS and RENTALS.

(a) What are the main advantages to **this** manager in storing the data in a relational database rather than a flat-file database? **(3 marks)**

(b) For each of the tables, identify the primary key field and also list the other fields for each table which would enable the manager to store the data with minimum redundancy. **(4 marks)**

4 Many organisations make use of a distributed database to hold their data.

(a) What is meant by a distributed database? **(3 marks)**

(b) What are the advantages and disadvantages in an organisation using a distributed database? **(6 marks)**

5 An organisation uses a computerised flat-file system for the storage of its data. The organisation is experiencing problems due to the use of this flat-file system.

(a) Describe **three** benefits that the organisation would gain by using a relational database rather than the flat-file system. **(6 marks)**

(b) The organisation currently has three files in use: Customer, Stock and Orders. During conversion to a relational database system these files would need to be normalised. Explain clearly what is meant by the term normalisation. **(2 marks)**

(c) Examples from the three files are shown below. Normalise these files, explaining any assumptions or additions you make to the files. **(5 marks)**

Customer file

Surname	Forename	Street	Town	City	Postcode
Chung	Rubana	21 East Street	Greengate	Liverpool	L44 6RR
Hughes	Amy	188 Morrison Rd	Greengate	Liverpool	L44 5RE

Orders file

Surname	Forename	Postcode	Order Date	Item Ordered	Quantity Bought	Price	Total Cost	Paid
Hughes	Amy	L44 5RE	02/01/09	Ruler	10	£1.50	£15.00	Yes
Hughes	Amy	L44 5RE	02/01/09	A4 Ream lined paper	20	£3.50	£70.00	Yes
Chung	Rubana	L44 6RR	03/01/09	Large stapler	4	£5.50	£22.00	No
Chung	Rubana	L44 6RR	03/01/09	Staples	5	£1.20	£6.00	No
Hughes	Amy	L44 5RE	05/01/09	Large stapler	10	£5.50	£55.00	Yes

Stock file

Item Name	Price	Quantity in Stock
Ruler	£1.50	120
A4 Ream lined paper	£3.50	1298
Large stapler	£5.50	438
Staples	£1.20	654
Photocopier paper	£2.85	1452

6 Most organisations use relational databases with Database Management Systems.
   (a) Explain the relative advantages and disadvantages of using a relational database rather than a flat-file approach for storage of the organisation's data. (4 marks)
   (b) Explain what is meant by a Database Management System and contrast its advantages and disadvantages. (6 marks)

7 A bank uses a data warehouse to hold details about customers and their banking transactions. Holding this large central store of data allows bank staff to use data mining to extract information about customers and their banking habits.
   (a) Describe what a data warehouse is and explain the advantages it might give this bank. (6 marks)
   (b) Explain what is meant by data mining and give an example of how the bank might use it. (3 marks)

8 Normalisation is the process undertaken to ensure that a database has no redundant or inconsistent data.
   (a) Explain what is meant by:
      (i) Redundant data (2 marks)
      (ii) Inconsistent data. (2 marks)
   (b) Explain the relevance of primary keys, foreign keys and relationships in a relational database. (6 marks)
   (c) Data in a database which has not been normalised raises a number of problems. Describe **two** problems that are caused by un-normalised data being stored in a database. (4 marks)

9 A company is developing a large database for use by everyone in the company. Staff who are developing the database are going to use a data dictionary.
   (a) Explain what is meant by a data dictionary and give **three** things it might contain. (4 marks)
   (b) Describe **one** reason why a data dictionary should be used when developing this database. (3 marks)

▶ Activity 1: Spot the primary key

A primary key is the unique field in a group of fields. Here are some fields in a table. You have to spot the primary key. The name of the table is shown along with a list of the fields that the table will hold. Also shown is a sample of the data which will be entered into the field.

For each of the tables shown, state with a reason the name of the field that is best chosen as the primary field. Remember to think about the purpose of the table when deciding on the primary key.

Student table	
Surname	Jones
Forename	Peter
Title	Mr
Gender	Male
Student ID	980006

Car Park Spaces	
Parking space number	190
Car registration number	DR08TGH
Employee number	180041
Department code	104

Patient table	
Patient surname	Graham
Patient forename	Julie
Title	Miss
NHS number	09-09809-8
Date of birth	16/12/91

Employee table	
Tax code	416L
Surname	Jones
Date of birth	15/06/88
National insurance no	AB100136Y
Department code	029

Product table	
Product description	A4 printer paper
Price per unit	£3.50
Number in stock	127
Product code	1381
Supplier number	2015

▶ Activity 2: Normalising data for a college database

For this activity you are required to fully normalise the data for a student database for a college. The principal of the college has identified the fields they want storing and has given you the following list:

Student number	Course number
Surname	Date of birth
Forenames	Course title
Address	Course cost
Tel no	Date enrolled
Lecturer name	Lecturer number

The principal has also given you the following information which you will need:
- Each student is allocated a unique student number when they join the college.
- A student can take more than one course.
- The same course (i.e., having the same course number) can be taught by one or more lecturers.

Using only the fields in the list supplied, go through the process of normalising this data.

You should show the processes of going through each stage of normalisation (1st, 2nd and 3rd normal form) and clearly indicate the primary keys in each table.

▶ Activity 3: A real-life data dictionary

The NHS service uses one of the biggest ICT systems in the country and many people are working on systems which use the huge amount of data held.

For consistency and to understand the existing system, they need to refer to the data dictionary. As so many people use this resource the NHS has produced it on-line and for this activity you are required to investigate it and produce a short paragraph outlining what their data dictionary consists of.

The website address for the NHS data dictionary is: http://www.datadictionary.nhs.uk/

▶ Activity 4: Normalising data for a college database

The following data items are in un-normalised form and need to be fully normalised (i.e., converted to third normal form) so that tables may be created which minimise the data duplication across the tables and thereby solving many of the problems associated with data redundancy.

The table name is in bold and all the fields are shown in the brackets.

CUSTOMER ORDER (<u>Customer-order-number,</u> Customer-number, Customer-name, Customer-address, Customer-tel-no, Depot-number, Depot-name, Product-number, Product-name, Product-quantity, Product-price)

Remember: Primary keys are underlined.

Go through the process of normalisation showing the various stages (1NF, 2NF and finally 3NF).

To help you through the processes, here are a few reminders:

1NF

A table is in first normal form if it contains no repeating groups.

2NF

The table must be in first normal form and then contain no non-key fields which are dependent on only part of the primary key.

3NF

The table must be in second normal form as well as there being no non-key fields which depend on other non-key fields.

Convert the data into third normal form, showing the intermediate steps.

▶ Activity 5: Normalising data for a car hire company

A car hire company uses a manual system at present but because of an increase in vehicles and rentals, it has now decided to store the data using a computerised database.

Someone in the company has been on a course at the local college but they have only been used to flat-file databases and have decided to store all the data in the one file which they intend to call VEHICLE. The fields that need to be stored are shown below the file name VEHICLE.

VEHICLE
Registration-number
Make
Model
Year
Customer-number
Surname
Initial
Address
Date-hired
Date-returned

Sometimes one customer may hire many cars at the same time so you will need to bear this in mind when going through the normalisation process.

(a) The person who has been on the college course has suggested that a flat-file database could be used to hold the data but you disagree.

Present a written argument, containing examples showing the likely problems, why storage of the data in a flat-file database would be unsuited to this application. Also, explain the advantages of storing the data in a relational database.

(b) You now have to go through the normalisation process until the fields have been placed in third normal form. You should explain and show how you arrive at your final arrangement.

Exam support

Worked example 1

1 The inpatients in a hospital have their details stored in a relational database. When a patient is admitted to the hospital they are allocated to a ward. As well as patients, staff are also allocated to a ward.

(a) Explain what is meant by a relational database. (2 marks)

(b) Relational databases hold the data in a number of tables. In the hospital inpatients system there is a table for Ward and this contains fields as outlined here:

WARD (WardID, NumberofBeds, StaffID)

In this table WardID is the primary key and StaffID is the foreign key.

(i) Explain the difference between a primary key and a foreign key. (2 marks)

(ii) Give **two** other suitable tables you would expect to see in this inpatients database, identifying any primary or foreign keys. (6 marks)

(iii) Relational databases are more secure that flat-file approaches. Explain why this is so. (3 marks)

(c) Most hospitals use distributed databases. Describe **two** advantages and **two** disadvantages in hospitals using distributed databases. (4 marks)

Student answer 1

1 (a) A relational database is a database with relationships between the tables.

(b) (i) A primary key is a key that is unique in a table whereas a foreign key is one that is not unique.

(ii) PATIENT, DOCTOR and NURSE
PATIENT primary key PatientID, foreign key WardID
DOCTOR primary key DoctorID, foreign key PatientID
NURSE primary key NurseID, foreign key WardID

(iii) The data is stored separately to the programs used to access it.
There is a hierarchy of passwords allowing people to only access that patient information necessary for them to perform their job.
You cannot copy a relational database.

(c) Advantages are that it is much faster to access the data over the network as the data can be spread over several servers and that it is easier to take backup copies of the data held because it can be copied onto any server.
Disadvantages are that the transfer of data along communication lines poses a security risk. If the one of the links to a server failed then the data could not be obtained from that server.

Examiner's comment

1 (a) No marks for this very superficial answer. Certain terms such as this one come up very often and students are best advised to remember the definition word for word.

(b) (i) The definition of a primary key is adequate for one mark but it is not clear what a foreign key is.

(ii) The students were given the table names (i.e. WARD) and the fields to help them with this part of the question. The student should have noticed that StaffID would refer to all those staff who are involved in the care of that patient and this would include doctors, nurses and other staff. This is the sort of answer that is quite difficult to mark. Clearly DOCTOR and NURSE could be appropriate tables and the student has written appropriate primary and foreign fields.
Three out of the six marks have been given here.

(iii) Two of these answers are correct but the answer about not being able to copy a relational database is incorrect.

(c) All these answers are correct, so full marks.
(10 marks out of 17)

Student answer 2

1 (a) It is a collection of data stored in two or more tables with links called relationships between the tables which means that the data contained in the table can be extracted. The applications software is able to use any of the data stored in the tables.

(b) (i) A primary key is a field that is unique in a row of a table. For example StaffID would be unique in the staff table as no two staff would be allocated the same StaffID.
A foreign key is a primary key in one table that is only a key in another and is used to supply the link between the tables. For example StaffID is a primary key field in the Staff table but a foreign key in the WARD table.

(ii) Two other tables are: STAFF and PATIENT
In STAFF table primary key StaffID and foreign key WardID
In PATIENT table primary key PatientID and foreign key WardID

(iii) Access to certain tables can be ensured using a hierarchy of passwords. This means the username and password can be used to determine which tables/files a user can access.
You can also decide whether a user can add a new record, only alter fields within a record or simply view and not alter records. This makes it harder for users who do not know what they are doing to accidentally alter data in the files.
Data is stored separate to the programs used to access it and this means alteration of the programs cannot corrupt the data held.

(c) The processing of the data is shared among the computers in different locations, so this means that the data can be all processed at the same time so it is quicker.

Examiner's comment

1 (a) Here the student has identified the main components of a relational database and although it is slightly different to the definition used in the specification, it is still an acceptable definition and worth full marks.

(b) (i) This is a very good definition of both terms and the student has related the definition to the application which clearly shows that they understand primary and foreign keys.

(ii) Both tables have been correctly identified as have the primary and foreign keys for both tables. Full marks for this part.

(iii) Three correct explanations have been given here so full marks.

(c) Unfortunately the student has given a reasonable description of distributed processing rather than distributed databases, which means no marks are awarded here.

(13 marks out of 17)

Examiner's answer

1 (a) Two marks max with one mark for each point.
Relational database – a large collection of data items stored in tables (1) containing links between the tables (1) so that the data can be accessed in many different ways (1) and by a range of different applications programs (1).

(b) (i) One mark for each correct definition similar to the following:
A primary key is a field that is used to uniquely define a particular record or line/row in a table.
A foreign key is a field of one table which is also the primary key of another. Foreign keys are used to establish relationships between the main table and the other subsidiary tables.

(ii) One mark each for the two tables, one mark each for correct primary key and one mark each for correct foreign key.
STAFF table (primary key StaffID and foreign key WardID)
PATIENT table (primary key PatientID and foreign key WardID)

(iii) One mark each for three reasons such as:
Hierarchy of passwords
Storage of data separate to programs
Access rights to parts of the program.

(c) One mark each for two advantages and one mark each for two disadvantages such as:
Advantages:
Faster response to user queries of the database
Non-dependence on one central huge store of data
Easy to back up and copy data from one server to another
If one server fails then the other servers can be used
Reduces network traffic as local queries can be performed using the data on the local server.
Disadvantages:
Heavy reliance on networks and communications which may not always be reliable
Security issues particularly if sensitive personal data is being transferred
If one of the links to a server failed then the data could not be obtained from that server
Increased costs owing to the use of expensive communication lines
Greater chance of data inconsistency
Harder to control the security of data spread in many different locations.

Worked example 2

2 Details of staff, students and courses are stored in a single file and an example of the contents of this file is shown below.

Student ID	Name	Date of birth	Sex	Course Code	Course Name	Lecturer ID	Lecturer Name
0022	G Wong	12/12/93	F	PHYS1	A level Physics	211	D Preston
0012	T Ash	09/08/93	M	MATH2	A level Maths	310	H Pearce
0022	G Wong	12/12/93	F	MATH1	A level Maths	211	D Preston

The data in the above file has not been normalised.

(a) By using the data in the above file to illustrate your answer, describe **two** different problems that the storage of the file in this way presents, owing to it not being normalised. **(4 marks)**

(b) The above data can be normalised and put into tables with primary and foreign keys and relationships between the tables.

Using **two** tables, normalise the data in this table and clearly indicate the primary and foreign keys needed. **(5 marks)**

Student answer 1

2 (a) You have to type in more data than you need to and this takes time and costs more money.
There is a chance that the data for the same person could be mistakenly typed in. For example G Wong could have her StudentID typed in as 0022 and 0020 which means that they look now as if they are two different students. If the data was normalised this would not happen as the StudentID would only appear once in the Student table.

(b) STUDENT (<u>StudentID</u>, Name, Date of birth, Sex, CourseCode)

Examiner's comment

2 (a) The first sentence is true about saving time and money but the student should have made it clearer by referring to the duplicated data in the table. It is also better if the student uses the correct terminology such as data duplication, data inconsistency, etc.
The second part of the answer was much better as the student has started referring to the data in the given file.

(b) The student has only given details for one of the tables and not the two asked for in the question. The table and its fields are correct and a primary key has been identified by underlining but no foreign key has been identified. Two marks are given here; one mark for the correct table and one mark for the correct primary key.
(5 marks out of 9)

Student answer 2

2 (a) Data duplication – details have to be keyed in more than once. For example, the details for the lecturer D Preston are stored more than once. This wastes time entering unnecessary data and also there is a higher risk of transcription errors.

Data inconsistency – data duplication means some of the same data can be found in the same file. If the data is changed in one of the files, then it must also be changed in the other file to ensure consistency. For example, the student details for G Wong appear twice and if a mistake is made with some details such as a typing mistake it would make it hard to know which one is correct.

(b) Two tables are used STUDENT and COURSE
STUDENT (StudentID, Name, Date of birth, Sex, CourseCode#)
COURSE (CourseCode, CourseName, LecturerID#, LecturerName)
In the Student table StudentID is the primary key and CourseCode# is the foreign key.
In the Course table CourseCode is the primary key and LecturerID# is the foreign key.

Examiner's comment

2 (a) This is a good answer as the student has used the correct terminology and has produced a good explanation. They could have better explained the data inconsistency using data in the table. For example, they could have given and example of how the data could become inconsistent, e.g. typing in the incorrect Date of birth for G Wong.

(b) This answer is very good and the student has identified the correct tables and the correct fields in each table. They have also identified the correct primary keys for each table by underlining them and have used the hash sign attached to the foreign key. To make it completely clear, they have stated the primary keys and foreign keys in a piece of text which is a good idea and makes it clear to the examiner. This is a perfect answer for this part of the question and therefore deserves full marks.
(8 marks out of 9)

Examiner's answer

2 (a) One mark for each advantage and example x 2.
Data duplication – data is duplicated in the file which means more data needs to be entered than is necessary, thus wasting resources. For example, the student with StudentID 0022 has their details duplicated in the table.
Data inconsistency – duplicated data means that a mistake can be made with one row of data and this means you do not know which version of the data is correct. For example, a mistake in the name would result in two different sets of data and it is difficult to know which one is correct.

(b) One mark for each correct table x 2, one mark for each correct primary key x 2 and one mark for each correct foreign key x 2 (to a maximum of 5 marks).
Examples similar to:
STUDENT (StudentID, Name, Date of birth, Sex, CourseCode#)
COURSE (CourseCode, CourseName, LecturerID#, LecturerName)
Primary keys are underlined and foreign keys contain the hash sign.
The identification of primary and foreign keys must be clear to gain maximum marks.

Summary mind map

Databases

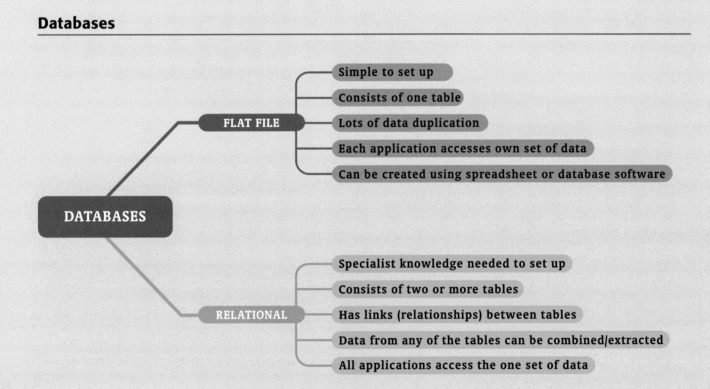

FLAT FILE
- Simple to set up
- Consists of one table
- Lots of data duplication
- Each application accesses own set of data
- Can be created using spreadsheet or database software

DATABASES

RELATIONAL
- Specialist knowledge needed to set up
- Consists of two or more tables
- Has links (relationships) between tables
- Data from any of the tables can be combined/extracted
- All applications access the one set of data

TOPIC 7: Management of change

When new ICT systems are introduced or existing systems undergo substantial modification, it places certain challenges on an organisation. The organisational structures may need changing, people may have to move departments or even locations, employees may have to work in different groups, most will need additional training and so on.

In this topic you will look at the issues involved in the management of change and how the change can be brought about in the least stressful way.

▼ The key concepts covered in this topic are:

▶ Consequences of change

CONTENTS

Consequences of change

Introduction

When organisations introduce new information systems there is the likelihood that they will cause a change in the working practices of the organisation and that the change will affect the staff in some way. The managers who will oversee the development of the new system will need to be skilled in the management of change to be able to gain the full cooperation of all the staff concerned.

There is no doubt that many people are resistant to change until it can be shown that the change may be to their advantage. After all, many staff will have seen the reduction in the number of staff as many of their jobs were computerised in the past.

The consequences of change

There are a number of consequences of change which need to be managed when new ICT systems are introduced to an organisation. In this topic you will look at the various consequences of change and how they can be managed.

The skills required and not required

New ICT systems need new skills and staff must be prepared to learn these skills. Old skills may not be needed, so it is necessary for staff to go on courses to ensure that they do not become unemployable. When new systems are introduced, staff will need to be trained to use the new system.

The increased use of ICT usually means that there is an increase in the number of skilled jobs (network managers, project managers, programmers, computer engineers, etc.) available, usually at the expense of less skilled jobs.

There are a number of jobs and skills that have now disappeared and these include:

- Typist – most people word-process their own documents.
- Filing clerk – data is now stored on computers in databases.
- Internal post clerk – these people delivered internal mail. Most internal mail makes use of e-mail now.

Changes to organisational structure

When a completely new system is introduced into an organisation, many organisations will see it as an opportunity to alter the structure of their organisation so that it fits in better with the new system. The introduction of new systems frequently means that the boundaries between the functional areas become more blurred and staff will be asked to do a greater variety of tasks. For example, a customer may place an order with the sales staff and at the same time ask about the balance of their account, which would normally have been dealt with by the accounts department. The sales person will probably do both activities.

Staff may be dissatisfied as working groups may have to be split up and staff may have to adapt to working in a completely different way with different people. Sometimes when organisations restructure, someone who has worked for years in a senior position may have someone much younger promoted above them.

Changes in work patterns

With the increased use of computers and communications, many organisations now operate in global markets and have to be able to react to customers' requests. This necessitates some operations having to run twenty-four hours a day. Flexibility can mean that more part-time work, and work outside normal office hours is also available. This will suit some people such as mothers with young children but others may not get time off at the same time as their partner.

Changes to internal procedures

Staff members are often asked to take on more responsibility and do a wider variety of tasks when ICT systems are introduced. For example, some staff who previously would have performed a purely admin role, now get more involved directly with customers and they may be asked to sell goods or services. Since with the new ICT systems their traditional job may be completed in much less time, they now have time available to devote to more profitable activities.

Ways of doing things will have to be reviewed and changed if necessary since the systems analyst will not usually fit the ICT system around the existing system but will prefer to always consider the best method of performing the task. Working procedures frequently change and this can cause stress to some staff unless they are consulted about the changes and are properly trained to deal successfully with the new procedures.

Many staff working with ICT systems have to obey a code of conduct that specifies what they can and cannot do with the ICT systems.

Effects on the workforce (the fear of change)

The adverse reaction of staff to the introduction of new systems is typified by the following:

- A fear of redundancy. Some systems are introduced to reduce the number of people needed to do a particular task, as the greatest cost is often the staff wages.
- Fear of reduction in status and job satisfaction. With the help of the management information supplied by computerised management information systems, managers

are able to get through more work and fewer of the middle levels are needed. Job satisfaction can be eroded owing to many of the tasks being performed by the computer. Some managers will lose power if all the data for the whole organisation is held centrally, as would be the case if the organisation made use of a data warehouse. This means that the data in the system, although originally supplied from their department, no longer belongs to them. This means that the data is a corporate resource and can be used, subject to the relevant security clearance, by anyone in the organisation.

- Fear of looking ridiculous. Some staff, especially the older members of staff, may feel that their lack of ICT knowledge could cause them to be ridiculed by the younger more ICT aware staff.
- Changes in location. Office space requirements are reduced, so this may result in the organisation moving to smaller premises to reduce the costs (rent, heat, light, etc.) and sometimes this will be away from the original location. Clearly any move will affect staff in some way.

Overcoming the resistance to new ICT systems

One of the greatest psychological problems concerning the introduction of new information systems is one of fear. The greatest fear is that of losing your job. Many staff may also be frightened that their conditions of service will worsen. Since these fears can lead to low morale and non-cooperation by the staff in introducing these systems, managers should identify the fears and be honest about the consequences of the new system. There are many steps that can be taken by managers and some of these are outlined below.

- All staff should be made aware of the need for the new system and they should be involved, even

if only in a small way, with the introduction of the new system. If the staff see the clear advantages of the system and can input their own ideas into its design, then they are less likely to oppose it. Managers should positively encourage staff to provide advice on the new system and acknowledgement should be made of their contribution.
- To make the learning process easy for staff, comprehensive training and retraining should be introduced. Many of these training sessions can be arranged off-site so that staff can stay in a nice hotel and the training becomes a social thing as well. Some companies make use of computer-based training (CBT) using multimedia and this can be conducted at the company's premises, so this minimises the disruption to the day-to-day business operations.
- Managers should explain the advantages that the new system has over the old system. Staff may well be pleased that things causing annoyance in the old

system were eliminated or improved in the new system. This will improve job satisfaction.
- Top management should spell out the implications of the new system before rumours start, particularly in relation to job security, pay, changes in contracts of employment, promotion prospects, changes in working conditions, etc. Above all, information about the new system must be communicated fully and frankly.
- Many of the staff using the new system will learn new skills which will improve their promotion prospects and could enable them to move to a better job outside the organisation if they so wished.
- Social groups, such as friends who have worked together for many years, should be kept together, if possible, since people who enjoy each other's company work together better as a team.
- Management should be willing to accept criticisms of the new system and should be prepared to act upon them.

"The reorganization still needs some fine tuning. Until further notice, you're a fern in our reception area."

Questions and Activities

▶ Questions 1 | pp. 110–111

1 When new ICT systems are introduced, staff have to cope with the changes that take place as a result of the new system.
   Describe how each of the following cause change for employees:
   (a) Work patterns (2 marks)
   (b) The skills required/not required (2 marks)
   (c) Internal procedures. (2 marks)

2 An organisation is introducing many new ICT systems in order to compete with other companies. This necessitates a lot of changes in the organisation and how it is run.
   (a) Explain the impact that these new ICT developments could have on jobs and the patterns of work. You should illustrate your answer with **three** appropriate and distinctly different examples. (6 marks)
   (b) The managers want to make the changes the least stressful to their employees as possible. Outline what managers can do in order that the changes the new ICT systems create cause the least possible stress to their employees. (4 marks)

3 An ICT system was introduced into an organisation and was considered a failure. The failure was due to the inability of the organisation to manage the change rather than for technical reasons.
   Describe **three** factors which influence the management of change within an organisation, illustrating your answer with suitable examples. (6 marks)

4 A large organisation is considering the introduction of an ICT-based system to log visitors. The current system is based on a manual log at reception. The new system will capture visitors together with details of their visit. The introduction of this system will cause considerable change for staff and visitors. In the context of this example, describe **four** factors that the management should consider when introducing this change. (8 marks)

▶ Activity 1: Fears of change

Imagine you are an employee of a large organisation and they are combining with another equally large organisation, resulting in a reorganisation of staff, procedures and ICT systems.
   Like most of the employees, you have a number of worries about this change.
   Write down a list of the likely worries you would have about the change.
   Write down some of the things managers of the organisation can do that would make the change less stressful for the employees of the organisation.

▶ Activity 2: New software being introduced

As people get older they sometimes find it difficult to cope with change. An organisation is introducing a completely new ICT system to replace the older one which has been running with minor amendments for the last 15 years. Naturally, many of the older members of staff who have used the old system for the last 15 years are worried about this new system, as from what they have heard about it, it seems very complex.
   Write a list of what managers can do to help the older members of staff to learn the new system.

Exam support

Worked example 1

1 An old established company has been bought and the new managers want to increase the profitability of the business by using the latest ICT systems. These new systems will have a great impact on the way the company works and also on the staff they employ.

   (a) Explain what is meant by the term 'management of change'. (2 marks)

   (b) Describe the impact that the new ICT system could have on job and work patterns. Illustrate your answer with **three** distinctly different examples. (6 marks)

Student answer 1

1 (a) Management of change means how the managers of the organisation manage the change brought about by the new ICT system.

   (b) People will lose their jobs due to the new system.
        People may have to move to different sites.
        Current teams of people who work together may need splitting up, forcing people to work with people they do not get on with.
        People will have to work more flexibly. For example, in an e-commerce system, if the website fails then it will need to be repaired very quickly otherwise the firm will lose orders.

Examiner's comment

1 (a) This is a superficial answer and typical of students who simply rearrange the words in the question to give an answer. No marks are given here.

   (b) Most of these points are valid but examples are not given except in the last part of the answer about e-commerce systems.
        People losing their jobs is not a suitable reason, as they need to be more specific on the type of staff who are at risk.
        The other answers are just about acceptable for a mark each with the last answer containing an example worth two marks. **(4 marks out of 8)**

Student answer 2

1 (a) This means how managers deal with the changes that will occur with the introduction of the new system. This would include the management of staff who may be concerned about work patterns, internal procedures, organisational structure and the new skills they will need.

   (b) Reorganisation of the organisation may mean employees have to move to a different location, which may be inconvenient for some staff.
        Older staff may not want to learn new skills and may feel intimidated when younger members of staff pick up how to use the new system more easily.
        Staff who used to do paper-based administration such as filing clerks, people who process orders, etc., may lose their jobs.
        Staff may have to change their hours of work and be more flexible in order to meet the needs of the business.

Examiner's comment

1 (a) This answer does not cover the detail of what is being managed, although it does mention the names of all the changes that affect employees. One mark is given for this answer.

   (b) The student has produced a good set of answers here and has added examples to most of the problems. Full marks are awarded for this section. **(7 marks out of 8)**

Examiner's answer

1 (a) No marks for answers that refer simply to the managers managing the change.
          One mark for mention of the following with a brief description:
          New skills required
          Changes to organisational structure
          Alteration of work patterns
          Changes to internal procedures
          Worries by the workforce.

   (b) One mark for each point to a maximum of six. Only a maximum of four marks should be given if there are no examples.
          May have to work in a different location (1) as downsizing of offices may occur owing to less paperwork/staff/
          computer space needed (1).
          Telecommuting/teleworking – it may be possible to work from home using computers and telecommunications (1)
          thus saving the employee travelling costs and time/fitting in with personal life better/environmental improvement (1).
          Retraining – may need to learn new skills (1) in order to use the new ICT systems such as database skills, use of e-
          mail, data mining skills, website updating skills (1).
          Job losses – new systems replace jobs (1) that were previously performed by humans such as filing clerks, data input
          clerks, post clerks (1).
          Different hours of work (1) – new system may operate 24/7 so staff may need to work more flexibly (1).
          New jobs will be created (1) such as web designers, systems analysts, help-desk staff, network administrators (1), etc.
          Some jobs will move abroad to call centres (1) owing to cheaper labour costs and the availability of well-qualified staff (1).

Worked example 2

2 (a) **When a new ICT system is introduced into the workplace, there are a number of changes the workforce has to
          cope with. Outline two such changes which are likely to be a cause of stress to staff and describe the worries
          that these staff might have. (4 marks)**

   (b) **Describe and give examples of three things that managers can do to alleviate any worries the staff have about
          the introduction of the new ICT system. (6 marks)**

Student answer 1

2 (a) The fear of unemployment. The new ICT system may replace
          some jobs that were previously done by people such as
          data input clerks who used to type in data but now direct
          methods of data capture are planned, so these people are no
          longer required. Once redundancies occur, many other staff
          worry that they could be next and this causes a lot of stress
          to all workers.

   (b) Staff should be re-trained so that they can take up the
          new posts that the new ICT systems create. For example,
          staff can learn database skills to enable them to extract
          information about customers so that they can be targeted
          for special sales promotions.
          Managers can explain that the changes will mean that
          many of the boring, more mundane jobs will be replaced by
          more highly skilled interesting ones and that the employees
          will be able to do these with suitable training.

Examiner's comment

2 (a) The student has not written about two changes
          but the change described is a good answer so
          two out of the four marks for this part of the
          question.
          After answering a question always go back to
          the question and check your answer fits exactly
          what is being asked.

   (b) Again this student has only supplied two
          answers rather than the three asked for. Both
          these answers are good.
          (6 marks out of 10)

Student answer 2

2 (a) Job losses. The new system may replace some of the tasks people used to do and this may cause redundancies or early retirement. The jobs at risk will be mainly admin staff and middle management.

More pressure on staff. Sometimes staff have to complete more work in less time and in some cases the computer can be used by management to monitor the amount of work being done.

Changes in work patterns. Staff may have to work more flexibly as customers demand 24/7 access to goods and services. Although these changes may suit some staff, others will have problems working shifts.

(b) Managers should outline the advantages the new system offers the organisation and how this might help them expand and create new promotion opportunities for staff.

Supply appropriate training so that staff know what they are doing.

Involve all staff in the development of the new system so they feel they have played a part in its design. This will make staff happier because the system will be the one that will help them most.

Examiner's comment

2 (a) In the question they were only asked to outline two changes and their answer contains three. All these answers are correct and well described so full marks are given for this part.

(b) This is a good answer with two points being fully described. The middle answer is not a full description and only gains one mark.

(9 marks out of 10)

Examiner's answer

2 (a) One mark for a statement of the change and one mark for an explanation of why it causes stress.

Job losses or fear of job losses (1) – new system may replace staff who performed manual processes such as data entry/filing/internal post/clerical work (1), etc.

Having to learn new skills (1). Older staff may be stressed by appearing to look stupid because they do not have the ICT skills younger people have (1).

Fear of change of organisational structure (1). Changes mean office may have to move which may make a much harder journey to work (1).

Changes in work patterns (1). Staff may have to work shifts/24/7, etc.

Changes in internal procedures (1). May make staff take on more responsibility for no extra pay (1).

Health fears (1). Staff may be worried about the health issues associated with prolonged use of ICT equipment (1).

(b) One mark for a brief description of the factor and one mark for further explanation or an example.

Appropriate training/re-training (1) to ensure all staff understand the new system and are not stressed wondering what to do (1).

Explanation of the advantages (1) so that staff can see how they will benefit by making their job easier/less frustrating/more interesting (1).

Spell out the implications of the new system (1) to help allay rumours which cause people stress (1).

Opportunity to learn new skills (1) will enable staff to improve their job prospects (1).

Involvement in the development of the new system (1) so that the staff can have a system which is straightforward to use (1).

Summary mind map

The consequences of change through the introduction of new ICT systems

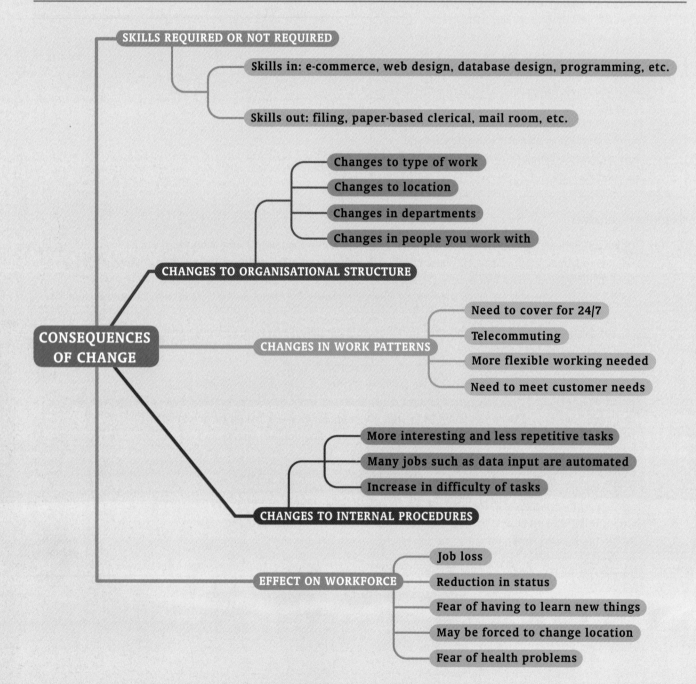

SKILLS REQUIRED OR NOT REQUIRED

Skills in: e-commerce, web design, database design, programming, etc.

Skills out: filing, paper-based clerical, mail room, etc.

Changes to type of work

Changes to location

Changes in departments

Changes in people you work with

CHANGES TO ORGANISATIONAL STRUCTURE

CONSEQUENCES OF CHANGE

CHANGES IN WORK PATTERNS

Need to cover for 24/7

Telecommuting

More flexible working needed

Need to meet customer needs

More interesting and less repetitive tasks

Many jobs such as data input are automated

Increase in difficulty of tasks

CHANGES TO INTERNAL PROCEDURES

EFFECT ON WORKFORCE

Job loss

Reduction in status

Fear of having to learn new things

May be forced to change location

Fear of health problems

Management information is the lifeblood of any business or organisation and it can range from a single report outlining the profitability of a range of goods to a whole document outlining the profitability of all areas according to region. There are many ways in which the material for these reports could be obtained but mostly this information will be obtained from operational information supplied by the computer system. Most often the management information is obtained by further processing of the data and information from the processing of the day-to-day transactions. It is important that any management information asked for contains the correct content, is in a form appropriate for the person who is to receive it and is presented at the correct time. Not all ICT systems supply management information. For example, a payroll system that calculates all the necessary figures for paying the employees along with details of deductions such as tax, National Insurance, pensions, etc., is quite capable of operating without the need to supply management with information.

▼ The key concepts covered in this topic are:

▶ Features of an effective MIS

▶ The flow of information between external and internal components of an MIS

▶ The success or failure of an MIS

▶ Features of a good MIS

▶ Factors which can lead to a poor MIS

CONTENTS

Features of an effective management information system (MIS)

▼ You will find out

▶ About the features of an effective management information system

▶ About the flow of information between external and internal components of an MIS

Introduction

Managers in organisations have to make decisions about their functional area in the organisation and to make sure these decisions are good, they need to be based on information. It is the purpose of the management information systems to supply this information.

Definition of an MIS

Systems that convert data from internal or external sources into information to be used by managers are called management information systems. These are organised collections of people, procedures and resources that support the decisions of managers.

Management information needs to be in an appropriate form to enable managers at different levels to make effective decisions for planning, directing and controlling the activities for which they are responsible. MIS are not a separate thing to information systems, since they are really only part of them. Information systems are routinely used by all staff. MIS are designed primarily with the information needs of managers in mind.

One of the main problems with many managers is that they do not understand the role of information. To a manager having lots of correct information reduces uncertainty when making decisions. These decisions can be reached quickly and with less worry because there is a much higher probability that the decision will be correct. If there was no uncertainty, then there would be no need for information, since it would be possible for a manager to predict things accurately. Unfortunately, in reality things are not like this, so it is necessary to gain as much management information as possible that is relevant to the decision being made.

It is important to note that many managers have specific jobs and responsibilities and any management information needs to be tailored for the individual manager's needs. Historically the manager would contact the data processing department or database manager with a request for this information and they were frequently met with the reply that the system could not produce the information in the way that they requested it. Many large database systems were quite inflexible when producing these sorts of ad hoc reports even though they were capable of producing routine information gained during data processing activities.

Now database systems are much more flexible and many managers are trained to be able to extract the information they need using a computer connected to the network.

Example of an MIS being used

In order to understand the importance of management information lets look at an example based on a barbeque manufacturing company. This company employs eight representatives who are given an area in which they operate. Their work is to visit, promote and make sales in these areas. Suppose the sales manager who is responsible for the representatives tells the managing director that salesman X, who is responsible for the north western region, has made £100,000 worth of sales in the last month. That sounds good to the sales manager, but is it? How can he decide? The obvious way would be to look at the sales the other representatives had made in the same period in order to make a comparison. You could also compare these sales with the sales made for the same region going back several years. This might reveal a trend in that having barbeques is becoming more popular. Management information systems are popular because they make getting information such as this as easy as possible and they take away the need for specialist staff to extract the information from the computer system. There are clear advantages in letting the person who understands the business make the decision about the information they need to extract. Things are not quite that simple since quite a bit of training will be required before staff can extract the information in this way.

Other examples of MIS

A chief executive of a supermarket chain may extract financial information about each supermarket in the chain in order to identify those making the least profits. This is so that they can be sold and the money used to open new supermarkets in areas that are likely to be more profitable.

A manager of a nationwide parcel delivery company uses the MIS to look at the distances each vehicle travels to make a decision on whether another depot is required.

What makes an MIS different from a data processing system?

Management information systems:

- produce information beyond that normally needed for routine data processing
- produce information where the timing is critical

- are used to supply information to management in order to help make decisions
- are based around databases.

Features of an effective MIS

Effective MIS will:

- Include information that is relevant and accurate. Too much detail is almost as bad as too little because managers have to spend time picking out the information they need from the mass of irrelevant information. Accuracy of the information depends on the accuracy of the data input into the system. Validation and verification must take place to make sure that incorrect data is not processed.
- Give the information when required. Some information systems only produce certain output at a certain time. For example, reports may be produced at the end of a monthly run for processing payments. Managers have to make decisions quickly and so should not have to wait for information. As MIS are used by the managers themselves, the information can be extracted whenever they need it.
- Be accessible to a wide range of users. Managers in different areas of the business will need information relevant to their area. This means that the MIS must be able to use all the data held by the corporate database and supply it to the full range of users. For managers to take advantage of the MIS they must be trained in its use.
- Present the data in the most appropriate format. Managers should be able to choose the way the information is presented. For example, in tables or the types of graphs used. They may choose to save the information in file formats that can be used for production of spreadsheets or presentations.
- Be flexible. Many managers complain that the MIS fails to give them the information they require in the format they choose. A good MIS will therefore allow complete

flexibility in the information it can produce and the way it is presented. The system should therefore fit in with the managers and not the other way around.

MIS should present information in the correct format: here charts and tables are used

The flow of information between external and internal components of an MIS

MIS use data that is both internal and external to the organisation. For example, an MIS to produce information about the effectiveness of a marketing campaign may include information about competitors as well as information about costs and sales from their internal ICT systems.

Schools use MIS in various ways. For example, for long-term planning they would need to ensure they had the resources to cope with increases in the population.

Internal information might include admission figures from previous years, details of brothers and sisters of existing pupils who will eventually start at the school, details of resources such as staff, rooms, desks, etc.

External information sources could be figures from primary schools, census details (for indications of population), details of immigration, local authority data, etc.

The following diagram shows the sources of information and the information flows. The entities (i.e., suppliers or receivers of information) are shown in oval boxes and the processes are written inside the shaded box. The overall box marks the internal system boundary.

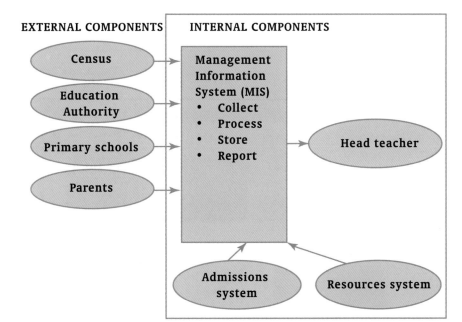

The flow of information from external and internal components of an MIS

The success or failure of a management information system

▼ **You will find out**

▶ About the reasons for failure of an MIS

▶ About the complaints managers might make about their MIS

Introduction

In this section you will look at the features of a good MIS and those factors that can lead to a poor information system.

The reasons for failure of an MIS

Many MIS are not successful in either giving the managers what they want or producing a working system at all. In some cases, the project goes out of control with the costs escalating and the progress of the project falling behind. Lack of project control can occur for a number of reasons: key personnel can leave; managers do not keep a grip on the schedules and costs and so on. Some MIS fail to live up to their expectations and some of the problems that managers have when using poor management information systems are summarised in the diagram below.

Features of a good MIS

The features which will lead to a good MIS include the following:

- Accuracy of the data – the data used from the transaction systems that supply data to the management must be accurate.
- Flexibility of data analysis – different managers have different requirements and the MIS must be able to cope with this.
- Providing data/information in an appropriate form – managers will need the data/information presented according to their requirements. Some will want it tabulated and others will want trends displayed in graphs and charts.
- Accessible to a wide range of users – managers have a wide range of skills and knowledge of ICT systems but MIS need to be used by all managers.

This means the MIS should make it easy for all managers to extract the information they need.

- Improves interpersonal communications – amongst management and employees: managers can get precise information which allows them to communicate this information with managers in other areas. They are also more capable of communicating with their subordinates because their decisions are based on sound information.
- Allows individual project planning – part of any manager's job is to plan for the future. The information from MIS can be used to help plan new developments such as opening of new branches, the provision of a new distribution network, the positioning of new stores and so on.
- Avoids information overload – MIS must not produce any superfluous information as this can waste time and sometimes make the essential information harder to use.

'I'll never get the hang of this MIS'

'This information tells me all sorts of things but does not tells me what I really needed to know'

COMPLAINTS MANAGERS MIGHT MAKE ABOUT THEIR MIS

'Every month I have to wade through these reports to extract the information I need'

'This information would have been really useful if I'd had it at my sales meeting yesterday'

Factors which can lead to a poor MIS

Factors which can lead to a poor MIS include:

- Complexity of the system – systems need to be complex enough to be able to deal with the detail some managers will require from the system but the system should not be too complex from a usability point of view. MIS need to be simple to use so that all managers are capable of using them in their day-to-day work.

- Lack of formal methods – there are many different ways in which a system can be developed and each method is called a methodology. What all these methodologies have in common is that the system is developed in a formal way. This avoids systems analysts taking short cuts and ending up developing a less than perfect system. Proper systems analysis does take time and effort but the resulting MIS is much better than MIS developed using less formal methods.

- Inadequate initial analysis – if the initial analysis is done by someone inexperienced, they might not appreciate the need to fully analyse the information requirements of management. Such an analysis will be based on incomplete information and will never produce a flexible and fully functional MIS. Inadequate analysis usually manifests itself when the system is unable to perform a key task or the system does not behave in a manner that is consistent with the original objectives.

- Lack of management involvement in the design – ICT specialists usually take charge of the development of the information system, since they have the knowledge about how to perform a rigorous systems analysis, although their actual business knowledge about the areas they are looking at is much weaker than the managers who are in charge of these areas. It is therefore important that these managers should be part of the development team and that there is constant consultation between them and the developers of the system. The result of the involvement will hopefully be a technically good system that meets management needs.

- Inappropriate hardware and software – the hardware, e.g. the speed of the file server, the speed of data transfer all affect the speed at which management information can be extracted from all the data held. If the system is too slow then managers will only use the system when absolutely necessary. The MIS software should make it easy for managers to construct conditions for the extraction of the information they need and they should be able to choose how the information is presented.

- Lack of management knowledge about ICT systems and their capabilities – management may not be aware of the latest developments in ICT and they usually place their trust in ICT specialists who they assume will have the latest knowledge. However, the ICT specialists cannot possibly be experts in all parts of the business, so management will also be expected to keep up-to-date with the latest developments in their particular area of management. For example, the personnel manager will probably subscribe to professional magazines and in these there will occasionally be articles on the latest developments in this area and many of these will involve the use of ICT. Management should go on training courses to equip them with the skills to extract management information and teach them the value in having this information.

- Poor communications between professionals – managers and ICT professionals should work together to produce a management information system that meets the demands of the managers who will be using the system. Poor communication between managers and ICT staff may result in a system that does not meet the needs of the managers. Such systems may not extract the information needed, or may be cumbersome to use which puts off managers from using them.

- Lack of professional standards – the British Computer Society (BCS) sets minimum standards of practice to be observed by all its members. Many ICT professionals are members of the society and membership shows the employer or the person paying for their services that the job will be performed in a professional manner. Not all computer professionals are members of the society and so do not have to conform to their standards. Some computer professionals are motivated by their own career progression and everything they do has this aim in the background. For example, if they need experience in a certain new area of computing, such as in the use of intranets, they may then try to persuade their organisation to get one, regardless of whether one is needed, simply so that they can put that they have had experience of using one on their CV. Some 'computer professionals', especially those engaged in contract work, may take on jobs for which they have little experience in the hope that they will 'get the hang of it' once they start work.

Case study, Questions and Activities

▶ **Case study**   pp. 118–119

Schools Information Management System (SIMS)

Running a school or college is very complex as there are many people and events to manage. It is not surprising that there are management information systems available for them to do this and the most popular one is called Schools Information Management System (SIMS).

The SIMS system is able to produce information at different levels, from information needed by the head teacher at a strategic level to tactical information needed by managers, and operational information needed by teachers and schools administration staff.

Schools information management systems help schools in many ways:

- They reduce the workload in every area of work in the school by automating many of the tasks undertaken by teachers and support staff.
- Tactical managers such as heads of department can use the system to plan what is taught in their department.
- The head has to make strategic decisions about staffing. The MIS can help them do this by being able to analyse what impact an additional

teaching assistant might have on the budget, the class size, and the pupils' achievements, based on what has happened in the past. They can then make the decision more easily because it is based on facts.

- Teachers can supply operational information about pupils' good or bad behaviour in lessons and this can be used by staff to identify patterns of behaviour.
- Strategic staff such as the head and assistant heads can use the MIS to plan timetables making the best use of staff and resources.
- At an operational level, classroom teachers can reduce the time it takes to write pupil reports by using a comment bank where a wide selection of comments can be selected and used to produce the report.
- The head can plan long- and short-term finances and make informed budget decisions.
- Head of years can strengthen school-home links by sharing information about pupils using the reporting tools and by sharing this information with parents using text messaging and e-mails.

1 There are three levels of staff in a school:
   Operational
   Tactical
   Strategic
   For each of the following staff explain which of the three levels is most appropriate for them. (8 marks)
   (a) Head teacher
   (b) Classroom teacher
   (c) Teaching assistant
   (d) School office clerk
   (e) Head of department
   (f) Head of year

   (g) Deputy or assistant head
   (h) Caretaker

2 Schools and colleges make use of management information systems (MIS). Different levels of staff have different requirements from the system.
   (a) Explain what is meant by a management information system (MIS). (3 marks)
   (b) Describe, by giving an example, a task that a head teacher would use the MIS for at a strategic level. (2 marks)
   (c) Describe, by giving an example, a task that a head of department/manager would use the MIS for at a tactical level. (2 marks)

▶ Activity 1: Management information needs at different levels

A company manufactures barbeques and these are sold through the large DIY stores and garden centres throughout Britain. At present there are 10 models ranging in cost from the cheapest model at only £55 to a top of the range model costing around £1400.

Your task is to look at the management information the production manager might need and compare and contrast their information needs with those of the managing director who is in overall charge of the business.

1 Management are the people who have the responsibility in organisations for the making of decisions. Information systems used to supply information for managers on which they can base decisions are called management information systems (MIS). Management information systems go hand in hand with data processing systems but are used for different purposes.

  (a) By giving a suitable example for each, explain the difference between a data processing/transaction processing system and a management information system (MIS). (4 marks)

  (b) Management information systems (MIS) are used in most organisations such as hospitals and schools. Describe, by giving a relevant example in each case, a use to which an MIS can be put in these two organisations. (4 marks)

2 (a) Most organisations make use of a management information system (MIS). Explain the purpose of an MIS. (3 marks)

  (b) Explain why an MIS is particularly useful to managers. (2 marks)

  (c) Give an example of one MIS that you have come across and explain briefly how it was used. (3 marks)

3 A management information system (MIS) converts the data from internal and external sources into information.

  (a) Explain what is mean by 'internal' and 'external' sources. (2 marks)

  (b) Describe briefly an MIS you have seen or read about and describe the data input into the system and how it is output to give the management information. (4 marks)

4 Management information systems (MIS) are used by many organisations.

  (a) Management sometimes complain about their MIS for a variety of reasons. Describe **four** factors which can lead to a poor MIS. (8 marks)

  (b) Describe **four** features of a good MIS. (8 marks)

5 One factor in the production of a good management information system (MIS) is management understanding and involvement. Describe **three** things the managers could do to increase the chance of an MIS being successful. (6 marks)

▶ **Activity 2: Is it a data processing/transaction processing system or a management information system?**

You need to be able to distinguish between a data processing system and a management information system. Basically, if the system processes raw data to produce routine information, then it is likely to be a data processing system. However, if the data produced is communicated to managers at different levels, in an appropriate form, to enable them to make effective decisions for planning, directing and controlling the activities for which they are responsible, then it is a management information system.

Here are some systems and your task is to say into which category they fall: data processing systems or management information systems.

- A payroll system for processing time sheets and printing pay slips.
- A system that compares the sales made of the same make of car over the same month for the last five years.
- Production of a list of all the main dealers in the country with a certain colour and model of car in stock to be given to a customer.
- A list of the items to be ordered from the suppliers produced from an EPOS system.
- A sales analysis system to investigate trends in sales over a certain time period.
- Production of a list of debtors (customers who owe money) to be sent to the managers for their decision on what further action to take.
- The sales figures for previous similar periods for the planning of production levels.
- A system that analyses competitors' prices for similar products.
- A system producing a report outlining the frequency of the calls to a help-desk and the average time each problem took to resolve.
- A system for producing a list of students who have paid their course fees, to be given to a course tutor.

Exam support

Worked example 1

1   Management information systems are used in most organisations.

Explain what a management information system is and support your explanation with two examples of how it can be used.

Describe those features/factors which make a management information system either good or poor. Your answer should include examples to aid your description. **(13 marks)**

Student answer 1

1   A management information system is a system used by managers to help manage the business or organisation. The managers can use the system to help them run the business. They can get lots of useful information from the system.

A good management information system is fast because managers do not want to wait too long for the information to be displayed.

The information from the MIS must be relevant so they do not have to wade through loads of unnecessary information to get at the information they need.

They may need to do some further processing of the information, so it must be able to be exported in file formats that other software such as spreadsheet software can use.

The information supplied by the MIS must be accurate otherwise any decisions made by the manager will be more risky.

A poor MIS is cumbersome to use. MIS needs to be easy to use otherwise managers will not use the system.

Examiner's comment

1   The answer for the description of an MIS is typical of those produced by weak students who have not understood or remembered the main points. Instead they have waffled on using words in the term. No examples of how an MIS can be used are given. This answer gains no marks.

This answer on factors and features is better but it is a bit general in parts. **(5 marks out of 13)**

Student answer 2

1   A management information system is a computer system that supplies the information in a form that managers can easily understand and use that will allow them to make good business decisions. Such information can reduce the risk in making decisions.

A good MIS will supply relevant information so that managers do not have to spend time having to extract the data they need. For example, if the manager wanted sales figures for a particular product each month for the previous year, they should not be given a list for all the products.

The information must be accurate, as the data being captured was accurate and suitably validated and verified. This will enable more accurate decisions to be made by the managers.

A good MIS will be easy to use by all managers, even those with poor ICT skills, so that they can all make use of the information the system provides. The organisation should support managers by providing training sessions and help-desks.

A poor MIS is one that has been produced without the involvement of the managers who will use the information. Insufficient initial analysis of the user needs means the system does not satisfy the user requirements.

Poor management information systems often arise due to the use of inadequate hardware and software. The software chosen or developed cannot give the information needed by managers.

Examiner's comment

1   The first part, the definition of the MIS, is good but fails to mention that the MIS includes people and procedures as well as ICT systems. The rest of the definition is good but two examples required by the question are not given.

There are three good descriptions of a good MIS with associated examples given.

The section on poor management information systems gives two good answers.

On the whole this is a good, well thought out and constructed answer and the student clearly understands what MIS are and how they are used and by looking at the mark allocation in the examiner's answer you can see this answer meets criteria for the top band of marks. **(10 marks out of 13)**

Examiner's answer

1 A management information system (MIS) is an organised collection of people, procedures and resources designed to support the decisions of managers.

Examples of use similar to the following:

A head teacher in a school analysing those pupils who are falling behind in their work as evidenced by test results and whose attendance is poor so that interviews with parents can be arranged.

A production manager of a company using the MIS to make predictions as to how many of a certain product to make based on the sales from the same quarter in previous years.

Features of a good MIS include the following:

Accuracy of the information produced (usually dependent on the accuracy of the data input).

Ability to allow managers to set up their own queries flexibly.

Presents the data in an appropriate form to make it easy to understand.

Avoids the giving of any information that is not necessary.

Able to be used by managers who have differing experience and skills in the use of ICT.

Ability to be transferred to other packages for further processing/analysis such as a spreadsheet package.

Factors which can lead to a poor MIS:

Inadequate consultation with managers during the analysis of the system to find out what their requirements from the system are.

Lack of training for managers means many managers do not use the system as they should.

Inappropriate hardware or software being used. For example, the network may run slowly when processing the information needed when producing MIS reports.

Poor communications between professionals. Staff have failed to cooperate during the setting up of the MIS.

Inadequate initial analysis. The system does not do exactly what it should do.

10–13 marks Candidates have given an accurate definition for MIS and have given clear examples of two uses. The candidates have given clear and coherent answers that accurately compare and contrast four features/factors giving relevant examples. They use appropriate terminology and accurate spelling, punctuation and grammar.

5–9 marks Candidates have given a partially correct definition for MIS and have given one correct example. The candidates give a few features/factors but they lack clarity or examples. There are a few errors in spelling, punctuation and grammar.

0–4 marks Candidates give a superficial definition of MIS and no examples. They list four features but add no explanation or simply describe more fully two features/factors. The response lacks clarity and there are significant errors in spelling, punctuation and grammar.

Worked example 2

2 **Management information systems are used by organisations to convert data from internal and external sources into information.**

One feature of an effective management information system is that the information should be communicated to managers in an appropriate form.

Other than the feature given in the example, give three distinctly different features of an effective management information system, supporting each answer with a suitable example. (6 marks)

Student answer 1

2 Here are the three features:

It improves personal communication between the management and employees.

Accuracy of the data.

Managers with wide ranging skills and knowledge about ICT and MIS can easily use the system.

Examiner's comment

2 The student has listed three features of management information system but has not included any examples or further explanation.

The student should have read the question more carefully and used the marks to work out that more is required here. **(3 marks out of 6)**

Exam support *continued*

Student answer 2

2 The MIS gives the data/information in an appropriate form. For example, trends in sales are more easily spotted when a graph is drawn rather than simply giving a table of numbers. The MIS should allow the manager to choose how the information is presented.

There should only be the information that the manager wants and this means they do not have to pick out the information they need from a mass of information. The system should not require managers to do further processing to get the information they need. For example a list of sales figures of one product over the last five years should be produced on its own rather than with the details of all the other products.

The MIS should be easy to use. It should make it easy for a manager to select what information they need from the system. For example, a manager can select the fields they want displaying and any grouping and ordering simply by clicking on a list. Managers with widely differing skills and knowledge should be capable of using the MIS.

Examiner's comment

2 This is a very good answer in all parts. This student has stated clearly the feature and added further explanation and supported their answer with a correct example.

Full marks are given here. **(6 marks out of 6)**

Examiner's answer

2 One mark given for the feature, one mark for further explanation and an example.

Accuracy of the data (1) processed by the MIS (1) to give information that can be relied upon so that correct decisions can be made (1).

Flexibility of data analysis (1) such as being able to provide comparisons between two sets of figures (1) by using differences, percentages, percentage increases/decreases (1), etc.

Providing the data in an appropriate form (1) such as producing graphs rather than tables of numbers (1) in order to see trends more easily (1).

Accessible to a wide range of users and support a wide range of skills and knowledge (1) so that all managers are capable of extracting the information (1) they need to make decisions in their area using the MIS (1).

Improves interpersonal communications amongst management and employees (1) by giving them precise information to discuss at meetings (1) and to ensure that the decisions made are as accurate as they can be (1).

Allows individual project planning (1). This means managers can plan future sales drives, staffing, budgets (1), etc., using information they can get from the MIS such as sales trends, costs of staff (1), etc.

Avoids information overload (1). The MIS will allow the manager to extract very specific information (1) which does not include any superfluous information which wastes time reading (1).

Summary mind maps

Features of an effective management information system

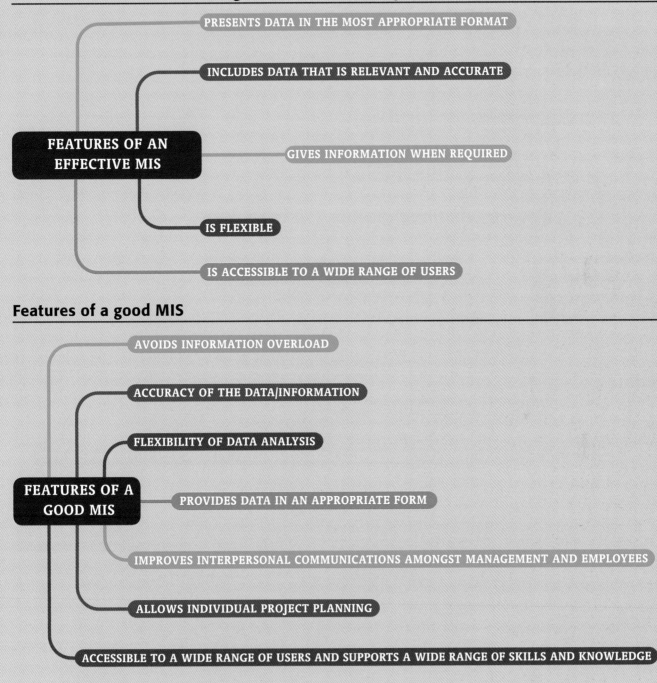

PRESENTS DATA IN THE MOST APPROPRIATE FORMAT

INCLUDES DATA THAT IS RELEVANT AND ACCURATE

FEATURES OF AN EFFECTIVE MIS

GIVES INFORMATION WHEN REQUIRED

IS FLEXIBLE

IS ACCESSIBLE TO A WIDE RANGE OF USERS

Features of a good MIS

AVOIDS INFORMATION OVERLOAD

ACCURACY OF THE DATA/INFORMATION

FLEXIBILITY OF DATA ANALYSIS

FEATURES OF A GOOD MIS

PROVIDES DATA IN AN APPROPRIATE FORM

IMPROVES INTERPERSONAL COMMUNICATIONS AMONGST MANAGEMENT AND EMPLOYEES

ALLOWS INDIVIDUAL PROJECT PLANNING

ACCESSIBLE TO A WIDE RANGE OF USERS AND SUPPORTS A WIDE RANGE OF SKILLS AND KNOWLEDGE

Factors that can lead to a poor MIS

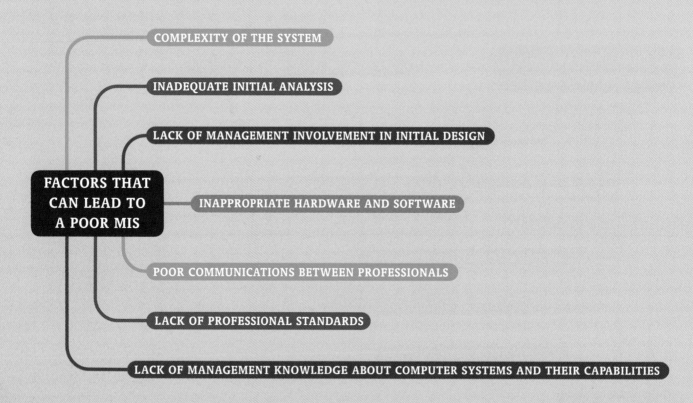

TOPIC 9: System development life cycle

If systems are to live up to expectations, they need to be developed in a formal manner. The system development life cycle (SDLC) is a series of steps that are taken when developing a new system or altering an existing system.

In this topic you will learn about the steps involved in the system development life cycle and how they are applied to the development of a new computerised system.

▼ The key concepts covered in this topic are:

▶ The main components of the SDLC and how they may be applied to the development of a computerised solution

▶ System investigation

▶ System analysis

▶ System design

▶ System implementation

▶ System maintenance

▶ System evaluation

CONTENTS

Unit IT3 Use and Impact of ICT

System investigation

▼ You will find out

▶ About what a system is

▶ About the activities involved in the system development life cycle

▶ About the first stage of the system development life cycle called system investigation

▶ About the feasibility study and the feasibility report

Introduction

In this section you will look at what a system is, the system development life cycle (SDLC) and why new systems are needed and the initial stage, called the system investigation.

What is a system?

A system is a way of doing things. Another way of describing a system would be as a complex whole, the component parts of which are arranged for a common purpose.

Organisations have various systems to deal with the different functional areas. There needs to be systems for paying staff, purchasing stock or raw materials, controlling how much stock is kept, keeping accounts, ensuring compliance with legislation, keeping records of staff employed and so on.

The system development life cycle (SDLC)

The SDLC is a sequence of activities which are performed when a system is analysed, designed and implemented. Look at the diagram and you will notice that it is cyclic. This is because once the system has been completed and is working, it is usual to periodically look at what improvements can be made to the system. This results in the activities shown in the diagram being repeated.

```
Investigation
    ↓
Analysis
    ↓
Design
    ↓
Implementation
    ↓
Maintenance
    ↓
Evaluation
```

System development life cycle

The tasks involved in system investigation

Before work can start on analysing the system, it is necessary to find out many facts about the organisation and the tasks they want the new system to do. You therefore need to investigate the existing system and also the requirements for the new system so that the analysis can be performed.

In order to improve an existing system it is essential to understand how it works. The process of finding out is called investigation or fact finding. There are a number of different ways information about the existing system can be found out and these are:

- interviews
- observation
- inspection of records
- questionnaires.

Interviews – interviews with managers will normally reveal how their particular department works and any problems they are having with the existing system. They will be able to offer information about how they would like the new system to work and they will be able to tell you about information that they would like the new system to provide.

Operational staff are those members of staff who perform the majority of the day-to-day work of the organisation and their knowledge of the organisation is usually restricted to their own area of work. They will be able to supply the fine detail about particular ways that jobs are done.
Collection of information using interviewing is time consuming.

Observations – if you wanted to take someone else's job over then the best way to learn what you have to do is to either sit for a few days with the person whose job you are taking over or sit with someone else who does a similar job. Observation involves sitting with a person and observing what they do in order to understand the information flows and processes they perform.

Inspection of records – many organisations still use and generate paper-based documents which are used in their business. By examining these documents you can understand what information is held and the way it is communicated between different departments or between the organisation and suppliers and customers.

Documents giving general information would include:

- organisation charts (this is a chart showing the hierarchy in the organisation and can be used to find out who reports to whom)
- staff CVs – useful to assess the skills or training needs of employees
- job descriptions – give details of the tasks undertaken by different people
- policy/procedure manuals – useful to understand the way the organisation works
- previous systems documentation – paper documents when previous systems have been produced.

Documents giving specific information would include:

- product catalogues
- order forms
- invoices
- despatch notes
- picking lists (for warehouse staff).

By looking at CVs you can find out what skills employees have and the likely training needed

Organisation charts help you understand the structure of the business

Questionnaires – at first sight, questionnaires seem an ideal way of collecting information about a company. You do not have to spend time interviewing people and a questionnaire sticks to the important points without digressing, which can occur in an interview.

However, questionnaires have drawbacks. Many people forget to fill them in, which can result in an incomplete picture of a system. Respondents may misunderstand some of the questions, if the forms are simply posted to them and no personal help offered.

Nevertheless, questionnaires are useful when information needs to be collected from a large number of individuals, as they consume a lot less staff time than interviews.

When compiling questionnaires, the following should be borne in mind:

- Make sure that the questions are precisely worded so that the users do not have to interpret the questions.
- It is best for respondents not to have to put their name on their questionnaire, as otherwise you may not get honest answers.
- Structure the questionnaire so that general questions are asked first, followed by more specific ones. It is also worth dividing the questionnaire into functional areas, so for example, one part could deal with sales order processing, another with stock control. Obviously this approach will vary depending on the type of organisation.
- Avoid leading questions (questions which suggest a preferred answer).
- At the end of the questionnaire, always add the question: 'Is there anything I have missed that you think I ought to know about?'.

Feasibility and the feasibility report

Feasibility is an initial investigation to look at the likelihood of being able to create a new system with stated aims and objectives at reasonable cost. The results of this exercise are summarised in a document called a feasibility report and it is this document that is used by senior managers/directors to assess the project's feasibility. Once the feasibility has been assessed, the project can either go ahead or be abandoned.

Feasibility is an important activity because it makes sure that new systems are not developed that have little chance of success. There are many examples of new systems being abandoned after a significant amount of work has been done on them.

Feasibility will normally involve the following:

- An initial fact find which will give information on what is required from the project.
- An investigation into the technical, legal, economic, operational and schedule implications.
- Identifying the costs and benefits of the new system and weighing them against each other.
- Making recommendations as to the feasibility of the project.
- A draft plan for the implementation of the project.

What should be included in the feasibility report?

After the initial analysis of the existing system, a report, called a feasibility report, is produced on which a decision to go ahead with the project or whether to abandon it is made.

A feasibility report will normally contain some or all of the following:

- User requirements – the user requirements of the system should be identified, agreed with the analyst and written as a list. Any developed system will be judged on how closely it matches these requirements.

- Details of existing hardware and software – it may be the case that existing hardware and software can be re-used or new or additional hardware or software is needed.
- Definition of the scope of the present system – this is so that everyone is clear what the system does and also what it doesn't do. The scope will determine the size and complexity of the proposed project. Included in the scope are details of organisation charts, sources of data and methods of data capture.
- Major data processing functions and processes – this is best illustrated as a context diagram which is a special data flow diagram which represents the whole system as a rectangle and shows how the information flows to and from the systems to the external organisations and systems. You will learn how to draw a context diagram a little later on in this topic when the full range of data flow diagrams (DFDs) will be looked at.
- Identification of problems with the present system – here you would list the problems with the existing system with a view to building a new system capable of solving them.
- Analysis of costs and benefits of the new system – costs will be incurred such as staff, equipment, hardware, software, licences, communication systems, training, etc. These will have to be weighed up against the benefits of the new system such as fewer errors, more management information, ability to complete transactions in less time, increase in business owing to greater satisfaction among customers.

> **KEY WORDS**

Fact finding – initial investigation of a system before a feasibility study is carried out

Feasibility study – a study carried out before a new ICT system is developed to see whether a new system can be developed at an acceptable cost to realise user benefits

Topic 9: System development life cycle

System analysis

▼ You will find out

▶ About the tasks that are involved in the analysis of the existing system

▶ About high-level (contextual view) data flow diagrams (DFDs)

▶ About the levelling of data flow diagrams

▶ About decision tables

▶ About entity-relationship diagrams

▶ About the data dictionary

Introduction

After the system investigation has taken place and the decision has been made, on the basis of the feasibility report, to go ahead with the new system, further understanding of the system being developed is needed. The process of finding out and documenting the existing system is called systems analysis and this is performed by a systems analyst. There is a variety of tools and techniques that produce diagrams and charts which are used to document a new or existing system and these are covered in this section.

Analysis of the existing system

Analysis looks in detail at the current system or the requirements for a task that has never been performed before. The systems analyst (or just analyst, for short) investigates the requirements for the new system.

Some initial analysis is performed during the system investigation, as it is necessary to determine information about the system being developed (aims and objectives, size, scope, re-use of existing hardware and software, etc.) as this will be needed to produce the feasibility report.

Analysis will normally involve the following:

- understanding the existing system
- understanding the proposed system if there is no existing system
- gathering and analysing different user requirements
- setting out the solution in a logical way using tools and techniques such as data flow diagrams, data models, process specifications and systems diagrams
- producing a specification.

Identifying and understanding tools and techniques used to understand a system

There are a number of tools and techniques used to help understand and analyse systems and these are covered here.

Analysis documentation is used repeatedly in systems analysis at different levels in the system. Usually we work from an overview of the whole system, but as the system is developed, more detail is added. In order to describe and understand the system, several techniques and diagrams are used.

Data flow diagrams (DFDs)

It is important, when explaining an existing system, to look at the data/information flows within an organisation. This is often done diagrammatically using DFDs. These are used as a first step in describing a system and they look at inputs, what processes are performed on the inputs and the outputs produced.

Unfortunately there are many different ways of drawing DFDs and it can all get very confusing. The method shown here is the method used with SSADM (Structured Systems Analysis and Design Methodology).

An initial investigation of the system is performed in the feasibility study. This looks at the inputs to the system, what processes are performed on them and the outputs from the system. The scope of the system is also specified in this phase. To help further analysis, DFDs are drawn. DFDs are used to consider the data, while ignoring the equipment used to store it. They are used as a first step in describing a system.

A series of symbols is used in these diagrams; unfortunately different authors use different-shaped symbols, which can be very confusing.

A process or action – is a rectangular box and it represents a process that does something with the data (it could manipulate it in some way or perform calculations on it, for example). The box is divided into three parts, the top left box having a number in it which identifies the box. The main body of the box is used to record a description of the process and the top right of the box is used to record the person or area responsible for the process.

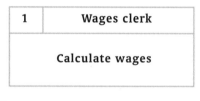

1	Wages clerk
	Calculate wages

A process

External source of data (where it comes from) or an external sink of data (where it goes to)

This is an oval box which is used to describe where, outside the system, the data comes from and goes to. We are not concerned with what happens to the data before it reaches the box (if it is a source) or what happens to it when it goes past a sink.

Customer

External object

EXAM TIP

There should only ever be one process box in a context diagram and no stores.

KEY WORDS

Context diagram – a diagram which represents a system as a single DFD process

Data flow diagram (DFD) – shows the flow, storage and processing of data in a system

Data flow

Data flow is shown by an arrow pointing in the direction of the flow. Usually it is advisable to put a description of the data flow on the arrow to aid understanding. By convention, we never use a verb on a data flow.

Credit card details

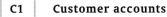

Data flow

A store of data

The symbol for this is shown in the diagram. A data store can be anywhere data is stored; it could be a drawer where you keep letters, file boxes, folders, books, a filing cabinet (or a certain drawer of a filing cabinet), magnetic disk, CD, etc. Again, the symbol bears a number which is used to reference the store when describing it, but there is also a letter placed in front of the number. M is used for a manual store and C for a computer store.

C1	**Customer accounts**

This data store contains customer account details and is on a computer

Levels of DFDs

When analysing systems it is usual to draw DFDs at different levels. The level used reflects the depth in which the DFD looks at the system being investigated.

The context diagram

The first DFD drawn is called the context diagram, because it puts the system being investigated into context. It is a high-level DFD showing the entire system under investigation as a single box and the information flows between external entities such as suppliers and customers. The diagram might show the flow of orders from the customers (an external entity) to the sales department and goods being despatched from the warehouse to the customers.

The aim of the context diagram is to show the scope of the system.

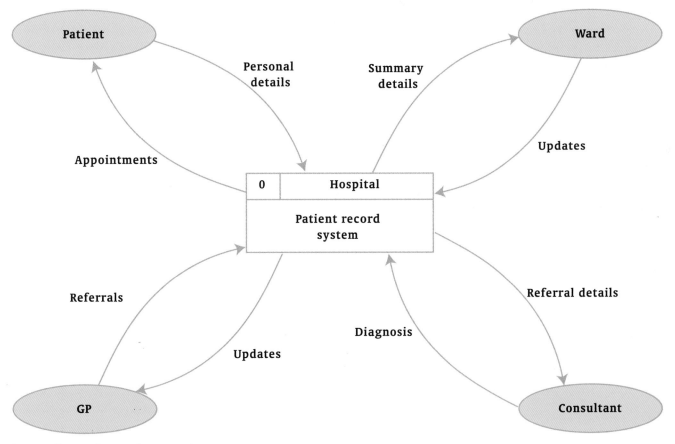

Context diagram for a patient records system

Level 1 DFD

The level 1 DFD shows the main processes in the system and presents a more detailed view of the data flows in the system. You should aim for no more than about six process boxes in this diagram.

Level 2 DFD

A level 2 DFD breaks down the process boxes in the level 1 DFD and thus presents an even more detailed view of the processes. To do this, one of the process boxes (i.e., the rectangular ones) from the level 1 DFD is taken, and the process it represents is, if possible, broken down into a series of more detailed sub-processes.

The advantage of this 'zooming in' approach is that by looking at each level starting with the outline DFD, we can gradually build up a complete picture of the information flows through the system. Instead of having a single DFD with a large number of processes shown, we end up with a whole family of DFDs showing different levels of detail.

High-level DFDs can be broken down into further diagrams showing greater levels of detail.

Using DFDs

DFDs can be used:

- during system investigation to record findings
- during system design to illustrate how a proposed system will work
- when outlining the specifications of new systems.

The decomposition (i.e., the levelling) of the DFDs

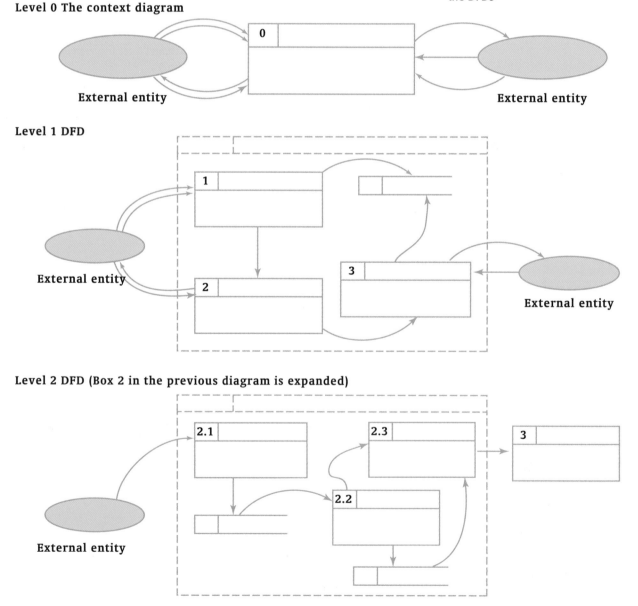

Level 0 The context diagram

External entity   External entity

Level 1 DFD

External entity   External entity

Level 2 DFD (Box 2 in the previous diagram is expanded)

External entity

Decision tables

A decision table provides a simple way of displaying the actions to be taken when certain conditions occur.

Looking at the diagram (right) you will see the following sections:

- Conditions stub: these are the situations or events which need testing. They are the cause of the actions which need to be taken in the actions stub section. A typical condition might be 'is person's age over 18?'.
- Actions stub: these are the actions which are taken depending on the combination of general conditions in the conditions stub that apply. For instance 'may be served alcoholic drink' could be an action.
- Conditions entries: these give an indication of which of the conditions apply. This is done by placing Y or N next to each condition depending on whether the condition applies or not.
- Action entries: these give the action to be taken depending on the conditions which apply. A cross is marked in the decision table to show which action or actions should be taken.

This all sounds complicated! However, they are much more difficult to describe than to do, so we will now look at a simple example with which you should be familiar.

Example: A decision table for a set of traffic lights

In order to understand how decision tables can be created, it is best to look at a non-ICT example (e.g., that of showing the operation of a set of traffic lights).

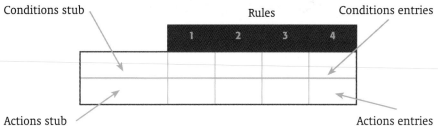

The standard way of laying out a decision table is shown here

The general conditions are obviously the colours of the lights and the general actions are whether to stop, carry on, etc.

The first step is to write in simple English the general conditions which here will be the colours of the three lights. We similarly write the general actions to be taken.

For the conditions in the conditions stub we have:

> RED
> AMBER
> GREEN

and for the actions in the action stub we have:

> STOP
> GO
> CALL POLICE (since lights aren't working properly)

We now need to set out the table, so we need to know how many rules there will be. Theoretically, we can work this out by putting two to the power of the number of conditions in the conditions stub, which will be 3 in this case. Hence there will be $2^3 = 8$ rules. For the sake of simplicity we will assume that all these rules are possible (there are in fact fail-safe systems in use in actual traffic light systems, so some of these rules will be impossible).

We can now draw the grid and fill in the conditions stub, actions stub and the combinations of Ys and Ns which make up the condition entries. When putting the Ys and Ns in, it is best to adopt a system so you could put all the Ys in first then the three combinations with two Ys and one N, then one Y and two Ns and finally all three Ns.

To fill in the action entries we look at the combinations to see what particular action or actions should be taken. We mark a cross in the relevant places to show the action or actions which should be taken.

Advantages of decision tables

The main advantages of decision tables are:

- You can make sure that all the combinations of conditions have been considered.
- They are easy to understand, since all the information needed is held in one table.
- There is a standard layout so everyone uses the same format.
- Programmers may use them to write programs and they are useful for working out logic conditions in spreadsheets and databases.
- They show cause and effect and are therefore understood by most people.

The rules for a traffic light can be set out in a decision table

	Rules							
	1	2	3	4	5	6	7	8
RED	Y	Y	Y	N	N	N	Y	N
AMBER	Y	Y	N	Y	N	Y	N	N
GREEN	Y	N	Y	Y	Y	N	N	N
STOP	X	X	X	X		X	X	X
GO					X			
CALL POLICE	X		X	X				X

Traffic light decision table

System analysis *continued*

Creating a carriage costs decision table

In some situations, there is no point in writing down and considering all the rules, since some of them may be impossible. Take the following example:

Suppose the carriage to be paid when ordering a CD from a club is as follows:

        1–3 CDs carriage is £2.50
        4–6 CDs carriage is £3.00
        7+ CDs carriage is £4.00

Since there are 3 general conditions there are 8 rules. If we look at some of these rules we find that some of them are impossible. For instance YYY would be impossible since the number of CDs ordered can only have one Y. We get impossible rules when the questions in the decision table are related to each other.

To take account of these impossible rules, we leave them out of the decision table.

By eliminating the impossible rules, the following decision table is obtained:

	Rules		
	1	2	3
1 – 3 CDs ordered	Y	N	N
4 – 6 CDs ordered	N	Y	N
over 7 CDs ordered	N	N	Y
Carriage of £2.50	X		
Carriage of £3.00		X	
Carriage of £4.00			X

Carriage costs decision table

Systems diagrams

Systems diagrams/flowcharts provide a pictorial representation of how an ICT system works by showing inputs to a particular part of the system, what actions are taken to process the data, and what moves out of this part to somewhere else. They also make clear the broad flow of the operations in a system and the hardware and media that are involved in these operations. The system flowchart also shows where the inputs originate and the mode (manual or computer-based) of processing is also made clear.

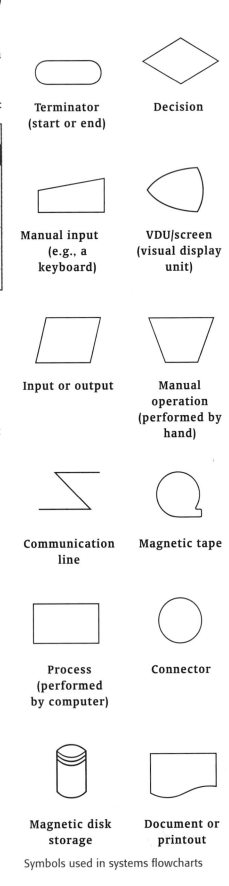

Terminator (start or end)

Decision

Manual input (e.g., a keyboard)

VDU/screen (visual display unit)

Input or output

Manual operation (performed by hand)

Communication line

Magnetic tape

Process (performed by computer)

Connector

Magnetic disk storage

Document or printout

Symbols used in systems flowcharts

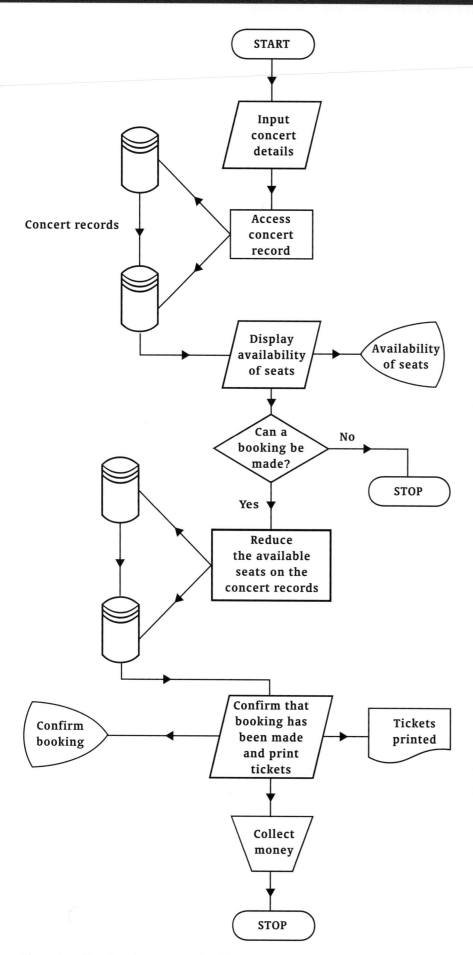

START

Input concert details

Concert records

Access concert record

Display availability of seats → Availability of seats

Can a booking be made? — No → STOP

Yes

Reduce the available seats on the concert records

Confirm booking ← Confirm that booking has been made and print tickets → Tickets printed

Collect money

STOP

The system flowchart for a concert booking system

Entity relationship models (ERMs)

Entity relationship modelling is a technique for defining the information needs of an organisation to provide a firm foundation on which an appropriate system can be built. Putting it simply, entity relationship modelling identifies the most important factors in the organisation being looked at. These factors are called **entities**.

Also looked at are the properties which these factors possess (called **attributes**) and how they are related to one another (called **relationships**). Entity models are logical, which means that they do not depend on the method of implementation. If two departments in an organisation perform identical tasks but in different ways, their entity models would nevertheless be identical, since they would be using the same entities and relationships. But their DFDs could be different, since their information flows may well differ. Entity models are particularly useful because they are independent of any storage or ways of accessing the data. They are thus not reliant on any hardware or software at this stage.

An entity model is an abstract representation of the data in an organisation and the aim of entity relationship modelling is to produce an accurate model of the information needs of an organisation which will aid either the development of a new system or the enhancement of an existing one.

An entity relationship model (ERM) describes a system as a set of data entities with relationships between them (one-to-one, one-to-many, many-to-many).

System analysis *continued*

Entity relationship diagrams

Entity relationship diagrams look at any components important to the system and the relationships between them.

So what is an **entity**? An entity can be anything about which data is recorded. It could include people, places, objects, customers, sales, payments or employees. Each entity has some associated **attributes**. An attribute is detail about an entity. Let us look at an example. In the following table the attribute for the entity 'customer' contains further details.

Entity	Attributes
CUSTOMER	Customer number
	Company name
	Postcode
	Telephone number
	Credit limit
	Amount owing

Each entity is represented in an entity diagram by a rectangle with the name of the entity written inside. The relationship between the entities is shown as lines between these boxes. The entity is always written inside the rectangle in capital letters and always in the singular because the use of plural would imply a certain type of relationship. So instead of CUSTOMERS we would need to use CUSTOMER.

The entity STUDENT could have the following attributes: student number, student address, telephone number, date of birth, tutor, course number. It is important, when developing databases, to check each attribute to decide whether it is possible to break it down further into more attributes. The attribute student address could be further broken down into the attributes; street, town and postcode. When attributes need not be broken down any further, they are said to be atomic. Hence street, town and postcode are atomic.

Breaking down attributes to produce atomic attributes allows the flexibility to manipulate the data. For example, we could search for students who have a certain postcode or sort students according to the town they are from.

Relationships

A relationship is the way in which entities in a system are related to one another. A relationship may be one-to-one (1:1), one-to-many (1:m), or many-to-many (m:n).

These three possible kinds of relationship between two entities A and B are shown here:

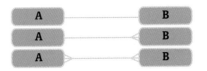

A one-to-one relationship, a one-to-many relationship and a many-to-many relationship

Entity relationship modelling for a CD e-commerce store

Here is how an entity relationship model can be constructed for a CD store that sells CDs by mail order using the Internet. The first thing to do is to identify those entities that are essential for this system. Four entities are used here:

> CUSTOMER
> CD
> ORDER
> DELIVERY

You now need to think about how these entities are related. It is a good idea to write these as a list like this:

- a customer places an order
- an order consists of one or more CDs
- delivery consists of the CDs in the order
- delivery is made to the customer.

It is now possible to draw the relationships between the entities like this:

A simple relationship model for the system but the orders (one-to-one, one-to-many, etc.) have not been added

The diagram is far from perfect. If an order consists of several CDs this is not indicated. In addition, if the club runs out of a popular CD, the part of the order that is in stock will be sent, with any out-of-stock CDs to follow.

Let us now look at the relationship between two of the entities: ORDER and CD. We need to examine the relationship from both ends. Looking in the direction from ORDER to CD we can see that one order can be for many CDs. Looking in the reverse direction we can see that a particular CD (that is a particular title) can be in many different orders. In other words, the relationship between ORDER and CD is many-to-many.

The diagram above shows the many-to-many relationship between ORDER and CD

We can see from the diagram that many members order many CDs. This would imply that an order is for many CDs but it is impossible to say which CD the order is for. There needs to be a way of linking the CDs to each order so that they can be cross-referenced. We do this by creating a new entity called ORDER LINE. This entity indicates the CD which is on a particular line in a particular order.

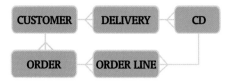

The ORDER LINE entity avoids having a many-to-many relationship

When you come to create your own entity relationship models, you will have to produce a new entity each time you come across a many-to-many relationship.

Once the new entity ORDER LINE has been created it is necessary to look at the relationships between ORDER and ORDER LINE. This relationship is one-to-many because one order may consist of many order lines. Looking at the relationship between CD and ORDER LINE we can see that this is also a one-to-many relationship because a particular CD can be in many different order lines.

Here is the entity relationship model for the system:

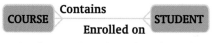

The complete entity relationship model for the system

Deciding on the type of relationship

In entity relationship modelling it is necessary to decide on the type of relationship between entities. This is best done by looking at the entity from both ends. Take the relationship between students and courses in a college. Looking at the relationship from the student end first we can see that a student could take more than one course. Looking at the relationship from the college end, we see that a single course can be taken by many students. So the relationship between COURSE and STUDENT is many-to-many.

COURSE [Contains / Enrolled on] STUDENT

Notice the use of words on the relationships

The entity relationship diagram tells us:

- one course contains many students
- one student can be enrolled on one or more courses.

As we have already seen, many-to-many relationships cannot be implemented, so in this case we need to create a new entity that would link a student to a course. In a college this is called an ENROLMENT. If a student takes several courses, there will be an enrolment for each course and the attributes of the enrolment record will include the student number (to identify the student) and the course number (to identify the course) as the primary keys.

The entities are now shown here.

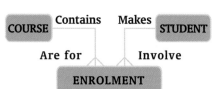

The final entity relationship diagram showing the relationships between the entities: COURSE, STUDENT and ENROLMENT

Using keys

You have already seen that each entity can be described by a number of attributes. Keys are attributes that have special significance. There are two main types of key: primary keys and foreign keys.

Primary key

A primary key is usually one or occasionally several attributes that can uniquely define a particular entity. For example, the CUSTOMER entity could be uniquely defined by a unique attribute such as customer number. The PAYROLL entity could be uniquely defined by the entity employee number.

Foreign key

When one of the attributes that is a primary key in one entity also appears in another entity, it means that there is a relationship between the entities. In the other entity the

attribute is not a primary key because it may no longer be unique. Instead it is known as a foreign key.

Suppose you supplied goods to other companies and you wanted to set up a system to keep the details of these contacts. There are two entities: the COMPANY and CONTACT. Here are the attributes for each of these entities:

CONTACT	COMPANY
Contact_ID	Company_ID
FirstName	Name
LastName	Address
Company_ID	TelephoneNumber

Each contact will be allocated a unique number so Contact_ID is the primary key for the CONTACT entity. In the COMPANY entity, the attribute Company_ID is unique and therefore the primary key. Notice that the attribute Company_ID appears in both the entities and that in the COMPANY entity it is the primary key. In the CONTACT entity Company_ID is a foreign key and since the attributes appear in both entities, we can link them. Hence the entity CONTACT has a relationship to the entity COMPANY.

You may be wondering why we have two entities rather than combine them and just have the one containing the contacts and the company they work for. If there was only a single contact for each company then it would be appropriate to put the company and contact details together. However, in reality there will be more than one contact in each company; if we store contact details, the name of the company and its address will appear in many different contacts' details. Hence the name and address of the company would be a repeating group of attributes. The main problem with this is that if the company changes address then it would be necessary to change the address for each contact working for that company. If two entities are used then if the address of the company changes, it will only need to be changed once in the company entity.

System analysis *continued*

Making sure that attributes are atomic

As well as making sure that repeating attributes are removed and placed in their own entity, you also have to make sure that all the attributes are atomic. Atomic attributes are attributes that do not need to be broken down any further.

For example, a beginner new to systems analysis and database design might use an attribute called Name to hold the following data items:

Mr Stephen Doyle

The trouble with this is that if a sort is now performed it will be done in order of title so names starting with Miss will appear before names starting with Mr. Additionally, if you want to search for the surname Doyle, then this can only be done if you know the title and forename. Using a single attribute called Name causes problems because the attribute is not atomic. Instead it needs to be broken down into three attributes which can be called Title, Forename and Surname.

Creating the database structure

After the normalisation process, we end up with several entities where previously we had just one, each with a list of associated attributes. Once this is done we are in a position to start thinking about the tables used to store the data. Each table can be given the same name as the entities and the field names can be the same as the names given to the attributes. We then have to plan out the structure of each table separately.

Important note

In a many-to-many relationship decomposed to a one-to-many and a many-to-one using a link table, the link table should have a compound key (e.g., in a rental table you might need a compound key of Cust_ID, Tool_ID, and Dateout).

Always make sure that the keys used uniquely define a row in the table.

Data dictionaries

A data dictionary system is a tool used during systems analysis and particularly during database design. The purpose of a data dictionary is to provide information about the database, its uses and participants in the system. A data dictionary could be said to provide 'data about data'.

The contents of the data dictionary

Data dictionaries usually contain some or all of the following features:

Entity names

Each entity needs to be given a name and these names need to be recorded and described in the data dictionary.

Relationships between the entities

The relationships between the entities can be described and then shown in an entity relationship diagram (ERD).

Attribute names

Each attribute should be given a name, and these names should be chosen so that they describe the data as fully as possible without being too long. It is best to avoid leaving spaces in field names, using - or _ to separate the words instead.

Synonyms

Synonyms are alternative names for the same thing. In many large organisations, a database is at the centre of the computer system and is used by different departments for various activities. It is therefore common to find users in different departments employing a different name for the same concept; this can be very confusing for systems analysts trying to design and build a new system. To prevent confusion, users should list any alternative names in the synonyms section of the data dictionary.

Data type

A data type needs to be specified for each attribute. It is very important that once an attribute's data type is set, it has the same data type wherever it occurs. In most cases, relationships can be made only between attributes with exactly the same attribute names and data types.

Format

Details of formats should be included in the data dictionary for those attributes which have formats set by the user. For instance, a numeric field can be a short integer, long integer, currency, etc., and dates can be given as 12 June 2001, 12/06/01, etc.

Description of the attribute

Each attribute should have a description, and these descriptions can be transferred to this section of the data dictionary.

Attribute length

Here we specify the length of the attribute for those attributes that can have their lengths set.

> **KEY WORDS**
>
> Data dictionary – a centralised collection of information about data such as meaning, relationships to other data, origin, usage, etc., used mainly in database design to ensure consistency

The names of other entities in which the attribute appears

An attribute may appear in more than one entity. For example the attribute Order_Number could appear in the entities ORDER and ORDER_LINE. If we wanted to change the name of an attribute then it is useful to know the entities where it is repeated.

Here is a data dictionary entry for an attribute called REORDER_QUANTITY:

Attribute name	REORDER_QUANTITY
Synonyms	None
Data type	Numeric
Format	0 decimal places (i.e. an integer)
Description of the attribute	The number of units of a stock item which can be ordered at any one time
Attribute length	4 digits
Entity names	STOCK_LIST
	STOCK_LIST_EXCEPTION
	REORDER

Data dictionaries ensure that all staff developing ICT systems adopt a consistent approach

Data dictionaries are always created when large commercial databases are being built, especially if the databases are to be used in many different applications. The purpose of the data dictionary is to make sure that data across the whole system is consistent. Large systems are built by large project teams, with each team working on a part of the whole system; in this situation, consistent terminology is vital, and the data dictionary is invaluable. The data contained in data dictionaries is often referred to as metadata.

Data dictionaries can be built as a manual system but there are clear advantages in maintaining a computerised data dictionary. Most relational database management systems have software which creates and maintains a data dictionary. It is kept as a separate database and automatically updated as changes are made to the structure of the main database.

Optional features of the data dictionary

In addition to the essential features listed above, some data dictionaries provide the following additional information:

- validation checks
- details of the validation checks performed on data entered for each attribute
- a key
- the type of key specified.

Most data dictionaries are stored on computer and on-line

System design and system implementation

▼ You will find out

▶ About the components of the design stage

▶ About the components of the implementation stage

▶ About the appropriateness of different changeover methods

Introduction

Once the old system or proposed system has been investigated and analysed, the new system will be designed using documents collected and created in the previous stages. The design work plans the system but is actually a planning stage, so the actual designs are not implemented at this stage.

Once the designs have been completed, the next stage of the SDLC can be started, which is the implementation. Implementation is where you take the designs produced and start actually creating the system using the hardware, software and data.

In this section you will also look at the appropriateness of the different changeover methods for changing over from the old ICT system to the new ICT system.

System design

To complete the design stage the analyst will start thinking about the system they have analysed and start to design the actual system to be built. All the pieces of documentation produced during the analysis stage will be used to design the system in line with user requirements.

System design will usually involve some or all of the following:

- Creating the design specification for hardware and software.
- Design of data and file structures that will enable the usable systems to be built. This would include the design of fields and table structure for the relational database.
- Design of input and output methods for information. This would include designs of forms used to input data and reports and queries used to

output information. Specialist documents such as invoices, pay slips, delivery notes, etc., would also be designed here.
- The design of information systems that will allow users to extract information on which decisions can be made.
- The design of networks and transmission issues such as topology, data transmission media, protocols, etc.
- Personnel issues. Completely new systems often mean that staff need training and departments need reorganising.
- Security processes and procedures. If personal data is being stored, its use needs to be registered with the Information Commissioner so there need to be procedures in place for this to happen. Consideration needs to be given to the security of the data stored and plans need to be made using levels of access, user-IDs and passwords to ensure the security of all data held.

It is important to note that in the design stage only designs are produced and it is not appropriate to produce the working version as this is only done in the next stage, the implementation stage.

EXAM TIP

You will be creating a relational database solution for your project work so you will experience many of the design skills listed above when producing your own design.

In the examination you should use the knowledge you have gained during your project to help answer questions and give examples.

System implementation

System implementation is the stage where the system is actually built according to the design produced in the previous stage. All the different staff in the project team will bring their particular expertise to the project and work together to produce the working system.

Implementation will normally involve the following:

- acquisition and installation of hardware and software and software re-training
- modifying existing software
- programmers producing any programming code need for the working solution
- installing software on operational hardware (NB systems are often developed on equipment not used on a day-to-day basis for operations for security reasons)
- producing the framework needed for databases
- training of users.

Most ICT projects involve lots of different people working on different aspects of the system. Each person in the team will be responsible for their own part of the project and they will have to test what they have done to make sure it works.

Testing will normally involve the following:

- testing at very detailed levels (i.e., individuals will thoroughly test their part)
- testing at a higher level (i.e., when the various parts of the system are joined together)

- testing at a systems level where all the parts are tested as a whole system
- testing each field using correct, erroneous and extreme data
- testing the system with real-life data.

Appropriateness of different changeover methods

In order to change from one system to another it is necessary to have a changeover strategy. There are several methods used and these are outlined here:

- **Direct changeover** – with direct changeover you simply stop using the old system one day and start using the new system the next day. The disadvantage of this method is that there is an element of risk, particularly if the hardware and software are cutting edge. If the system fails then it can be disastrous to the business. The advantage of this method is that it requires fewer resources (people, money, equipment) and is simple, provided nothing goes wrong.

- **Parallel changeover** – this method is used to minimise the risk in introducing a new ICT system. Basically, the old ICT system is run alongside the new ICT system for a period of time until all the people involved with the new system are happy it is working correctly. The old system is then abandoned and all the work is done entirely on the new system. The disadvantages of this method are that it involves a lot of unnecessary work (as the work is being done twice) and is therefore expensive in people's time. It also adds to the amount of planning needed for the implementation.

- **Phased conversion** – a module at a time can be converted to the new system in phases until the whole system is transferred. The advantage of this is that IT staff can deal with problems caused by a module before moving on to new modules. The disadvantage is that it is only suitable for systems consisting of separate modules.

- **Pilot conversion** – this method is ideal for large organisations that have lots of locations

or branches where the new system can be used by one branch and then transferred to other branches over time. The advantage of this method is that the implementation is on a much smaller and manageable scale. The disadvantage is that is takes longer to implement the system in all the branches.

Choosing a changeover method

Choosing a changeover method is based on a number of factors such as:

- Is there an existing system? If there is no existing system (either ICT or manual) then parallel changeover could not be used.
- Is the system cutting edge (new technology, newly written software etc.)? Parallel changeover will reduce the risk or pilot conversion will reduce the problems that could occur.
- Is the system to be implemented in lots of different locations? If so, pilot implementation would be ideal. You could get the system working in one branch and then transfer the implementation to other branches.

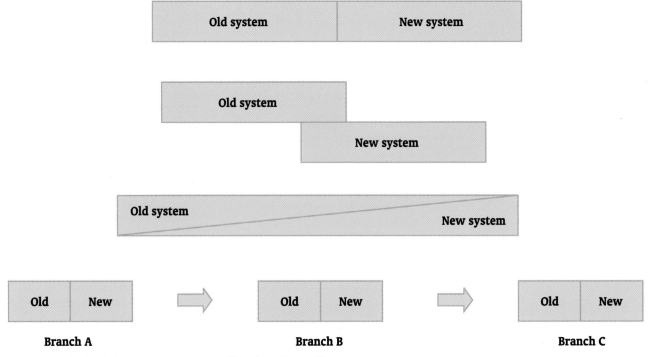

The four methods of changeover: direct, parallel, phased and pilot

System maintenance and system evaluation

Introduction

Once the system has been implemented it will need to be maintained. It is important to note that the people involved in the original project may leave the organisation, so new staff will need to familiarise themselves with and understand the new system. They will need documentation in order to do this, so the first stage of the system maintenance process is the production of both user and technical documentation.

In this section you will learn about the on-going system maintenance needed to satisfy the change in business needs and user requirements. Eventually there will come a point when the system no longer meets business needs and so a new system will need to be created and all the tasks involved in the system development life cycle will need to be repeated. You will also cover system evaluation, which is a reflection on how well the project went and how well the system is assessed to meet the needs of the users.

System maintenance

System maintenance of a new system will involve the following:
- training of all users who will use the system
- production of technical and user documentation to help people understand the system
- setting up help-desk facilities to help users who experience problems with the new system.

Systems cannot be left until a new system is developed to replace them. Changes in the way the business or organisation operates will need alterations in the system. Programs may need to be written or altered. For example, the rate of VAT could change, or changes in income tax could trigger the need for changes. Businesses change direction or get involved in

new ventures. For example, British Gas who supply gas to homes, now also supply electricity, and Anglia Water who supply millions of houses with water, now have a subsidiary that builds homes.

Maintenance will normally involve *(identify)* the following:

- extra functions that need to be added to the existing system are identified at the review meetings
- maintenance teams will alter existing programs or create additional ones
- any operational issues such as poor performance or software bugs will be identified at the review meeting and corrected by the appropriate staff
- any system crashes are investigated to find out the reasons for their occurrence
- managing interfaces with other systems, such as Internet, email and intranets.

The three types of system maintenance: perfective, adaptive and corrective

Maintenance of an ICT system (i.e., hardware, software and communications) can be classed as perfective, adaptive or corrective.

- **Perfective** – is maintenance that will improve the performance of the ICT system. Usually this will involve adding features not originally present to the software to make it produce the information from a database faster or to improve the speed of a network.
- **Adaptive** – the way of doing things changes in an organisation. For example, there may be new laws which mean that the system needs changing. Changes in the way the organisation operates may require a change in the system.

- **Corrective** – this is correcting faults or bugs that did not reveal themselves during testing. Sometimes the combination of new software and hardware causes the older software to crash. Software manufacturers often produce updates to deal with these issues and these have to be installed.

There are several maintenance issues in order to keep a developed ICT system working properly and these include:

- Identification of errors – no matter how thoroughly a system is tested errors can still crop up and will need to be dealt with. Usually they are caused by conflicts with other software, particularly virus checkers and firewalls. These errors must be identified and corrected.
- Security issues – certain programs (particularly operating systems) can present security weaknesses which were not envisaged when the software was originally created. Security issues are addressed by writing software code to alter the original software to close the security loophole.
- Changes in the business environment – business needs change over time and software will need to be altered to cope with these changes. Examples include changes to legislation, changes to taxation, etc.
- Dissatisfaction with hardware and software – users may become dissatisfied with the hardware and software, which may not function at an acceptable speed or give the information needed to keep the business up with the competition.

- Updating system – software often needs updating to cope with changes to operating systems or by adding extra functionality.

Technical and user documentation

There are two types of documentation: user documentation and technical documentation.

User documentation (or user guide) for the system

A user guide or manual is documentation that the user can turn to for learning a new procedure or for dealing with a problem that has cropped up. The guide should cover:

- minimum hardware and software requirements
- how to load the software
- how to perform certain functions
- how to save
- how to print
- frequently asked questions (FAQ)
- how to deal with error messages and troubleshooting
- how to back up data.

It is a good idea to include examples and exercises to help the user understand the system. Since users are usually non-technical, any specialist, technical language should be avoided.

The guide should detail what to do in exceptional circumstances. For instance, if the system fails to read a disk or data is sent to the printer without it being switched on, and the machine is locked, a user will need to know what they have to do. You should also include backing up and closing down instructions.

As always, users have the best view of a system and so should be asked to evaluate any proposed user guide. Their comments should be incorporated into the guide. You have probably tried to find advice in manuals, so you will realise just how important they are.

Technical documentation

It is important that systems are fully documented because the person who designed and implemented the system may no longer be around to help with problems. Someone else who may not be as familiar with the system may have to maintain it. In order to do this they will need to understand how the system was designed and implemented. Technical documentation is produced to help systems analysts and programmers understand the technical workings of the system.

You would expect to find the following included in the technical documentation:

- a copy of the system design specification
- all the diagrams used to represent the system (flowcharts, system flowcharts, dataflow diagrams, entity relationship diagrams, etc.)
- the data dictionary
- macro designs, spreadsheet formulae or program listings
- screen layout designs
- user interface designs
- test plan.

System evaluation

The evaluation and review stage normally takes place a few weeks after the implementation as it is only then that the users and others involved in the development of the system will find out about any problems or shortcomings.

Evaluation and review will normally involve the following:

- checking that the original user requirements have been fully met by the new system
- assessment of how happy the clients are with the development of the new system
- setting up a review cycle so that the system is checked periodically to make sure that it is still meeting requirements.

Criteria for evaluating a system

Before evaluating a new system it is useful to list some evaluation criteria such as:

- how closely the solution matches the user requirements
- how easy the new system is to use

- how satisfied users are with the information the system gives
- how well the system has been tested as evidenced by logs of user problems such as system crashes
- how reliable the system is
- how well the system ensures the security of data and programs.

Tools for gathering information for the evaluation report

There are a number of tools that can be used to gather information which can be referred to in the evaluation report and these include the following:

- **Quantitative test** – it is always easier to evaluate satisfaction with or the performance of a system if it can be expressed numerically. For example, the users could be asked to assess the overall satisfaction with the solution on a scale of 1 to 5 with 5 being the most satisfied. You can then apply statistics to the numbers (e.g., the average satisfaction among users was 3.8).
- **Error logging interviews** – all calls to help-desks are logged and these logs are an important source of information on such things as:
  - how easy the software was to use
  - how well the training given to the users met their needs
  - how often the software crashed.
- Interviews with managers of the help-desk to assess how well the new ICT system is working.
- **Questionnaires** – users can be given questionnaires to collect information about their satisfaction or otherwise with the new system. Users are more likely to give a more honest response to the questions if they are able to remain anonymous, and in order to simplify the processing of questionnaires, they can be assessed using automatic methods of input such as OMR or OCR.

It is a good idea to allow users to suggest limitations of the new system, and improvements that could be made.

System maintenance and system evaluation
continued

Methods of avoiding post-implementation cost

Once a system is built and is starting to be used, the costs of the system do not end and some of these costs include:

- Training costs – the initial training may not have covered all of the software, or new software modifications may be needed and this can lead to additional training.

- Modification costs – the software may not perform all of the tasks the user required, so additional modification to the system is needed. With better identification of user requirements these post-implementation costs can be reduced.
- Help-desk and other support costs – if training had been complete and the software had been easy to use then these additional costs can be minimised.

- Need to purchase additional hardware – organisations often expand so systems need to be made larger by the addition of more storage, faster processors, etc. Systems should be built with plenty of additional capacity initially to reduce these further costs.
- Correction of bugs – with comprehensive testing these should not occur or should at least be reduced.

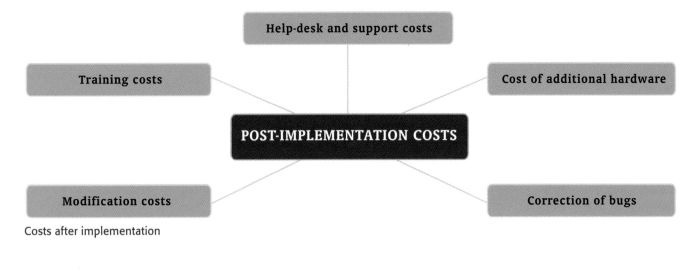

Costs after implementation

"Please listen carefully as some of our menu options have changed. For customer service, go fly a kite. For technical support, whistle in the wind until the cows come home. For repair service, wait for you-know-what to freeze over...."

If the solution is hard to use, then users can be in for long phone calls trying to get though to the help-desk

Questions and Activities

 Questions 1 | pp. 128–146

1 (a) Explain the meaning of the following terms, giving a suitable example for each:
   (i) Entity (2 marks)
   (ii) Attribute. (2 marks)
(b) Attributes should be atomic. Explain what this means. (2 marks)

2 (a) An ICT system has just been developed for an organisation. Compare and contrast the different methods they could use for conversion over to the new system. (6 marks)
(b) Once conversion has taken place, the system will need to be maintained.
   (i) Explain what is meant by system maintenance and give **two** examples of tasks that would normally be completed as part of this maintenance. (4 marks)
   (ii) Describe **two** different methods of system maintenance, giving an example in each case to illustrate your answer. (4 marks)

3 New ICT systems are developed for a variety of reasons.
(a) Explain **three** reasons for developing a new ICT system. (3 marks)
(b) Before a new system is developed, a system investigation will be carried out and this will lead to the production of the feasibility report.
   Outline the tasks involved in system investigation and explain the purpose of and what is normally contained in the feasibility report. (6 marks)

4 The main components of the system development life cycle are:
   System investigation
   System analysis
   System design
   System implementation
   System maintenance
   System evaluation
(a) Explain why system development is a cyclical process. (2 marks)
(b) Describe **three** different techniques used to analyse a system. (3 marks)
(c) Describe **three** tasks that are completed during the system design phase. (3 marks)

5 When one ICT system is being replaced by another there are a number of different methods of conversion.
(a) Give the names of **three** different methods of conversion from one ICT system to another and discuss the relative merits of each method. (6 marks)
(b) Once the system has been implemented, technical and user documentation will need to be provided. Explain the difference between these two types of documentation and give **three** examples of items which would be included for each of the two types. (8 marks)

6 A college library uses a relational database management system to operate a membership and loans system. Staff and students can borrow as many books as they wish at any given time.
(a) Name **three** entities that you would expect to find in this system and for each entity you have named, give a list of the attributes for each table, identifying in each case the primary and foreign keys. (9 marks)
(b) Draw an entity relationship diagram to show the links between the database tables named in (a). (3 marks)

▶ Activity 1: Creating a decision table

To pass a course in computer studies at college, a student must satisfy the following conditions:

- they must pass all the computing units
- they must pass English and Maths
- they must have at least 80% attendance (unless they satisfy this attendance rule, they will fail, even though they might have passed all the units).

The actions that can happen are:

- pass course
- re-do English or Maths or both
- re-do computing modules failed
- fail course.

Draw a decision table to show these rules.

▶ Activity 2: Entity relationship diagrams

Draw entity diagrams to show each of the following relationships:

1. Classes consist of many students.
2. One customer has many orders.
3. One tutor lectures on many courses.
4. Each module is taught by one tutor.
5. Many students enrol on many courses.
6. Many customers order many products.

▶ Activity 3: Which of these are atomic?

Which of the following attributes could be considered to be atomic?

- Video details
- Date of Birth
- Membership Number
- Member Name
- Enrolment
- Quantity in stock
- Product Number.

For each of the above attributes that are not atomic suggest suitable attributes which are atomic that can replace them.

▶ Activity 4: Creating an entity relationship model for an ICT system

A market research company takes on staff on a per job basis, although as one job finishes another one starts. It has asked a consultant to build a database system to store details about staff, jobs, rates and the hours they work. Initial analysis reveals the following entities:

> EMPLOYEE
> DATE
> HOUR
> JOB
> RATE

Further investigation revealed the following:

At a given moment one employee can work on only one job with that job having only one rate. The one job can have many hours and can be done over many dates. The one rate can also be paid over many hours and worked over many dates. Finally, one employee can work many hours over many dates.

Produce an entity relationship model to show this system.

▶ Activity 5: Deciding on attributes for entities

A college library borrowing system has been looked at and was found to have the following entities:

- MEMBER (a person who is a member of the library and eligible to borrow books)
- BOOK (a book which may be borrowed)
- LOAN (a link between a particular book and the person borrowing it)
- RESERVATION (books may be reserved by members, so that when brought back they are kept aside for another person).

The above system is only part of the whole library system.

For this activity you have to identify and list the attributes for each of the above entities. You will need some attributes which uniquely define the entities MEMBER and BOOK. Although the ISBN (International Standard Book Number) is used by bookshops to identify book titles, a library might have many copies of the same title, in which case the ISBN could not be used to distinguish each copy.

Produce your list and show it to your tutor.

Exam support

Worked example 1

1 No matter how well software is tested, software still needs to be maintained. Explain the types of maintenance that might be needed and why this maintenance is needed, illustrating your answer with suitable examples. (8 marks)

Student answer 1

1 Software may need to be upgraded, which will iron out any bugs or problems which were not discovered during the testing. Software will need to be changed as the needs of the business change.

The software may need to be able to supply files to another piece of software that has recently been bought. This will enable the data from the software to be sent to and used by another piece of software.

There may be new laws which will mean that the software will need to be changed. For example, new data protection laws may mean that the software works in a way that would be illegal under the new laws.

Examiner's comment

1 This answer has made some valid points but it would have been better to have identified the three types of maintenance: perfective, adaptive and corrective and then structure the answers accordingly.

There are five points made in this answer worthy of marks. **(5 marks out of 8)**

Student answer 2

1 Perfective maintenance means that the performance of the software or whole system is improved. An example would be where a new version is produced that runs faster than the previous version such as where management information is produced in a lot less time than before.

Corrective maintenance is where there are problems with the software that cause crashes, incorrect results, layout problems, etc. The software is corrected by the programmers or program manufacturers.

Adaptive maintenance may be required if the needs of the organisation have changed since the software was developed. The managers may decide that the software should work in a different way and produce more management information. Organisations merge so sometimes systems need to be changed so that they all produce output in a similar way.

Examiner's comment

1 This is a much better answer than the previous one. The student has structured their answer and this has led to them being able to supply good explanations and examples.

This is an excellent answer and there are many more points made than the eight needed for full marks. **(8 marks out of 8)**

Examiner's answer

1 One mark for each point to a maximum of eight. Students can only get a maximum of six marks if they have not given any examples.

Perfective maintenance (1) – improving the performance of the software (1).

Examples: Configuring the network management software (1) to improve performance such as improving access times to data, speed at which reports are produced, etc. (1).

Software may need to be modified to improve the user interface (1) upon feedback from users who are finding it more difficult to use than it needs to be (1).

Developing on-line tutorials and more help screens (1) to help new staff learn the software (1).

The software provider provides upgrades (1) which will improve the performance of the software (1).

Corrective maintenance (1) – bugs in the software which were not discovered during testing may need correcting (1).

Example: A piece of software may crash (1) when being used with another piece of software (1).

A piece of software may crash (1) when used with a particular item of hardware (1).

Software may present a security risk which needs correcting (1).

Problems with reports not being printed out properly (1). **continued overleaf**

Adaptive maintenance (1) – software may need to be changed owing to the changing needs of the business or organisation (1).

Example: Software may need altering so that it is more flexible in supplying the managers with information (1) which was not envisaged at the time of development (1).

Changes to values such as the percentage rate of VAT or changes to income tax rates will result in changes to the software (1).

The organisation expands (1) so the software needs to be altered so it is able to cope with an increased number of users (1).

Adapting the software to work with newly developed operating systems software or new hardware (1).

A virus threat/hacker threat (1) means that the software will need to be adapted to protect against this (1)

Worked example 2

2 Once a system has been investigated and analysed, resulting in the implementation of a new system, consideration needs to be given to the changeover strategy.

   (a) **Compare and contrast two alternative strategies for the changeover from an old ICT system to a new ICT system. (6 marks)**

   (b) **Discuss the reasons why users may become increasingly dissatisfied with an implemented ICT solution over time. (4 marks)**

Student answer 1

2 (a) You can run the two systems in parallel with each other until users are happy with the performance of the new system. They can make sure that there are no errors produced and then they can start using the new system. Another way is just to start using the new system. This way is easy because you do not have to waste any time.

   (b) The new system may not be as easy to use as they thought and the training might not be enough, so they are constantly being held up waiting for someone to help them.
   They may not like the speed of the network as it may take too long to get jobs done.
   They may find that the new system does not do all it was supposed to do, so is a waste of money.

Examiner's comment

2 (a) Although the student has mentioned parallel conversion they have not explained its relative advantages clearly enough. They need to say that it increases the workload on the staff because everything is done twice for the parallel period. The second part of the answer is superficial. It is always best to mention the name of the method of conversion (i.e., direct conversion/changeover) in this case. Much more detail is needed here and a comparison should have been made. Two out of the six marks have been given to part (a).

   (b) This answer is good but only worth two of the four marks.
   They should have made reference to more things that change over time such as a change in the nature of the business.
   (4 marks out of 10)

2 (a) Parallel conversion where the new system runs alongside the old system for a few days or weeks until the users are sure that the new system can be trusted to work as expected. This method increases the amount of work the user has to do, as for a period they are doing the work twice. The advantage is that you only have to give up the old system when you are completely happy with the new system, so this method is low risk compared to the next method.

The next method is called direct changeover, which means that the old system is stopped and immediately the new system is used. There is a lot of risk compared to parallel conversion as there is no old system to fall back on.

There is less work, though, and it is much cheaper in terms of the resources needed.

(b) There may be dissatisfaction due to the ICT system not meeting fully the user requirements meaning users find that there are things that cannot be done using the new system.

The business may expand and the new system may no longer be able to cope with the performance demands placed on it. For example, there may be more users, so the whole system runs very slowly.

Maintaining the system may cost too much.

Examiner's comment

2 (a) Both methods of conversion have been well described with their relative advantages and disadvantages mentioned and full marks are given for this excellent answer.

(b) Only three points have been adequately explained. The last point in the final sentence is not given a mark because it needs further explanation as it fails to mention any examples of maintenance.

(9 marks out of 10)

Examiner's answer

2 (a) One mark for the correct name and correct brief explanation for each strategy x 2.
One mark for the advantage or disadvantage of the method x 2.
One mark for a comparison of the method x 2.

Direct changeover – stop using the old system one day and start using the new system the next day (1). Element of risk particularly if the hardware and software are cutting edge (1). It the system fails then it can be disastrous to the business (1).
Requires fewer resources (people, money, equipment) and is simple, provided nothing goes wrong (1).

Parallel changeover – used to minimise the risk in introducing a new ICT system (1). Old ICT system is run alongside the new ICT system for a period of time until all the people involved with the new system are happy it is working correctly (1). The old system is then abandoned and all the work is done entirely on the new system (1). Disadvantages: lots of unnecessary work (as the work is being done twice) and is therefore expensive in people's time (1). It also adds to the amount of planning needed for the implementation (1).

Phased conversion – a module at a time can be converted to the new system in phases until the whole system is transferred (1). Advantage that IT staff can deal with problems caused by a module before moving on to new modules (1). Disadvantage: is only suitable for systems consisting of separate modules (1).

Pilot conversion – this method is ideal for large organisations that have lots of locations or branches where the new system can be used by one branch and then transferred to other branches over time (1). Advantage: implementation is on a much smaller and manageable scale (1). Disadvantage is that is takes longer to implement the system in all the branches (1).

(b) One mark for each point up to a max of three. Final mark for a point which applies to increasing dissatisfaction over time with the system. Example answers include:
The full range of user requirements has not been met, so the system does not live up to user expectations.
Change in business needs means system cannot deal with new demands placed on it.
Failure to supply users with the information they require.
User interface causes many user problems with increased help-desk use.
Problems with the software or system crashing owing to lack of rigorous testing.
Network performance or speed of access to stored data becomes unacceptable as more users are added to the system.
Modifications to the system are needed regularly and the system needs replacement with a new one.
Too much time is spent updating the new system.
The cost of user support is too high.
There are security breaches which were not envisaged when the system was first developed.

Summary mind map

The system development life cycle (SDLC)

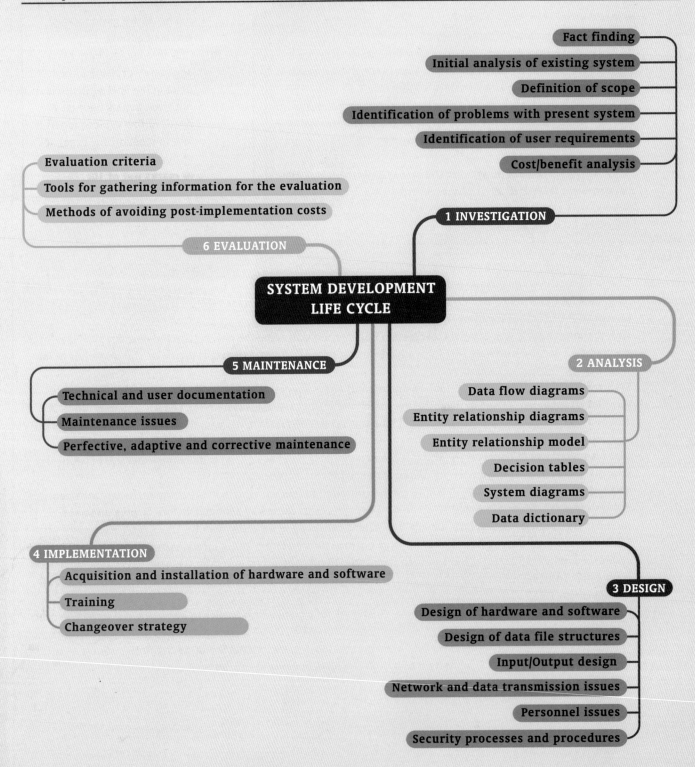

1 INVESTIGATION
- Fact finding
- Initial analysis of existing system
- Definition of scope
- Identification of problems with present system
- Identification of user requirements
- Cost/benefit analysis

6 EVALUATION
- Evaluation criteria
- Tools for gathering information for the evaluation
- Methods of avoiding post-implementation costs

SYSTEM DEVELOPMENT LIFE CYCLE

5 MAINTENANCE
- Technical and user documentation
- Maintenance issues
- Perfective, adaptive and corrective maintenance

2 ANALYSIS
- Data flow diagrams
- Entity relationship diagrams
- Entity relationship model
- Decision tables
- System diagrams
- Data dictionary

4 IMPLEMENTATION
- Acquisition and installation of hardware and software
- Training
- Changeover strategy

3 DESIGN
- Design of hardware and software
- Design of data file structures
- Input/Output design
- Network and data transmission issues
- Personnel issues
- Security processes and procedures

UNIT IT4: Relational Databases

In IT4, which accounts for 20% of the total marks for the A-level, you will be required to produce a solution to a problem of your choice that requires the use of a relational database. This solution will be a substantial piece of work that will involve the processes of analysis, design, implementation, testing and evaluation. You must also show that you have managed your work effectively.
The solution will be undertaken over an extended period of time and it is internally assessed (i.e., assessed by your teacher/lecturer) and moderated by WJEC.

▼ The key components of the assessment for IT4 are:

▶ Choosing a project

▶ User requirements

▶ Design specification

▶ Implementation

▶ Testing

▶ User documentation

▶ Evaluation

▶ Project planning

CONTENTS

Choosing a problem

▼ **You will find out**

▶ About what problem to choose

▶ About tips on getting ideas for projects

▶ About ideas for database projects

▶ About questions and answers on the project

▶ About the mark allocation for the main components of the project

Introduction

Choosing the right project for the creation of a database is essential for your success, so it needs to be given a lot of thought. If you get it right you will be able to produce a project that is completed in the time allowed and you will be able to supply evidence of all the components for assessment. If you get it wrong you could end up with all sorts of technical problems owing to the project being too complex and the time spent sorting this out may come at the expense of evidencing all the components for assessment.

This section gives you important advice on choosing your project.

What problem do I choose?

Before you even think about a problem, you need to read through the whole of this topic, because only then will you understand what is required. You must choose a problem that will allow you to demonstrate all the components. You do not want the problem to be too complex, yet it needs to be complex enough to satisfy all the criteria.

The choice of a suitable problem is essential to the success of the project. You must not be too ambitious and must realise your limitations. You do not want to get bogged down in the complexities of the database software and you need to realise that you only have a limited amount of time to complete this project.

Tips on getting ideas for projects

Make use of contacts

Find out what your parents, relatives, neighbours, friends, etc., do in the course of their jobs since they might be able to suggest an idea for you. If you are able to contact them to find out any information you might need, this will be a big help.

The best projects are those that have a real end user and which continually refer back to the end user for their reactions and input into the development. The end user will need to be consulted at all stages in the project.

Real projects are often better than artificial ones

There is nothing wrong with creating a new system from scratch rather than improving an existing system. Many people start up from scratch, so it is appropriate for you to design a system to cope with the many tasks they would have to perform. However, you will need quite a bit of prior knowledge of the type of business the system is for and there won't be an existing system to examine.

Use reference material to help with ideas

A quick look through any magazines or newspapers will give you ideas about business such as mail order businesses that advertise in such places. These all share common problems, so it should not be too difficult to think up a system for them.

Do not choose a system which is outside your experience or which you cannot easily find information about

For example, you may choose to create a system to keep records for dentists, but unless you know about, or can find out about, how dentists cope with their administrative tasks, then you could make things difficult for yourself and end up with a very unrealistic system.

Be realistic

It is important to be realistic about what you can achieve in the time. The better projects are usually the ones which comprise fewer tasks and which are better designed, documented, fully tested and evaluated and closely focused on the problem being solved.

Ideas for projects

If you cannot make use of contacts for a real system, you could create your own around one of the following ideas. You need to consult with your teacher/lecturer or perhaps make contact with someone who is prepared to help you in the type of business you choose.

Here are some ideas you could develop if you get stuck:

- A system recording borrowing of equipment in a school/college
- A booking system for a gym
- Simple system for storing pupil records in a school
- A dog boarding kennels or cattery
- A dentists' surgery
- A dating agency
- A job agency for contract workers in computing
- A tutor agency
- A driving school
- A doctors' surgery
- A small independent travel agency
- A car hire company
- A tool and equipment hire company
- A flat/house rental company
- A wedding dress hire company
- A mail order wine company
- A restaurant
- A mail order book shop
- A wholesaler
- A school management system
- A coach hire company
- A mail order computer components company
- A membership system for a sports club
- An estate agency
- A stock control system for a builders' merchant
- Villa rentals
- Function room hire
- An estate agency database
- A crime database for the police

- A database of pupil marks for a teacher
- Mail order companies (CDs, books, clothes, wine, household goods, cosmetics, gardening, etc.)
- Health centre
- Appointments system for a hairdresser/beautician
- Production of a stock control system
- Temporary staff agency
- Talent/model agency
- Dress hire company
- Database for the running of a riding school
- Fancy dress hire.

Questions and answers on the project

Do I need a real user?

No you don't, but if you do have one, it can be better because you are able to understand their requirements by interviewing them and you can also ask for their comments during the creation of the solution. It is also easier, in some respects, to produce your evaluation as they will be able to make comments about your work.

How much time is allocated for the project?

The project should represent 50 hours of supervised time.

What is the best way to start?

Before starting on your database project you will need to gain advanced database skills and knowledge. There is a tendency for projects to be developed in isolation and the only time the teacher sees the results is when the project is handed in at the end. Your teacher/lecturer should be kept up-to-date with the progress of the project so that if you are going off in the wrong direction you can be stopped and put on course again. Too many projects are handed in that are inappropriate for the requirements of the A-level and then there is no time to do anything about them.

Before you start the project work, your teacher may have given you booklets to work through with exercises to build up your knowledge of database software. You should make sure you know about

the advanced features of these. One way to learn about such advanced features is to get hold of some of the more advanced guides to the software, particularly those guides that concentrate more on the development of applications. It is important to note that plagiarism is not allowed and is easily detected!

It is best to have the database skills and knowledge in place before you start building your database

PROJECT TIP

For this project you need to develop a database in a relational manner. Do not use a single table and it is also an idea not to include lots of tables. At least three tables should be used but no more than about eight.

Some useful advice before you start the project

The following advice applies to all parts of the project:

- Do not waste time providing evidence that is not needed.
- Avoid cropping your work too much, as this sometimes destroys the evidence.
- Do not provide screenshots that are too small – the markers will need to be able to read them.
- You must produce proper design work – annotating (i.e., adding remarks) to implemented solutions is not proper design. Design must not be an afterthought.

Important notes about project work

Here are some important notes about the project work:

- Your project does not have to be complicated for you to get a good mark.
- Documenting your project is very important. It supplies your teacher with the evidence of your work and enables them to give your project an accurate mark.
- Make sure that you check your work for grammatical and spelling mistakes. Do not just rely on the computer to do this. You should always proof read your work thoroughly.

The mark allocation for the main components of the project

Below is a summary of the main components of the project and the marks allocated for each main component. In the following sections you will be looking at each component in turn and then looking at the tasks and evidence you need to complete for each section.

Components	Max mark
User requirements	12
Design	24
Implementation	25
Testing	16
User documentation	15
Evaluation	8
Total	100

Mark allocation table

Useful websites for learning about Microsoft Access

This is the Microsoft site for Access (all versions) and here you can find tutorials and lots of how to do sections: http://office.microsoft.com/en-us/access/FX100487571033.aspx

A summary of a variety of links to Access tutorials: http://www.techtutorials.info/appaccess.html

Useful sections on all the main features of the Access database: http://www.teach-ict.net/software/access/access.htm

User requirements

Introduction

Once you have chosen your project you have to identify the user requirements. It is better if you have a real user but this is not absolutely essential. The user requirements outline what needs to be produced. In this section you will look at what is involved in collecting information about user requirements and what documentation you need to provide for this component of the project.

Producing the user requirements

Before coming up with a list of user requirements you will have to perform some system investigation. You will need to collect information about what the new system has to do or what the old system being replaced did and the problems it caused.

Evidence of the user requirements will require you to produce documentation covering the following:

- A general background description of the organisation for which you are developing the solution.
- A description of the image and ethos of the organisation.
- A specification of the aims and objectives for the system.
- An outline of the user interface requirements.
- An outline of the security requirements.
- A specification of the hardware and software requirements for the new system.
- An entity relationship diagram for the existing system or proposed new system.

A general background description of the organisation for which you are developing the solution

At the start of the project you will need to describe the project. Your problem description could start like this:

'My father works in a garage and although they mainly sell and repair used cars, they also have a small car hire operation. They have around 20 cars to hire and this part of the business is rapidly expanding. He would like a way of recording and storing the details about the cars, customers and the rentals in a more professional manner. At present all the details are stored manually on cards held in filing cabinets or in diaries. This was fine when the garage only hired a couple of cars each week but with 20 cars and possible doubling of the fleet in the next year they need to obtain information quickly and present a more professional image to their customers.'

In this section it is a good idea to mention about the scope of the project. This means how far-reaching the project will be. For example, in this section, as well as saying what specifically the project will do, you can also mention what it will not do. If you make the scope of the project too wide, then you

may not have enough time to complete it or it may be too complicated. For example, the car hire example could just deal with the car, customers and rentals but it would be possible to expand the scope by adding details of services, MOTs, insurance, etc.

A description of the image and ethos of the organisation

Here you need to consider the image and ethos of the organisation, as this will influence the house style of the documents that are produced by the database system. The documents or screen designs will need to reflect the image and ethos of the organisation, so you need to write a short section on this.

Ethos

To understand what the word ethos means it is best to look at a dictionary definition: ethos is the fundamental character or spirit of an organisation; the underlying sentiment that informs the beliefs, customs or practices of the organisation.

Image

Image has a similar definition: image is the general or public perception of a company, organisation, etc., especially as achieved by careful calculation aimed at creating widespread goodwill.

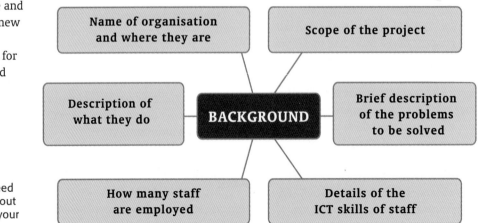

Things you need to find out about to include in your background

House style

House style

Many different people in an organisation produce documents and these documents need to look similar – almost as if the same person had produced them all. House style concerns the following:

- Use of logos – logos are used consistently (i.e., size, colour and position).
- Use of words – there are different ways to spell the same word, so there needs to be consistency.
- Use of colours – colour schemes can be identified and used consistently.
- Writing style – the way people express themselves needs to be consistent.
- Tone – certain documents need to adopt a certain tone.

A specification of the aims and objectives for the system

The aim of a system is its intention or purpose. For example, the aim of a system for a car hire company might be:

> 'To improve the record keeping of cars, customers and rentals so that customers experience a professional level of service from the business and thus improve the overall profitability of the business.'

An aim needs to cover the overall system and not just one part of it.

Objectives can be thought of as a series of desirable goals that the proposed system should aim for. Objectives for a system are a minimum list of what the system must do. For example, objectives for a system might be:

- To be capable of being used by people with widely differing ICT skills and knowledge.
- To reduce the number of errors made with bookings.
- To reduce the costs of postage owing to material being sent to the wrong customer address.

- To be able to identify those customers who use the service the most and target them for special discounts.
- To provide management information on which decisions can be made.
- To enable all staff to access pre-stored reports and queries on an ad-hoc basis.
- To keep regular customers informed of special promotions and deals by the use of the database and the mail merge facility of word processing software. This will help retain the main customers and prevent them using competitor car hire.

An outline of the user interface requirements

Users should not have to struggle to use the software, so you need to make it as easy to use as possible. You need to list the user requirements in terms of the expertise of the users of the system. There are a number of things you should consider when designing the user interface:

- Users should not have to move the mouse or enter data at the keyboard any more than is essential.
- The most important or the most often used items should appear first.
- The user should not be left wondering what they have to do next. Give them instructions to help them and make these instructions clear.
- Users should not be expected to enter their data directly into tables.
- You must keep your users away from the complexities of the software.
- There should be consistency between menus. They should all have a similar appearance.

You should consider:

- Using switchboards. Switchboards simplify the process of starting the various forms and reports in a database.

- Using data entry forms to add data to your database or view, edit or delete existing data.
- Creating custom dialogue boxes for when the computer needs to act on user input. For example, you can create search dialogue boxes that prompt users for search parameters, and then return data that match those parameters.

An outline of the security requirements

Here you need to consider with the user the security requirements for the system, which would include:

- how the database can be secured using passwords
- how archive versions of the data can be kept
- how and when data is backed up.

A specification of the hardware and software requirements for the new system

The hardware needed depends on the database software you are using. The main thing here is to check on the minimum requirements for the software from the software manufacturer's website. You will need to specify the system software under which the database software will run.

Remember to include such things as Internet connection and equipment if necessary and virus checkers and any other utilities you consider essential.

Entity relationship diagram

A diagram should be drawn showing the entities and their relationships to each other in either the old system or the proposed new system if the old system does not exist.

Design specification

▼ You will find out

▶ About the design of reports/ queries

▶ About the design of inputs

▶ About the design of processes

▶ About the design of the user interface

Introduction

Once the user's requirements have been identified, the next stage is to produce a design specification. The purpose of the design specification is to design various components of the solution, leaving the actual production of them to the next stage, the implementation stage.

Design of reports/queries

It is best to first look at the design of the output because the output determines what processing and inputs are needed. If a field needs outputting then it needs to be either input or calculated from other fields that are input.

Important note

Do not include screenshots showing the implementation in this section. Only designs should be included.

For the design of reports you need to provide evidence of:

- reports from tables or from queries
- suitable headers and footers
- sorted data grouping
- calculations, totals or statistical fields that clearly display the fields and the data – any of the numeric fields stored in the tables can have calculations performed on them.

For the design of queries you need to provide evidence of:

- Queries (single and multiple field) for specified reasons/purposes – when extracting information from your database you must always add a context by clearly stating the reason for the query.
- Queries using relational links and logic between tables for specified reasons/purposes – the Boolean AND, OR and NOT are used in the queries and fields from several tables are combined.

- Queries using parameters for specified reasons/purposes – for example, you could find pupils in a class whose date of birth lies between two dates.
- Append, delete or update queries for specific reasons/purposes – for example, you could use a query to increase all the prices in a product table by 5%.

Designs of inputs

In this part of the design you should produce documentation for the following:

- data dictionary
- normalisation
- design of validation techniques
- design of password protection techniques
- design of on-screen data entry forms.

Data dictionary

The purpose of a data dictionary is to explain to others (e.g. co-developers or people who modify the database after you) what tables, fields and field properties have been used.

You can start off with a list of the fields that will be included in the database. This should not be put into tables at this stage because normalisation (i.e., where the data is put into the tables) is started after the data dictionary has been completed.

Field Name	This is the field name
Data type	Data may be numeric character, date or logical (Y/N), memo, etc.
Format	Currency, number of decimal places, standard form (a way of storing very large or small numbers).
Description of the field	Information about what the field is and how it is used.
Field length	The number of characters needed for the text or the number of digits used for numbers.
Validation checks performed on the field	Details of input masks, range checks, restricting users to a list of data, etc.
Whether the field is required	Some fields have to be filled in with data and others do not.

Here is what should be included in the data dictionary

Field Name	REORDER_QUANTITY
Data type	Numeric
Format	0 decimal places (i.e., an integer)
Description of the field	The number of units of a stock item which can be ordered at any one time
Field length	4 digits
Validation checks performed on the field	>0
Whether the field is required	No

A data dictionary entry for a field called REORDER_QUANTITY

Field names – these need to describe the data fully but should not be too long, since they appear as the column headings and in turn will determine the width of the columns, which will then determine how much data can fit onto the screen at a time.

Avoid leaving spaces in field names, using - or _ to separate the words instead, e.g. stock-item, qty_in_stock, etc.

Data type – each field needs to have a data type specified which is sometimes set automatically by the software and at other times the user needs to select the type from a list. It is very important that once a field has its data type set, all occurrences of the field in different tables will have the same data type. Relationships, in most cases, may only be made between those fields with exactly the same field names and data types.

Format – details should be included of the formats used for those fields that can have their formats set by the user. For instance, a numeric field can be a short integer, long integer, currency, etc.; dates can be given in a variety of formats, e.g. 12 June 2009, 12/06/09, etc.

Description of the field – a full description of the field can be included if the field name is not self-explanatory.

Field length – the length of the field for those fields which can have their lengths specified is included.

Validation checks performed on the field – details of validation, such as the use of input masks, range checks, lists of allowable data, etc., should be included

Whether the user always has to enter data into the field – some fields always have to contain data, whereas other fields such as mobile_phone_number do not always have to be filled in.

PROJECT TIP

Entities, their attributes and the relationships should be designed using entity relationship diagrams and normalisation processes. Do not use intuition to create the tables, as you will be marked for evidence of entity relationship diagrams and normalisation.

Designs of validation checks

Validation checks can be designed here on the basis of the information in the validation check section of the data dictionary.

Data validation checks should be on fields where their use is appropriate and steps should be taken where possible to restrict a user's choice of data. It is best to use built in lists (lookup lists) if the user can only choose a limited number of items.

Design of processes

For the design of processes you need to evidence the following:

- design of automated routines using programming code
- design of calculations that are performed in reports or forms.

You will probably have included calculations in your designs for reports or forms and so you can simply mention here what the calculations do and then reference them to the page number where they appear on the design of reports and forms.

For each automated routine you can structure the actions required like this:

```
PROCEDURE macro name
Action
Action
Action etc.
ENDPROC
```

Design of password protection techniques

Just a couple of sentences are needed here to sketch out the designs for a password system to prevent unauthorised access and also to prevent users from accidentally or deliberately altering the database structure.

Algorithms for individual routines which enhance solutions using the programming capabilities of the software package (e.g., a password routine) can be included here.

Design of on screen data input forms

Remember here that you are only designing the forms so you can provide

rough hand-drawn sketches or rough versions produced using word-processing software. All you have to do here is to position the organisation's logo, a heading for the form, user instructions, positions of the fields along with the table name where the field can be found.

Here are some things you need to consider:

- The use of sub-forms within forms for when data needs to be entered into more than one table.
- Details of logo (box to mark size, file name, position) and details of other graphics used.
- Font, font size and font colour used.
- Headings marked.
- Field captions/labels (to inform users what data they have to input).
- Field boxes to mark the position of each field.
- Command buttons to allow user to move to next record, previous record or to close the form, etc.
- The fields that have drop-down lists to allow the user to select from a list.

Design of user interface

You need to supply evidence of the design of your interfaces here. Again you must remember that this is design, so you should not use screenshots of your implemented menus and forms for this. Hand-drawn sketches are fine for this.

Here are some things you should consider in your designs:

- Splash screens – these are screens that are visually appealing, that appear when a program is loading.
- Menu systems – designs of all the menus used and also details of any menus that are linked and how they are linked.
- Colours used – this applies to background and text.
- Fonts and font sizes – need to identify these on your designs.
- Labels/captions – instructions to the user telling them what a command button does or what they have to enter.
- Command buttons – to allow user to move to next record, previous record or to close the form or to run a macro.

Implementation, testing, user documentation and evaluation

▼ You will find out

▶ About the tasks involved in implementing the relational database solution

▶ About the tasks involved in testing the relational database solution

▶ About the tasks involved in providing user documentation for the relational database solution

▶ About the tasks involved in evaluating the relational database solution

▶ About the project planning which must take place throughout the solution

Introduction

Implementation is where you take your design and build the solution using the database software. It is important that your implementation should match your design as much as possible; however, if you have had to change the design in some way (usually because you lack the skills to do what you originally wanted to do) you need to annotate your design with the changes.

Testing is a process that takes place throughout the implementation and after the solution has been built. It checks not only such things as validation checks, forms, reports and queries but also that the solution meets the user requirements.

User documentation involves the development of support for the inexperienced user and is an important component of the solution.

The evaluation reviews the solution and reflects on how well the solution met the user requirements and an outline of the problems encountered during the development and how well they were solved.

The tasks involved in implementing the relational database solution

Here are the tasks you would need to supply evidence of to obtain the marks for the implementation section. Do not worry if your order is not quite the same as this, as in some cases the tasks are completed in parallel:

- creation of tables and links
- include data validation techniques
- create forms
- include calculations
- create forms with sub-forms
- create user-friendly interface
- create macros

- perform single table queries (remember to state the context, i.e. why they are being produced)
- perform multiple table queries
- perform multiple table queries using relational links
- parameter queries
- append, delete or update queries
- reports
- individual enhancements of solutions using the programming capabilities of the software package.

Testing

The database solution you produce must be thoroughly tested by first of all producing a test plan which tests expected outcomes against actual outcomes. There should be clear evidence of all outcomes in the form of screenshots or printouts wherever appropriate.

In your test plan you need to ensure that you test:

- the user interface and all the routes through the system
- all data entry forms with valid, invalid and extremes of data
- all validation procedures
- all reports
- all queries

- security systems
- all individual and automated routines
- that all calculations are correct.

Your test plan can be set out as follows with each test numbered, and when evidence of the results of testing are included, you can refer to the number of the test to which it refers.

> **PROJECT TIP**
>
> If you provide diagrams of the tables and their relationships using screenshots from the database software, make sure that the tables are opened out so that your teacher/moderator can see all the fields in the tables and can identify the primary keys and foreign keys.

Test plan

Number of test	Description of what is being tested	How the test is conducted	Test data used	Expected results	Actual results	Corrective action taken
1	Validation checks for fields in customer table	Test data is entered into those fields with validation checks	Set 1 page 20	Validation checks should accept or reject the test data according to Set 1 table	Field for postcode did not work properly – all other validation checks worked	The input mask was adjusted to accept the full range of acceptable formats for postcode
2						
3						
4						
Etc.						

User documentation

User documentation is used to enable users to understand and use the system effectively. The user documentation you supply should show:

- details of where to find the database (i.e., the directories where the data is stored)
- how to start up the database
- details of how to enter passwords or other security procedures
- details of how to navigate the user interface
- details of how to add, delete, edit, print and save the data in records via examples given in screenshots of data entry forms
- examples of validation text to support validation procedures
- instructions about using different types of queries and producing reports
- instructions about disaster recovery techniques.

© 2001 by Randy Glasbergen.
www.glasbergen.com

"It took us five days to figure out how to finish our project two days early. That's why we're three days late."

Use screenshots to illustrate your user documentation and ensure that it is written with the skills of your average user in mind.

Evaluation

Evaluation involves you critically evaluating your solution against:

- The user requirements – here you need to discuss how close a match your solution was to the user requirements. This is best done in a table along with a brief explanation.
- Problems encountered and the strategies used to solve them – here you need to mention how you got around any problems. For example did you manage to solve them by reading books, using on-line help, etc., or did you have to simplify the system slightly to get around the problem? A full explanation needs to be given here.

You should avoid comments made by yourself like this:

'I thought it worked well and really enjoyed doing the project.'

If you used an end user (your teacher, a friend or relative, someone you know with a business or problem to solve) then they can be given questionnaires to complete. If you do use a questionnaire, then include it in your evidence.

You need to manage the time for your project carefully

Gantt chart

	Tasks	WEEKS												
		1	2	3	4	5	6	7	8	9	10	11	12	13
1	User requirements													
2	Design													
3	Implementation													
4	Testing													
5	User documentation													
6	Evaluation													

Project planning

This section is not placed at the end because it is done at the end. Project planning should occur throughout the project. Throughout the project you will need to show that you have:

- used suitable names for the database, tables, forms, queries, reports and automated routines such as macros
- saved work regularly
- kept dated backup copies of files on other removable media and kept in another location or used online backup
- worked to a time plan – you should also include evidence of successful time management (Gantt charts, timetables, diaries, etc.)
- protected confidentiality and observed copyright laws.

Gantt charts

Gantt charts are really just horizontal bar charts which are used to schedule jobs and are used to show using a diagram when the tasks that make up the whole job start and finish. They have a timescale going across the page and a list of the activities to be done going vertically down the page. The blocks which show the duration of the activities are shaded to show the time taken on each task. They are used as a planning tool, since it is possible to use a ruler placed alongside the chart to determine which jobs are late and which jobs are running ahead of schedule.

It is usual to construct Gantt charts on squared paper so that times may be accurately read off. A transparent ruler placed at the present time aids reading off those activities that are behind schedule. Most project management software makes use of Gantt charts in some way.

Useful project advice, tips and how the project is assessed

▼ You will find out

▶ About things you should watch out for

▶ About frequently asked questions

▶ About how the project is assessed

Introduction

The project work is an important component of A-level ICT so it is worth spending some time looking at some useful advice and tips. Also included is detail about how the project is assessed.

Things you should watch out for

There are a number of things you should be aware of when working on your project and these are outlined here:

Plagiarism (i.e. copying) – It goes without saying that all project work must be your own work. It is no use copying parts of examples in textbooks or specimen project material supplied by the examination board, since your teacher will probably have seen it before and the moderator will almost certainly be familiar with the material. Do not buy A-level projects off Internet auction sites such as e-Bay.

In cases where copying has been proved, the student could be disqualified from entering the examination in ICT and possibly any other subjects they are taking. Both you and your teacher will have to sign a declaration to confirm that the work you have submitted is your own and this is why your teacher/lecturer needs to see you completing the vast majority of your work during class time.

Take regular backups – As Advanced level ICT students, you should be aware of the dangers in having only one copy of your work. Regular backup copies should be taken and these should not be kept near the original. It is also a good idea to print out your work occasionally and keep the printout.

Pace yourself – There is a tendency amongst ICT students to get on with developing the system and to leave all the documentation to the end, when they hopefully have a system that works. This should be avoided and you should provide the documentation as you go along. If you need to make changes as you go along, then this is OK provided these changes are explained along with the reasons for the changes. Time management is an important skill throughout life and you should manage your time and avoid attending school or college without having some idea as to what you hope to achieve during the practical sessions.

Document everything – Although the teachers/lecturers who mark your work will be familiar with the software you have used, the moderators may not have used it before or have a copy of the software themselves. This means that the moderators can only mark your projects on the basis of the documentation you have supplied. If, for example, you have included a very innovative on-line help system as part of a database project, then the moderator would not know about it unless you have provided evidence in the form of screen designs and screen dumps. If any of the documentation is missing then you will lose marks no matter how clever the ICT solution is.

Frequently asked questions

Here are some answers to questions students frequently ask about project work.

Who will mark my project work?

Your project work will be marked by your teacher/lecturer and in turn a moderator will check that the work has been marked to a comparable standard to other schools/colleges. The moderator is normally a person with expertise in ICT (usually another teacher/lecturer) but they will not necessarily have any expertise in the particular database software you are using for your project. It is important to note that there are many other software packages that can be used to create databases besides the very popular Microsoft Access. What this means is that your work will have to be clearly explained and documented so that they are able to see clearly what you have done and this will enable you to receive the maximum mark possible for your efforts. You may have done a spectacular project, but unless you have supplied proper documentation and evidence, you will only get a low mark for it.

What software can I use?

It obviously makes sense to use the database software that you are most familiar with. Any database software may be used but the software must be business quality and therefore not too simplistic. Most integrated packages are suitable but those containing a non-relational database (i.e. a flat-file database), such as Works, would not be considered appropriate. Only use specialist relational database software for this project.

Please note that you can use Microsoft Access for this project but there are many other equally good and even better database packages around and your teacher/lecturer can tell you which one to use.

How much help can my teacher/lecturer give me?

Your teacher/lecturer should have given you enough practice at using some of the advanced features of database packages to be able to identify those features that would be useful in solving a particular problem. Your teacher is allowed to use the project as a vehicle for teaching, so you will learn how to use the software but the teacher has to teach the database in general terms, so you will have to adapt what you have learnt to your own solution. If your teacher has to directly help you because you are going completely off track, then they will record this on the assessment sheet which may reduce the mark you get for your project.

Can I do the work at home?

Your teacher must be able to supervise your work so that they can be sure that it is your own. You can still do work at home but enough of the work must be seen to be done at your school or college to satisfy the teacher that it is your own work.

Can I do programming?

You can do a small amount of programming as part of the project but for some students the nearest they will get to programming is to produce a macro or to produce SQL instructions when extracting data.

You are allowed to do a very small amount of programming if you need to

Presentation of the projects

It goes without saying that all the project documentation should be word-processed, and diagrams (usually screen dumps) should be incorporated into the documents. Although many of you will be able to produce 'glossy', high-quality finished work, if there is very little evidence of analysis, design and testing, then you will not obtain high marks. In other words, the examiner will not simply be looking at the presentation of the project.

What general points about documentation should I bear in mind?

All projects should have a signed cover sheet and a project sheet identifying the Centre, your name and the project title. Make sure that your documentation includes: a contents sheet, headers (suited to your project) and a footer indicating the page numbers to which the contents refer.

What is the best way to keep the pages of my project together?

Projects must be securely bound in such a way as to reduce bulk and make it easy for the material to be marked. When binding your project you should not use the following methods:

- Ring binders or lever arch files, since this makes the material far

too bulky and causes storage and transport problems for both your teacher and the moderator.
- Slide binders which tend to inhibit the reading of the text or diagrams and which also tend to come off in the post or when being read.

Do not put any of your material in plastic covers or plastic presentation folders. Your teacher may need to put marks or comments on your work and removing lots of pages from the plastic is time consuming and also annoying. In addition the use of plastic covers makes the projects much heavier than they need to be. It is best to use one of the following:

- a thin folder
- punched holes with treasury tags.

Do I get marks for spelling, punctuation and grammar?

In order for you to get the marks for each component of the project it is necessary to convey meaning clearly. This means you must:

- use the spellchecker
- obey all the rules of punctuation
- proof read anything you have written several times before handing it in
- use the grammar checker
- get other people to look through your work to see if it makes sense.

Do not put your project work in lever arch files like this or ring binders as they take up too much space. Remember you poor teacher/moderator has to transport your projects to meetings

Useful project advice, tips and how the project is assessed *continued*

How the project is assessed

In order to gain the maximum marks, you need to cover as many of the criteria given in the following table as soon as possible. Your teacher and the moderator will use these criteria to mark the various sections and components of your project. You should work through this and check that you have sections in your project corresponding to the sections and components in the table. You can also use the marks allocated to the components to work out how much evidence you should produce for each component.

Detailed scheme of assessment

Compontents	Criteria	Mark
User requirements		
Background	Show a clear understanding of the background to the problem	2
Expected outcomes / aims and objectives	A clear statement of the aims and objectives of the system, along with the expected outcomes and house style and ethos of the organisation	6
User interface requirements	Details of specific user interface requirements for the system	1
Hardware	Details of the minimum hardware requirements for the system to function.	1
	Entity Relationship Diagram	2
Design		
Design of inputs	Data dictionary Normalisation Design of validation techniques Design of password protection technique Design of on screen data entry forms	4 2 2 1 3
Design of user interface	Design of user-friendly, menu driven, front end interface Design of queries (including purpose and structure)	1 6
Design of outputs	Design of report	2
Design of processes	Automated routines using programming code Design calculations in reports or forms	2 1
Implementation	Create tables and links Data validation techniques Calculated field Create forms Create forms with subforms Create user-friendly interface Macros Single table queries Multiple table queries Multiple table queries using relational links Parameter queries Append, delete or update queries Reports Individual enhancement of solutions using the programming capabilities of the software package	4 2 1 2 1 1 2 2 1 1 1 1 4 2
Testing to a test plan	Test user interface and test all routes through the system Test with valid data and extremes of data Test all validation procedures with invalid data Test report Test all queries Test security systems Test all individual and automated routines Test all calculations are corrected	1 2 2 1 6 1 2 1
User documentation	Details of where to find the database (directories) and how to start up the database Details of how to enter passwords or other security procedures Details of how to navigate the user interface Details of how to add, delete, edit, print and save data in records via examples given in screenshots of data entry forms Examples of validation text to support validation procedures Instructions about using different types of queries and producing a report Instructions about disaster recovery techniques	1 1 1 5 2 4 1
Evaluation	Against user requirements Problems encountered and strategies used to resolve them	4 4

Glossary

Acceptable use policy Document making it clear to all employees or users what is acceptable use of ICT systems and what isn't.

Access rights Restricting user access to only those files they need in order to perform their job.

American Standard Code for Information Interchange (ASCII) A code for representing characters in binary.

Analysis Breaking a problem down so that it is easier to understand and solve.

Append Users can add new records but they will be unable to alter or delete existing records.

ASCII Code for representing characters in binary.

Audit Keeping a record of who has done what on the network in order to identify abuses of the systems by authorised staff and also to investigate instances of unauthorised access (i.e., by hackers).

Back up Keeping copies of software and data so that the data can be recovered should there be a total loss of the ICT system.

Backup file A copy of a file which is used in the event of the original file being corrupted (damaged).

Bandwidth A measure of the amount of data that can be transferred using a data transfer medium.

Binary code Code made up from a series of binary digits – 0 or 1.

Bit Binary digit 0 or 1.

Bookmarks Storage area where the URL (i.e. the web address) of a website can be stored so that it can be accessed later using a link.

Broadband A fast connection to the Internet which does not use a modem.

Bug A mistake or error in a program.

Bus Type of network topology where all the computers are connected to a common shared cable called the bus.

CAD (computer-aided design) A method of using the computer to produce technical drawings.

Client server A network where several computers are connected to one or more servers.

Coding Producing a shorter version of the data to aid typing in and validation of the data.

Computer Misuse Act 1990 The Act which makes illegal a number of activities such as deliberately planting viruses, hacking, using ICT equipment for fraud, etc.

Cookie A small text file downloaded to your computer used by websites to collect information about how you use the website.

Copyright, Designs and Patents Act 1988 An act, which amongst other things, makes it an offence to copy or steal software.

CPU (central processing unit) The computer's brain. It stores and processes data. It has three parts; the ALU, the control unit and the memory.

Crime An illegal act.

Cybercrime Crimes committed involving ICT systems as a major part.

Data Raw facts and figures or a set of values, measurements or records of transactions.

Data capture Term for the various methods by which data can be entered into the computer so that it can be processed.

Data controller The person whose responsibility it is in an organisation to control the way that personal data is processed.

Data Protection Act 1998 Law to protect the individual against the misuse of data.

Data subject The living individual whom the personal information is about.

Data type check Check to ensure the data being entered is the same type as the data type specified for the field.

Desktop The working area of the GUI and where all the icons are situated.

Dialup modem A device which converts the digital signals into a series of sounds which are then passed along a telephone line. The sound signal is converted back to a digital signal at the other end of the wire. Provides a slow connection to the Internet.

Distributed computing Where a series of computers are networked together and they each work on solving the same problem. Each computer shares data, processing, storage, and bandwidth in order to solve a single problem.

Double entry of data Two people use the same data source to enter the details into the ICT system and only if the two sets of data are identical, will they be accepted for processing.

Dpi (dots per inch) A measure of the resolution of images. The more dots per inch in an image, the higher the resolution.

Drag and drop Allows you to select objects (icons, folders, files, etc.) and drag them so that you can perform certain operations on them such as drag to the recycle bin to discard, add a file to a folder, copy files to a folder and so on.

Driver A short specially written program that understands the operation of the device it controls/operates. It is needed to allow the systems or applications software to use the connected device properly.

Encoding Process of putting information/data (e.g., text, numbers, symbols, images, sound and video) into a specified format that allows effective transmission or storage by an ICT system.

Encryption Coding data whilst it is being sent over a network so that only the true recipient is able to decode it. Should the data be intercepted by a hacker, then the data will be in code and totally meaningless.

Ergonomics An applied science concerned with designing and arranging things people use so that the people and things interact most efficiently and safely.

Erroneous data Data that is ridiculous or totally unsuitable.

Evaluation The act of reviewing what has been achieved, how it was achieved and how well the solution works.

External threat A threat to an ICT system that comes from outside the organisation.

Extranet An external network that can be used by the customers, suppliers and partners of an organisation as well as the organisation itself.

Favourites Storage area where the URL (i.e. the web address) of a website can be stored so that it can be accessed later using a link.

Federation Against Software Theft An anti-piracy organisation who protect the work of software publishers.

File attachments Files that are transferred along with an e-mail.

File compression Used to compress files before storing or before being sent over a network.

File management software Part of systems software used to create folders, copy folders/ files, rename folders/files, delete folders/files, move files/folders, etc.

File/Table lookups Used to make sure that codes being used are the same as those used in a table or file of codes.

File transfer protocol (FTP) A standard Internet protocol (way of doing things) providing a simple way of transferring files between computers using the Internet. Used to transmit any type of file: computer programs, text files, graphics, etc., by a process which bunches the data into packages.

Firewall Either hardware and/or software that work in a network to prevent communication that is not allowed from one network to another.

Flash/pen drives Popular storage media which offer cheap and large storage capacities and are an ideal media for photographs, music and other data files. They consist of printed circuit boards enclosed in a plastic case.

Footer Text placed at the bottom of a document.

Format checks Checks performed on codes to make sure that they conform to the correct combinations of characters.

Forward If you are sent an e-mail that you think others should see, you can forward it to them.

Freedom of Information Act 2000 Act giving the right of access to information held by public authorities.

Generic software Applications package that is appropriate for a wide range of tasks and can be used in lots of areas of work.

GIGO Abbreviation for Garbage In Garbage Out. It means that if you put rubbish into the computer then you get rubbish out.

Grammar checker Used to check the grammar in a sentence and to highlight problems and suggest alternatives.

Graph plotter A device which draws by moving a pen. Useful for scale drawings and is used mainly with CAD packages.

Graphics tablet An input device which makes use of a large tablet containing many shapes and commands which may be selected by the user by moving a cursor and clicking. Basically it moves the toolbars onto the tablet rather than clutter up the screen when doing large technical drawings using CAD software.

Groups Lists of people and their e-mail addresses.

GUI (graphical user interface) An interface that allows users to communicate with ICT equipment by making use of icons and pull-down menus.

Hacker A person who tries to or succeeds in breaking into a secure ICT system.

Hacking The process of trying to break into a secure computer system.

Hard copy Printed output on a computer which may be taken away and studied.

Hardware The physical components of a computer system.

Hash total Meaningless total of numbers used to check that all the numbers have been entered into the computer.

Header Text placed at the top of a document.

Health & Safety (Display Screen Equipment) Regulations 1992 Regulations making it law for employers to take certain measures to protect the health and safety of their employees who use ICT equipment.

Health and Safety at Work Act 1974 Law making sure that employees have safe working conditions and methods.

Hotspot A region where the Internet can be accessed wirelessly.

Icons Small pictures used to represent commands, files or windows.

ICT systems Hardware and software working together with people and procedures to do a job.

Identity theft/fraud Stealing your banking/credit card/ personal details in order to commit fraud.

Implementation The process of producing the working version of the solution to the problem as identified by the client.

Information Output from an ICT system or data which has been processed and gives us knowledge.

Information Commissioner The person responsible for enforcing the Data Protection Act. They also promote good practice and make everyone aware of the implications of the Act.

Ink-jet printer A printer that works by spraying ink through nozzles onto the paper.

Input Act of entering data into an ICT system.

Input device The hardware device used to feed the input data into an ICT system such as a keyboard or a scanner.

Input media The material on which the data is encoded so that it can be read by an input device and digitised so that it can be input, processed and turned into information by the ICT system.

Input message A message which when the field or cell is selected, gives the user some advice on the kind of data that should be entered.

Integrated software An application package consisting of software for several distinct applications. There will always be two or more applications packages in integrated software.

Interactive Where there is a constant dialogue between the user and the computer.

Interface The point where two objects meet. In ICT this is usually between a device such as a computer, printer, scanner, etc., and a human.

Internal threat A threat to an ICT system that comes from inside the organisation.

Internet A huge group of networks joined together.

Internet service provider (ISP) The organisation that provides your Internet connection.

Intranet A private network used within an organisation that makes use of Internet technology.

Kilobyte or 1024 bytes Sometimes abbreviated as KB. A measure of the storage capacity of disks and memory.

Laser printer A printer which uses a laser beam to form characters on the paper.

Length check Checks to make sure that the data being entered has the correct number of characters in it.

Log-in Identifying yourself to the network in order to gain access.

Log-out Informing the network you want to close access to the network facilities until the next log-in.

Macros Used to record a series of keystrokes so that, for example, your name and address can be added to the top of the page simply by pressing a single key or clicking on the mouse.

Magnetic ink character recognition (MICR) Input method making use of numbers printed onto a document such as a cheque in a special magnetic ink, which can be read by the magnetic ink character reader at very high speed.

Magnetic media Media such as tape and disk where the data is stored as a magnetic pattern.

Magnetic strip Data is encoded in the magnetic strip and when the card is swiped the data from the card is used to record the transaction.

Magnetic strip reader Hardware device that reads the data contained in magnetic strips such as those on the back of credit cards.

Mail merge Combining a list of names and addresses with a standard letter so that a series of letters is produced with each letter being addressed to a different person.

Malpractice Improper or careless use or misconduct.

Memory cards Thin cards you see in digital cameras used to store photographs and can be used for other data.

Menus Allow a user to make selections from a list.

Mesh Type of network topology where there are many paths data can take between the computers.

MIDI (Musical Instrument Digital Interface) Used mainly to communicate between electronic keyboards, synthesisers and computers. MIDI files are compressed and the files are quite small.

Mind map A hierarchical diagram with a main idea, or image, at the centre of the map surrounded by branches that extend from the central idea.

MP3 Music file format that uses compression to reduce the file size considerably and this is why the MP3 file format is so popular with portable music playing devices such as i-Pods.

Multimedia A means of communication that combines more than one medium for presentation purposes, such as sound, graphics and video.

Natural language interface An interface that allows the user to interact using natural written or spoken language (e.g. English) as opposed to computer language and commands.

Network A group of ICT devices (computers, printers, scanners, etc.) which are able to communicate with each other.

Networking software Systems software which allows computers connected together to function as a network.

Non-volatile memory Memory stored on a chip which does not lose data when the power is turned off.

Normal data Data that should be acceptable.

Notification The process of letting the Information Commissioner's Office know that an organisation is storing and processing personal data.

OCR (optical character recognition) This is a combination of software and a scanner which is able to read characters into the computer.

Off-the-shelf software Software that has not been developed for a particular use.

OMR (optical mark reader/recognition) Reader that detects marks on a piece of paper. Shaded areas are detected and the computer can understand the information contained in them.

Operating system Software that controls the hardware and also runs your programs. The operating system controls the operations of handling: input, output, interrupts, storage and file management.

Optical character recognition (OCR) Input method using a scanner as the input device along with special software which looks at the shape of each character so that it can be recognised separately.

Optical mark recognition (OMR) Input method using paper-based forms or cards with marks on them that are read automatically by a device called an optical mark reader.

Output The results from processing data.

Package software A bundle of files necessary for a particular program to run along with some form of documentation to help a user get the program started.

Password A series of characters which need to be typed in before access to the ICT system is allowed.

Peer-to-peer Network arrangement with each computer of equal status.

Peripheral A device connected to and under the control of the central processing unit (CPU).

Personal data Data about a living identifiable person, which is specific to that person.

Personal skills Those skills a person possesses, which are transferable to any job or task.

Phishing Tricking people into revealing their banking or credit card details.

Piracy The process of illegally copying software.

Pixel The smallest dot of light on the computer screen which can be individually controlled.

Podcasting Creating and publishing a digital radio broadcast using a microphone, computer and audio editing software. The resulting file is saved in MP3 format and then uploaded onto an Internet server. It can then be downloaded using a facility called RSS onto an MP3 player such as an iPod.

Pointer This is the little arrow that appears when using Windows.

Presence checks Check to make sure that data had been entered into a field.

Primary storage Storage in chips inside the computer.

Print preview Feature that comes with most software used to produce documents. It allows users to view the page or pages of a document to see exactly how they will be printed. If necessary, the documents can be corrected.

Printer driver Software that converts commands from the systems or applications software into a form that a particular printer can understand.

Privacy Being able to choose to keep aspects of your life private.

Process Any operation that transfers data into information.

Processing Performing calculations or arranging the data into a meaningful order.

Programmer A person who writes computer programs.

Proof reading Carefully reading what has been typed in and comparing it with what is on the data source (order forms, application forms, invoices, etc.) for any errors, which can then be corrected.

Protocol A set of standards that allow the transfer of data between computers on a network.

Proxy server A server which can be hardware or software that takes requests from users for access to other servers and either forwards them onto the other servers or denies access to the servers.

RAID (redundant array of inexpensive disks) A system used by networks to keep backups.

RAM (random access memory) Used to hold the data temporarily whilst the computer is working on it. Contents are lost when the computer is switched off.

Range check Data validation technique which checks that data input into the computer is within a certain range.

Read only A user can only read the contents of the file. They cannot alter or delete the data.

Read/write A user can read the data held in the file and can alter the data.

Real-time processing The input data is processed immediately as it arrives. The results have a direct effect on the next set of available data.

Relational database management system (RDMS) Database system where the data is held in tables with relationships established between them. The software is used to set up and hold the data as well as to extract and manipulate the stored data.

Relationship The way tables are related to each other. Relationships can be one-to-one, one-to-many or many-to-many.

Reply Allows you to read an e-mail and then write the reply without having to enter the recipient's e-mail address.

Resolution The sharpness or clarity of an image.

Ring A type of network topology where all the computers are of equal status and are arranged in a circle.

ROM (read only memory) Memory stored on a chip which does not lose data when the power is turned off.

Router Hardware device which is able to make the decision about the path that an individual packet of data should take so that it arrives in the shortest possible time.

RSI Repetitive strain injury. A painful muscular condition caused by repeatedly using certain muscles in the same way.

Scams Setting up bogus companies with bogus websites and then making off with the money from customers' orders.

Scanner Input device that can be used to capture an image and is useful for digitising old non-digital photographs, paper documents or pictures in books.

Search engine Program which searches for required information on the Internet.

Secondary (or backup) storage Storage outside the computer.

Security Making sure that the hardware, software and data of an ICT system does not come to any harm.

Software Programs which supply the instructions to the hardware.

Software licence Document (digital or paper) which sets out the terms by which the software can be used. It will refer to the number of computers on which it can be run simultaneously.

Sorting Putting data into ascending or descending order.

Spam Unsolicited bulk e-mail (i.e., e-mail from people you do not know sent to everyone in the hope that a small percentage may purchase the goods or services on offer).

Specific software Software that only performs one function.

Spellchecker Facility offered by software where there is a dictionary against which all words typed in are checked.

Spyware Software which collects information about the user of a computer connected to the Internet without their consent.

Star Type of network topology where the computers are connected to a single connection point.

Storage capacity How much data the storage device/media can hold. Usually measured in MB or GB.

Systems software Any computer software that manages and controls the hardware thus allowing the applications software to do a useful job. Systems software consists of a group of programs.

Taskbar Shows the programs that are open. This facility is handy when working on several programs together.

Technical skills Those skills that are necessary in order to complete a specific job in ICT.

Telecommunications The field of technology concerned with communicating at a distance (e.g., telephones, radio, cable, etc.).

Telecommuting Performing job-related tasks by using telecommunications to send and receive data to and from a central office without having to be physically present.

Teleworking Using communications to save a journey. For example, you could save a journey abroad by using videoconferencing.

Templates Used to specify the structure of a document such as fonts, page layout, formatting and styles.

Test plan The approach that will be used to test the whole solution and consists of a suite of tests.

Thesaurus Allows a word to be chosen and the word processor will list synonyms (i.e., words with similar meanings).

Toner Black plastic particles used by laser printers as the 'ink'.

Topology The way a particular network is arranged. Examples include ring, star and bus.

Touch screen Screen that allow a person to make selections by simply touching the screen.

Transaction A piece of business, e.g. an order, purchase, return, delivery, transfer of money, etc.

Transaction processing Processing of each transaction as it arises.

Transcription error Error made when typing data in using a document as the source of the data.

Transmission medium The material which forms the connection between the computers in a network (i.e., air in the case of wireless; metal wire, optical fibre).

Transmission rate The speed of data flow in bits per second (bps) through a transmission medium.

Transposition error Error made when characters are swapped around so they are in the wrong order.

Trojans Lines of computer code that are stored in your PC without you knowing.

Uninstallers Software used to remove all the files put onto the computer when a piece of software was installed.

UPS (uninterruptible power supply) A backup power supply (generator and battery) which will keep the computer running should the mains power supply fail.

URL (uniform resource locator) The web address used to locate a web page.

User log A record of the successful and failed logins and also the resources used by those users who have access to network resources.

Username A way of identifying who is using the ICT system in order to allocate network resources.

Utility Part of the systems software that performs a specific task.

Utility programs Software which helps the user perform tasks such as virus checking, file compression, etc.

Validation checks Checks a developer of a solution creates, using the software, in order to restrict the data that a user can enter so as to reduce errors.

Validation expression/rule Command that a developer must type in order to set up the validation for a particular field/cell.

Validation message A message which appears if the validation rule is breached.

Verification Checking that the data being entered into the ICT system perfectly matches the source of the data.

Videoconferencing ICT system that allows face-to-face meetings to be conducted without the participants being in the same room or even the same geographical area.

Virus A program that replicates (i.e. copies) itself automatically and usually carries with it some payload which causes damage.

Voice recognition Voice recognition systems allow you to enter data via a microphone directly into a computer.

Volatile memory Memory which loses data when the power is turned off.

WAV Used with Windows for storing sounds. Files in this format are not highly compressed.

Web browser The software program you use to access the Internet. Microsoft Internet Explorer is an example of a web browser.

Webcam A small video camera used as an input device to send a moving image over an intranet or the Internet.

Webpage Single document on the World Wide Web.

Wi-Fi A trademark for the certification of products that meet certain standards for transmitting data over wireless networks.

WIMP (Windows Icons Menus Pointing devices) The graphical user interface (GUI) way of using a computer rather than typing in commands at the command line.

World Wide Web A means of accessing information contained on the Internet. It is an information-sharing model that is built on top of the Internet.

Worm A program that keeps replicating itself automatically, and as it does so it takes more and more disk space and also uses a greater proportion of the system's resources for each copy.

Index